Applied Theatre and Gender Justice

Applied Theatre and Gender Justice is a collection of essays highlighting the value and efficacy of using applied theatre to address gender in a broad range of settings, identifying challenges, and offering concrete best practices.

This book amplifies and shares lessons from practitioners and scholars who use performance to create models of collective solidarity, building upon communities' strengths toward advocating for justice and equity. The book is divided into thematic sections, comprising three essays addressing a range of questions about the obstacles, learning opportunities, and benefits of applied theatre practices. Further exploring the themes, issues, and ideas, each section ends with a moderated roundtable discussion between the essays' authors.

Part of the series *Applied Theatre in Context, Applied Theatre and Gender Justice*, this book is an accessible and valuable resource for theatre practitioners and the growing number of theatre companies with education and community engagement programs. Additionally, it provides essential reading for teachers and students in a myriad of fields: education, theatre, civic engagement, criminal justice, sociology, women and gender studies, environmental studies, disability studies, and ethnicity and race studies.

Lisa S. Brenner is a professor of theatre at Drew University, where she teaches dramaturgy, theatre history, and applied performance. Her theatre experience includes dramaturgy, devising, directing, and playwriting.

Evelyn Diaz Cruz is a professor of theatre at the University of San Diego, where she teaches playwriting, acting, theatre of diversity, and theatre and community. Her theatre experience includes playwriting, directing, and acting.

Applied Theatre in Context

Routledge's *Applied Theatre in Context* series documents the potency of the performing arts to provoke and disrupt the status quo, and ignite social change. The array of essays and conversations engages critically with a range of theories and current practices.

Each book is divided into thematic sections that include essays and moderated roundtable discussions, further exploring the themes, issues, and ideas introduced in the anthology.

This series will be a valuable resource for practitioners and the growing number of theatre and dance companies with education and community engagement programs. In addition, the collection demonstrates how the performing arts can innovate one's pedagogy and enliven the practice of multiple disciplines.

Applied Theatre with Youth
Education, Engagement, Activism
By Lisa S. Brenner, Chris Ceraso and Evelyn Diaz Cruz

Applied Theatre and Gender Justice
Imagination, Play, Movement
By Lisa S. Brenner and Evelyn Diaz Cruz

For a full list of titles in this series, please visit: www.routledge.com/Applied-Theatre-in-Context/book-series/ATIC

Applied Theatre and Gender Justice

Imagination, Play, Movement

Edited by Lisa S. Brenner and Evelyn Diaz Cruz

LONDON AND NEW YORK

Designed cover image: The CURIOUS Ensemble (Ryn Mercado, Ray Anderson, S.C Mott, and George Hagelstein) embodies the prompt: "How does it feel to be queer for you today?" Directed by Alejandro Batien and Sofia Kencken. Spring 2023, Escalante Multi-Generational Center. Tempe, Az. Photo by Jacob Buttry.

First published 2025
by Routledge
4 Park Square, Milton Park, Abingdon, Oxon OX14 4RN

and by Routledge
605 Third Avenue, New York, NY 10158

Routledge is an imprint of the Taylor & Francis Group, an informa business

British Library Cataloguing-in-Publication Data
A catalogue record for this book is available from the British Library

ISBN: 978-1-032-37764-3 (hbk)
ISBN: 978-1-032-37763-6 (pbk)
ISBN: 978-1-003-34180-2 (ebk)

DOI: 10.4324/9781003341802

Typeset in Optima
by KnowledgeWorks Global Ltd.

Access the Support Material: www.routledge.com/9781032377636

Contents

Figures

Acknowledgments

We wish to acknowledge all of our families who have contributed to our sense of purpose. As stated in our first book, they include our immediate and extended families as well as kindred spirits: ancestors, children, colleagues, mentors, and the families yet to come. Most significantly, this book was made possible by the many open-hearted, creative authors, facilitators, participants, and community members in our programs.

Special thanks: The Association for Theatre in Higher Education (ATHE), Lisa Biggs, Bomba Liberté, Bringing Theory to Practice, Capuli Mexica, the Centro Cultural del la Raza, ChangeMaker Hub at University of San Diego (USD), Chris Ceraso, Peter Cirino, Odesma Dairymple, Danza Coatlicue, Dean's Office of the College of Liberal Arts at Drew University, Dean's Office of the College of Arts and Letters at USD, Jessica Delvecchio, Josen Diaz, Kevin Guerrieri, Ethnic Studies at USD, Eunice Ferreira, Kimani Fowlin, John Loggins, Marcelle Maese, the Mulvaney Center, Gail Perez, Alberto Pulido, Eva Sandoval, Judy Tate, the Theatre & Dance Department at Drew University, the Theatre Department at USD, Women & Gender Studies at Drew University, Women & Gender Studies at USD.

We would also like to thank Lucia Accorsi, Stephanie Hines, Claire Margerison, and Nancy Rebecca who helped shepherd this book from idea to publication.

About the Editors

Lisa S. Brenner (she/her) is a professor of theatre arts and an affiliate faculty member of Women and Gender Studies at Drew University, where she received the President's Award for Distinguished Teaching, the Civic Engagement Faculty Leadership Award, and the Mellon Periclean Faculty Leader in the Humanities Award. Together with Chris Ceraso and Kimani Fowlin, she co-directs the applied performance minor and is a co-leader of AdvantageArts, a theatre and college-readiness program for Newark youth developed with the late Rodney M. Gilbert. She also designed and teaches a course on applied performance and sexual consent. Brenner holds an MA and PhD in theatre from Columbia University and a BA from Barnard College and has studied with seminal theatre artists Augusto Boal, Anne Bogart, Moisés Kaufman, and Holly Hughes. She is a past editor of *Theatre Topics*, an official journal of the Association for Theatre in Higher Education, published by Johns Hopkins University Press. Additionally, she is the co-editor of *Applied Theatre with Youth: Education, Engagement, Activism* (Routledge), *Represent! New Plays for Multicultural Youth* (Bloomsbury), and *Katrina on Stage: Five Plays* (Northwestern UP). She's currently the dramaturg on the musical *Airborne: the Bessie Coleman Story*. Brenner has published in *The New York Times. Theatre Topics, Transformations, Praxis, Theatre Survey,* and *Theatre Annual*.

Evelyn Diaz Cruz (she/her) is a professor of theatre and affiliate faculty of Ethnic Studies at the University of San Diego. She earned her MFA in playwriting from the University of California at Los Angeles and her BA in theatre from San Diego State University. Professor Cruz teaches the capstone course, Theatre and Community, which partners with local community organizations toward a final theatrical performance. As a professor, she has been recognized for her high-impact, innovative teaching and community engagement practices, which garnered her the highest honor bestowed upon a faculty, with a University Professorship in 2019–2020, as well as the 2023 Anti-Racism Transformation Award. Past honors include The Moxie Theatre Award for Women, a KPBS Local Heroes Award in The Arts, a USD Innovations in Experiential Education, and featured in her university's magazine as one of "The Best and Brightest Professors." Originally from the Bronx, New York, her vision as a playwright is Latina-centric. She has been produced in San Diego, New Jersey, and New York City and has published two of her short plays in the anthology, *Represent! New Plays for Multicultural Youth* (Bloomsbury).

Contributors

Megan Alrutz (she/her) is a professor at the University of Texas at Austin, where she teaches in the Drama and Theatre for Youth and Communities area. She works nationally and internationally as a theatre-maker, as well as an applied theatre facilitator. Megan's research and practice focus on the role of performance, storytelling (live and digital), and drama-based pedagogy in building intentional communities of practice. She creates and directs theatre for the very young and is a long-time producer and dramaturg for award-winning author, artist, and playwright Mo Willems. She leads interactive workshops in K-12 schools and higher education, as well as with organizations focused on community engagement, professional development, and curriculum innovation. Megan is the author or co-author of three books: *Devising Critically Engaged Theatre for Youth: the Performing Justice Project; Digital Storytelling, Applied Theatre & Youth: Performing Possibility*; and *Playing with Theory in Theatre Practice.*

Quenna Lené Barrett (she/her), EdD, is a Chicago-based theatre artist and practitioner, whose work gathers folks of diverse backgrounds, centers marginalized identities, learns from Black radical wisdom, and then dreams collectively to act boldly through those learnings. Quenna is an associate professor of applied theatre at Governors State University. She has developed participatory, theatre-based programs at the University of Chicago's Arts + Public Life and Goodman Theatre. She is a member of the leadership circle of the *Center for Performance and Civic Practice*, Quenna received her BFA from NYU Tisch in drama, MA in applied theatre from the University of Southern California, and EdD in educational theatre from NYU Steinhardt. Recent publications include work in *Contemporary Black Theatre & Performance: Acts of Rebellion, Activism, & Solidarity,* Methuen Drama, and the forthcoming *Every Great Dream, Theatre for Young Audiences Anthology*, Dramatic Publishing.

Alejandro Bastien-Olvera (he/him) is a teaching artist and creative placemaker with queer communities. He is originally from Mexico City, where he studied Theatre at UNAM and trained in physical theatre and Playback Theatre at La Cabra Salvaje. Alejandro learned theatre philosophy and arts management in Buenos Aires and recently completed an MFA in theatre for youth and community at Arizona State University, where he collaborated with Rising Youth Theatre and Childsplay. He worked at The New Children's Museum as a creative youth coordinator, where he helped transform the museum into a space of belonging for diverse communities in San Diego. Recently, he founded the Queer theatre company Xuir Mexico. His work focuses on devised theatre with queer communities, Playback Theatre, and creative youth development. Social media @bastienalejandro

Lisa Biggs (she/her), PhD, is a performance studies scholar, actress, and playwright. Originally from the South Side of Chicago, she currently serves as an assistant professor at Brown University in the Department of Africana Studies/Rites and Reason Theatre. Her original stage plays have been produced at the National Black Theatre Festival, Links Hall, Shadowbox Theatre, Cultural Odyssey, the NY Hip Hop Theatre Fest, DC Arts Center, Drew University, Amherst College, and the Baltimore Theatre Project. In addition to her artistic work, she is the author of the award-winning ethnography, *The Healing Stage: Black Women, Incarceration, and the Art of Transformation* (Ohio State University Press, 2022). Her work has been supported by grants and fellowships from the Knight Foundation, DC Commission on the Arts and Humanities, Ellen Stone Belic Foundation, Michigan Humanities Council, the Pembroke Center, and the Center for the Study of Race and Ethnicity at Brown University.

Trevor Boffone (he/him) went viral in 2019 and hasn't looked back. His work using TikTok and Instagram with his students has been featured on *Good Morning America*, *ABC News*, *Inside Edition*, and *Access Hollywood*, among numerous national media platforms. His work as a social media expert has been featured in the *New York Times*, *Washington Post*, *LA Times*, *Forbes*, *The Atlantic*, and *NPR*. Trevor has published two books on social media and popular culture and has two forthcoming books exploring theatre marketing on social media. He is the co-editor of *Shakespeare & Latinidad* and is currently co-writing a book on Yassified Shakespeare.

Kit Bothum (they/them) has been involved in The ART Project since 2021. They are seventeen years old and a high school senior. They hope to go to college for communications to further a career as a novelist or screenwriter. They love music, writing, film, cartoons, and trashy reality TV. The biggest inspirations in their artistic career are Bjork (mother), Mitski, Fiona Apple, their older sister, and their mom and dad.

Veronica Burgess (she/her/ella) is a resident teaching artist for the Old Globe Theatre's Arts Engagement Department. She has brought her applied theatre practice to communities such as unaccompanied minors seeking asylum, veterans in recovery, people experiencing homelessness, men currently incarcerated in state prison, and students in middle and high schools with underfunded arts education. She has recently joined OnStage Playhouse (the only professional theater in SouthBay San Diego) as a new board member. Veronica is also a working comedian and actor who can be seen regularly in comedy clubs and playhouses. Prior credits include her work with the Playwrights Project, Circle Circle dot dot, and Teatro Izcalli, whose mission is to educate on issues of inequity and social justice in the border region. Veronica earned her BA in Theatre, with a performance emphasis from San Diego State University.

Jasmin Cardenas (she/ella) is a theatre arts activist, educator, facilitator, cultural worker, bilingual storyteller, and proud daughter of Colombian immigrants. Jasmin studied Theatre of the Oppressed with Augusto Boal then spent fifteen years amplifying youth voices through devised work. Inspired by El Teatro Campesino, she devises original scenes with precarious adult workers and co-founded WorkersTEATRO for labor justice in Chicago, IL. An article about this work was published in the *PTO Journal*. Jasmin is an International LAB Fellow at The Laboratory for Global Performance and Politics at Georgetown University and a Civic Facilitator for the University of Chicago's Office of Civic Engagement. She gave the US Emergent Artist Address for UNESCO's 2022 World Theater Day. Commissioned by 1st Stage Theater, VA, Jasmin wrote *Disposable*, a documentary-style solo play about the temp/contractor community. A featured storyteller at the National Storytelling Festival, TN, her recently released album Cuentos from the Americas won the 2024 Storytelling World Award. Jasmin is a proud SAG-AFTRA Member & stage actress. www.jasmincardenas.com/

Zachary A. Dorsey (he/him) is a scholar specializing in LGBTQ+ art and activism. Prior to his arrival at Montclair State University, he taught at James Madison University and at St. Lawrence University. Zachary is a production dramaturg and new work dramaturg, and he has contributed to theatre, dance, and musical theatre productions at universities, as well as shows at Austin Shakespeare, Jump Start Performance Company (San Antonio), State Theatre Company (Austin), and Pendragon Theatre (Saranac Lake), among others. He is a graduate of the Performance as Public Practice program in Austin's Department of Theatre and Dance at the University of Texas. He was also a co-creator of Virginia's first regularly recurring Drag Storytime series.

Dana Edell (she/her), PhD, MFA, is an activist-scholar-artist-educator. She has produced and co-directed over eighty original plays written and performed by teenage girls and nonbinary youth addressing social and racial justice issues. Edell has worked as a teaching artist with people of all ages in public and private elementary, middle, and high schools, adult prisons, and youth correctional institutions. She's the co-director of The ART (Anti-Racism Theater) Project where she collaborates with multiracial groups of teenage girls and nonbinary youth in Delaware to create activist theatre and collaborates with feminist Jewish teens and Jewish organizations in arts-based activist projects. She has published chapters and articles in more than a dozen academic books and journals and currently serves as Co-Editor of *Youth Theatre Journal*. Her book, *Girls, Performance and Activism: Demanding to Be Heard* was published by Routledge in 2022. She is an assistant professor of applied theatre at Emerson College.

Laura Epperson (she/her) is a theatre artist, educator, and collaborator with over fifteen years of experience working in schools and communities in the U.S. and internationally. She uses storytelling, embodiment, play, and inquiry to create community-engaged projects and performances that imagine vibrant futures and abundant possibilities. In her practice-based research, Laura explores how aesthetic approaches support healing, cultivate belonging, and shape change. Recent publications include *Our Voice is Powerful: Toward an Aesthetics of Healing in the Performing Justice Project* (recipient of the 2021 Distinguished Thesis Award from the American Alliance for Theatre and Education) and a co-authored essay in *Devising Critically Engaged Theatre: The Performing Justice Project* (Alrutz and Hoare, 2020). Learn more at www.lauramwepperson.com.

Sarah Fahmy (she/her), PhD, is an assistant professor of theatre and performance research at Florida State University. Sarah is a decolonial scholartist, whose work intersects Middle East North African identity politics, community-based performance, digital humanities, and ecofeminist art-science devising. She is co-founder and current chair of the Middle Eastern Theatre Focus Group at ATHE and has served on the conference planning committee of the MENA Theater Makers Alliance. Her publications appear in a range of journals and books ranging from *Theatre Topics*, *RiDE*, and *PTO Journal*, to *PLoS ONE*; and she is on the Environmental Communication editorial board. Sarah has devised multi-disciplinary site-specific pieces and facilitated applied performance and Playback with hundreds of participants internationally, ranging from creative climate communication with scientists to youth-centered workshops for the UN Commission on the Status of Women. Her current book project explores decolonial MENA-specific, feminist praxis with young women. https://sarahfahmy-scholartistry.com/.

Jasmine Games (she/her) is a Black and queer spoken word poet and theatre practitioner based in Austin, TX. With a BA in English and performance studies from Texas A&M University (2018) and an MFA in drama and theatre for youth and communities from The University of Texas at Austin (2022), Games is an award-winning poet and practitioner, including the 2021 Sexton Prize for Poetry and the 2021 Winifred Ward Scholarship. As the Director of Education and Social Justice Activation at The VORTEX, she utilizes drama, creative writing, and devised performances to address social (in)justices with participants of all ages. Her first full-length poetry collection, *Somebody's Daughter,* is set to be released in March 2024. Learn more about Jasmine at jasmineigames.com and follow her on social media @jasminegamespoetry.

Sarah Ashford Hart (she/her) is a socially engaged performance practitioner/scholar from a Canadian-Venezuelan-American background. She completed her BA in theatre at Barnard College, Columbia University, her MA in devised theatre at Dartington College of Arts, Falmouth University, and her PhD in performance studies with a designated emphasis in human rights at the University of California, Davis. Recent publications address contemporary performance in Latin America, devised theatre methodology, the importance of affect to applied theatre in contexts of immigrant incarceration, and embodied approaches to witnessing testimonial performances. Research areas include applied theatre, decolonial theory, affect theory, migration studies, carceral studies, embodiment, trauma, and memory. https://sarahashfordhart.com/.

Faith Hillis (she/her), is a dedicated teaching artist, poet, and performance maker hailing from Houston, Texas, currently serves as the Senior Specialist of University and Professional Learning at the Museum of Fine Arts Houston. In this role, Faith brings her rich expertise to the intersection of education and the arts. Faith completed her BFA in acting and directing at Sam Houston State University and her MFA in drama and theatre for youth and communities at the University of Texas at Austin. Beyond her artistic pursuits, Faith is passionately involved in communities that prioritize justice, equity, and love as essential elements of embodied practice. https://www.faithalyce.com/.

Kristin Horton (she/her) is a director who works primarily on new plays, reimagined classics, and community-centered practices. She is committed to collaborating with playwrights and artists whose work disrupts and unsettles notions of race, gender, and class through imaginative and theatrical storytelling. Additionally, she collaborates with researchers from a multitude of fields at the intersection of theater practice and scientific research. She is currently working with an international art-science research team on the development of transdisciplinary approaches that examine and communicate future volcanic risk in Campi Flegrei (Italy). Horton teaches at New York University's Gallatin School where she received the Dean's Award for Excellence in Teaching and served as chair of the Interdisciplinary Arts Program from 2017 to 2022.

Radhika Jain (she/her) is an applied theatre and expressive arts therapy practitioner from India. She is the co-founder of First Drop Theatre, a Bangalore-based applied theatre company. An accredited Playback Theatre trainer,

Radhika is a visiting faculty for Playback Theatre at the renowned Azim Premji University, Bangalore, and at the Applied Theatre India Foundation. She is the co-editor of the *International Playback Theatre Network* (IPTN) journal and the Secretary (Executive Committee) at the Centre for Playback Theatre, USA. She specifically uses Playback Theatre, Theatre of the Oppressed, and Applied Improvisation for self and social awareness, for opening up conversations and for enabling deep reflections in the area of healthcare, for mental health awareness, for addressing issues of diversity and inclusion, for community outreach, and for the holistic development of organizations.

DeVante Love (they/them) is an Olympic martial artist, movement therapist, Buddhist monk, and performer who travels the world helping queer people of color fight for their inner peace. They founded Healing Kung Fu, an online queer martial arts-dance academy that shares Chinese Healing Dances, Meditation, and Spiritual Philosophy to help folks overcome conditioning and courageously embrace their true selves. They have a masters in psychology from Columbia University and have written immersive ritual plays that have been performed in the United States and Asia. They are now pursuing a PhD in theatre, dance, and performance studies at Tufts University, where they investigate queer world-making through ecstatic dance and ritual combat.

Pranab Kumar Mandal (he/him) is an assistant professor in the Department of English of Ramakrishna Mission Residential College, Kolkata, India (affiliated with the University of Calcutta). His research interests include the intersections of performance and ecology, ecology and spirituality, and gender and performance. He is the recipient of John McGrath Scholarship 2021 (from Scottish Universities International Summer School, University of Edinburgh), Asian Graduate Student Fellowship 2023 (from Asia Research Institute, National University of Singapore), Charles Wallace Research Grant 2023 (from Charles Wallace India Trust, British Council), and Research Fellowship 2023 (Utrecht University, The Netherlands). His edited book *Theatre Practice: Text and Performance, Interpretation and Experimentation* was published by the Jadavpur University Society for American Studies (JUSAS) in November 2018.

Natalie Y. Moore (she/her) is an award-winning journalist based in Chicago, whose reporting tackles race, housing, economic development, food injustice, and violence. Natalie's acclaimed book *The South Side: A Portrait of Chicago and American Segregation* received the 2016 Chicago Review of Books award for nonfiction and was Buzzfeed's best nonfiction book of 2016. She is also co-author of *The Almighty Black P. Stone Nation: The Rise, Fall* and *Resurgence of an American Gang* and *Deconstructing Tyrone: A New Look at Black Masculinity in the Hip-Hop Generation*. For the 100th anniversary of the 1919 Chicago riots, she co-wrote a thirty-minute audio drama with Make Believe Association that aired on WBEZ. 16th Street Theater adapted portions of *The South Side* in 2019. Haymarket Books published *The Billboard* in March 2022. *The Billboard* was produced by 16th Street Theater in July 2022. It won a Jeff Award for best new work, short run. Natalie collaborated with the Make Believe Association on the fictional *Lake Song* podcast.

Aviva Helena Neff (she/her), PhD, is the Director of Youth & Community Learning at Columbus College of Art & Design and an adjunct faculty member with Otterbein University Department of Theatre and Dance. An honors graduate of Goldsmiths College (MA, applied theatre), Dr. Neff enjoys working in devised theatre and theatre for social change with participants aged 1–100. She is an ensemble member with Teatro Travieso, which premiered her solo performance, *Blood, Earth, Water* in 2021, written as part of a practice-as-research PhD at the Ohio State University. Dr. Neff has recently published works on mediatized race and identity, mixed-Black women in Reconstruction-era New Orleans, and inclusive theatre pedagogy. Dr. Neff is very fortunate to serve as a freelance intimacy coordinator and director within the incredible theatre community in Columbus.

Kailyn Oates (she/her) is a junior at Conrad Schools of Science in Wilmington, Delaware. She wants to go to school to study nursing and become a nurse anesthetist. She is passionate about the arts and has studied dance since a young age. This is her third year doing the ART Project Activist Theatre program, and each year she has been excited to pursue this form of art and self-expression further. She currently runs a small business, Big Heart Crafts and Design, which she truly loves and uses as a vehicle to support other causes she is passionate about such as Heart Health Awareness.

Stephen Oghenеruro Okpadah (he/him) is a Chancellor International PhD Candidate in the Department of Theatre and Performance Studies, University of Warwick, United Kingdom. He is the co-editor of *Decoloniality and Topicality* (eTropic: Electronic Journal of Studies in the Tropics 2023), *Towards a Praxis in Decolonizing the Tropics*. (eTropic: Electronic Journal of Studies in the Tropics 2023), *Intercultural Encounters, Historicity and Cultural Communication for Development in Nigeria*. (Germany, Galda Verlag 2023), and editor of *Ecological Resistance in the Postcolonial Text* (Lamar Journal of the Humanities, Lamar University Literary Press 2023). He is currently researching participatory theatre and climate justice in the context of the environmentally degraded Niger Delta region of Nigeria. His project draws on theatre for development to create community-based performances that advocate for climate justice. He won the 2021 Janusz Korczak/UNESCO Prize for Global South in the emerging scholar category, and he is also a Director at the Theatre Emissary International, Nigeria. Okpadah is a non-resident research associate at the Centre for Socially Engaged Theatre, University of Regina, Canada.

Nicole Perry (she/her) is a *Silver Palm* award-winning intimacy director, as well as intimacy coordinator and dance choreographer in South Florida. Career highlights include two Broward County Artist Investment Grants for *KINesphere* (site-inspired dance works), intimacy coordination for *God Forbid* on Hulu, and a Carbonell nomination for the intimacy direction of *To Fall in Love* at Theatre Lab. Nicole is a Certified Laban/Bartenieff Movement Analyst. She holds an MFA from Goddard College. She apprenticed with Intimacy Directors International and is certified by Intimacy Directors and Coordinators (IDC). Nicole is a visiting assistant professor of dance at Florida Atlantic University. Memberships: Stage Directors and Choreographers Society, Dance Studies Association, National Dance Education Organization, Association of Theatre Movement Educators TikTok and IG: @intimacychorefl. https://nicoleperry.org/.

Winter Phong (open pronoun) an assistant professor of arts administration at the University of Kentucky, works and researches in areas of community-based arts practice and engagement and arts administration. She employs "IDEAS for Change," expanding on DEI/EDI principles to consider accessibility and sustainability. In 2021, this effort informed a partnership while teaching at Oklahoma State University to reflect on the 100th Anniversary of the Tulsa Race Massacre. Her past commitments include serving internationally in the Peace Corps in China, where she produced a performing arts festival highlighting marginalized groups, Tibetans, Uyghur, and Yi people. In Cambodia, she led student teachers to develop arts programming to support children who had been orphaned, recovered from dump sites, and/or rescued from sex trafficking. Dr. Phong earned her PhD from Texas Tech University, MBA and MFA in theatre management from California State University, Long Beach, and a BA in drama from the University of Washington.

Alyea Pierce (she/her) is an award-winning poet. With over twenty years of poetry and performance experience, Pierce has collaborated with Disney, National Geographic, NPR, and TEDx. Her dynamic passion for poetry, history, and culture has led her to share her expertise with museums and institutions, including The Smithsonian Center for Folklife and Cultural Heritage and Planet Word in Washington, DC. As a National Geographic Explorer and Fulbright alumna, Alyea Pierce was featured on National Geographic's podcast series *Into the Depths* as well as *The Soul of Music*, using spoken word poetry and audio to amplify lost voices of history across the African Diaspora. Pierce has performed internationally, as well as at colleges and universities across the country, Off-Broadway venues, and Poetry Slam spaces. Her poetry has been published online and in print, including Obsidian, The Caribbean Writer, and The Guardian, to name a few. Alyea is a lecturer at Rutgers University-New Brunswick. Social Media @alyeaspierce.

Alyssa Vera Ramos (she/ella) is a Chicago-based director, deviser, intimacy director, and cultural strategist dedicated to dreaming and practicing a liberated world. Alyssa co-wrote *The Sex Ed Playbook: Participatory Theatre for Health Education* and contributed to the forthcoming *Into Abolitionist Theatre: A Guidebook for Liberatory Theatre-making.* She stewarded the Illinois Caucus for Adolescent Health through its "re:Birth" process as co-director and helped win the repeal of Illinois' parental notification of abortion law. As a director of socially engaged, often participatory theatre, original work includes *You Can't Cover the Sky with Your Hand* by Marisel Vera (Pivot Arts), *Meeting Our Desires* (Chicago Night Out in the Parks), *Epic Tales from the Land of Melanin* (Latinx Theatre Commons' International TYA Festival), and *Expectation* (For Youth Inquiry- FYI Performance Company, where she previously served as artistic director). Alyssa is also a curator of Swarm Artist Residency, shaping community experiences of racial and healing justice for Midwest artists.

Danielle Rosvally (she/her) is an assistant professor of theatre at the University at Buffalo. Her forthcoming monograph (*Theatres of Value: Buying and Selling Shakespeare in Nineteenth-Century New York City,* State University of New York Press) considers the commodification and economization of Shakespeare's work in America's nineteenth century. Danielle's interest in the digital has fueled past work on database methodologies in humanist text, social media, and the personification of Shakespeare by performers/users. Her work has been seen in *Theatre Topics,* The *Early Modern Studies Journal, Studies in Musical Theater, Shakespeare Bulletin,* and *Fight Master* Magazine. She is the co-editor of *Early Modern Liveness* (Bloomsbury 2023), and the forthcoming special issue of *Shakespeare* dedicated to contingency titled "Inessential Shakespeares: Contingency, Necessity, and Marginalization in Early Modern Drama." She's co-writing a book about Yassified Shakespeare.

Soroya Rowley (they/she) is an adjunct professor of theatre at the University of San Diego and a resident teaching artist for the Old Globe Theatre's Arts Engagement department. Soroya has been practicing community-based theatre since 2008 and is a co-founder of the theatre company Circle Circle dot dot (CCdd), which produced original community-based theatre between 2011 and 2020. CCdd has worked in residence at the La Jolla Playhouse in San Diego and Arizona State University. Soroya's creative scholarship is focused on using theatre to address global conflicts at the intersections of racial justice, gender, climate crisis, and rising authoritarianism. Soroya has earned an MA in peace and justice studies, and a BA in theatre from the University of San Diego.

Editors' Introduction

Lisa S. Brenner and Evelyn Diaz Cruz

This book documents the vital work of international applied theatre practitioners committed to gender justice. Several paramount concerns compelled this focus. For one, we felt the need to respond to the dangers facing ciswomen and women-identified persons. The global organization, UN Women, defines gender equality as a human rights challenge, noting that the COVID pandemic, geopolitical conflicts, poverty, and climate disasters disproportionally affect women and those on the social and economic margins (2023). In addition, the World Health Organization has identified violence against women and girls as a public health problem: "Across their lifetime, 1 in 3 women, around 736 million, are subjected to physical or sexual violence by an intimate partner or sexual violence from a non-partner – a number that has remained largely unchanged over the past decade" (2021). In response to these perils, advocates "propose a shift towards a green economy and care society that amplifies women's voices" (UN Women, 2023).

Compounding this distress is an urgent need for access to healthcare and bodily autonomy. In the case of reproductive justice, public health consultants and bioethicists Onwuachi-Saunders et al. maintain that the agenda has been "polarized to a choice or abortion issue without any alignment to other issues that predominantly impact women of color within the reproductive health framework" (Onwuachi-Saunders et al., 2019). For instance, the Center for Disease Control reports that Black birthing people are two to three times more likely to die from pregnancy-related complications than white people, with most of these deaths being preventable (Winny and Bervell, 2023). As coined and defined by a group of Black women in Chicago, the term "reproductive justice" can be better understood as "the complete physical, mental, spiritual, political, social, and economic wellbeing of women and girls, based on the full achievement and protection of women's human rights" (Onwuachi-Saunders et al., 2019). This expanded framework articulates the need to approach gender justice from an intersectional lens that recognizes the impact of social, political, and economic factors (Onwuachi-Saunders et al., 2019).

Our choice of topic also sprang from alarm over discrimination based on sexual orientation, and gender identity and/or expression. Human Rights

DOI: 10.4324/9781003341802-1

Watch has determined that in addition to bans against gender recognition, LGBTQ2S+ people have been made vulnerable to attacks across the globe, including being forced out of their homes, subject to humiliating punishments, and denied access to healthcare (Reid, 2020). In the United States, over 500 anti-LGBTQ2S+ bills were introduced in state legislatures in 2023 (three times the number introduced in 2022). In addition to banning gender-affirming care, this legislation has focused on regulating public school curricula regarding discussions around gender identity and sexuality (Choi, 2024). We wanted to showcase practitioners who initiate dialogue, problem-solving, and social change around these issues and more, through the arts. This coverage of gender justice and applied theatre is not meant to be definitive; rather, we hope it will be a valuable contribution to a larger movement.

As of this writing, Donald Trump has returned as the president of the United States after the stunning defeat of Kamala Harris. While many factors contributed to Trump's victory, as journalist and editor Errin Haines argues, "We definitely saw former President Trump coming back into the White House on a message of his particular brand of masculinity. I think that we cannot have a conversation about this election without having a conversation about the role — the ongoing role of gender in our politics" (Nawaz, Corkery, & Young, 2024). In the face of these challenges, the work offered in this anthology reanimates us and will be all the more critical in the years to come.

This anthology is the second in a trilogy entitled *Applied Theatre in Context*. The first book, *Applied Theatre with Youth: Education, Engagement, Activism* (2021), which we co-edited with our colleague Chris Ceraso, stemmed from our personal experiences in the field and our desire to connect artists, educators, and activists. We were encouraged by the book's reception, especially within interdisciplinary contexts, and the formation of new collaborations across the United States. Therefore, when Routledge proposed expanding the work into a series, we agreed and accepted the offer to be series editors and extended the coverage of the next two books to include an international praxis.

We are fortunate to welcome esteemed scholar-practitioners Lisa Biggs and Eunice S. Ferreira as the book editors of the forthcoming third collection in the series: *Applied Theatre and Racial Justice: Radical Imaginings for Just Communities*. All three books document artistic communal responses to issues of our time while simultaneously interrogating the marker used to describe this work: "applied theatre." Biggs and Ferreira emphasize that community-generated and engaged work existed before practitioners in the United Kingdom coined this label. Their anthology thus highlights "the importance of knowledge and cultural practices developed by historically marginalized communities (including social activists, community organizers, artists, religious leaders, and teachers) who have been doing the work long before academic training programs developed the terminology applied theatre" (2025).

As the editors of *Applied Theatre and Gender Justice*, we likewise strove to foreground community-based performance and to scrutinize the terminology, aims, and methods of the field.

Several authors in this series also have questioned the qualifier "applied," arguing that it creates a binary relationship between mainstream theatre and applied theatre that delegitimizes the latter. Still, a key distinction for us lies in the intention, the process, and the participatory nature of the work. In our previous book, *Applied Theatre with Youth*, we cited Tim Prentki and Sheila Preston's definition:

> [Taking] participants and audiences beyond the scope of conventional, mainstream theatre ... The work often, but not always, happens in informal settings, in non-theatre venues in a variety of geographical and social settings... that might be specific or relevant to the interests of a *community*. Applied theatre usually works in contexts where the work created and performed has a specific resonance with its participants and its audiences and often, to different degrees, *involves them in it*.
>
> (Prentki and Preston, 2009, p. 9, our emphasis)

This distinction focuses on theatre as a means toward a larger communal, educational, or political goal rather than an end in and of itself (especially if it entails commercial gain). More specifically, this anthology investigates theatre created in community partnerships. Alternative designations include "community-based performance," and "community-engaged theatre," among others. Our definition of applied theatre thus prioritizes a dynamic synergy between practitioners and community members, and the creative process and product.

With this spirit in mind, we approached *Applied Theatre and Gender Justice*. As with our previous book, we have followed an interactive format to generate discussion. The anthology is divided into six thematic sections. Each section contains three essays and culminates with a roundtable discussion with the contributors. Rather than assign rigid categorization (several essays fit into multiple categories, and many practitioners approach their work intersectionally), we designed groupings to spark conversation and spur further exploration. Moreover, we strove to widen the theatre tent to include disciplines such as dance, spoken word, ritual, drag, digital storytelling, and martial arts.

This book begins with what is arguably the most pressing matter of our time: climate change. Ecojustice is also a form of gender justice: "Women and girls experience the greatest impacts of climate change, which amplifies existing gender inequalities and poses unique threats to their livelihoods, health, and safety" (UN Women, 2022). Writing from a Global South perspective, the authors in Part 1 foreground Indigenous women's resistance to ecological devastation. In "Decolonizing the Conversation: Sustainable Development Performances in Egypt," Sarah Fahmy reflects on the facilitation and outcomes of an applied theatre program involving young women in Alexandria and Aswan, Egypt. Encouraged by Fahmy to challenge neocolonial and Eurocentric biases, the young women grew to confidently and creatively express their opinions on environmental activism. Pranab Kumar Mandal's scholarship focuses on Subodh Patnaik, whose company, Natya Chetana (Theatre for Awareness), dramatizes the plight of the rural people of Odisha, India, and engages audiences to take action on issues such as water scarcity and pollution. Mandal focuses on the effectiveness of Patanaik's intersection between gender and eco-justice, illuminating women's "double layer of marginalization at the patriarchal and environmental levels" (p. 27). Stephen Ogheneruro Okpadah likewise emphasizes the role of women in combating environmental degradation. In particular, Okpadah spotlights the Beni Kamai Festival Theatre in the Niger Delta, which holds a religious-ritual purpose while also serving as a site of protest against what he calls "ecopower."

Part 2 continues exploring the potential sites and practices of applied theatre forms, particularly those taking place decidedly outside traditional theatre venues. In "Picking up the Sequins: Drag Storytime Performances, Applied Theatre, and Queer Joy," Zachary A. Dorsey responds to gender discrimination on the frontline of culture wars. Amidst proposed legislation in dozens of US states to ban drag performers from reading to children and to defund libraries that host these events, Dorsey presents Drag Storytimes as a mode of applied theatre "that speaks to who should be able to experience joy, and when, where, and how …" (p. 57). Next, Radhika Jain examines gender dynamics in the workplace in India. Jain delineates the practices of First Drop Theatre, which uses interactive techniques, particularly Playback Theatre, to examine power structures in the workplace and implicit biases that enable misconduct and inequity. Expanding where and how applied theatre occurs, in "Yassified Shakespeare: the Case for TikTok as Applied Theatre," Trevor Boffone and Danielle Rosvally argue that the digital platform creates like-minded communities, provides a forum to produce queer and femme-centered content, and helps reach a wider audience.

Part 3 exemplifies how the impact of applied theatre must go beyond *effect* to value the role of *affect*. Sarah Ashford Hart initiates this examination with her stirring essay on Patricia Ariza's work with female victims of Colombia's armed conflict. Depicting an alternative perspective to Global-North-centric applied theatre conversations, Hart's essay bears witness to Ariza's practice of Afecto, which shifts "normalized violent relations into life-affirming relations based on an ethics of radical care" (p. 87). Director Kristin Horton and playwright Lisa Biggs continue the theme of care in their essay, "Moving Women from the Margins to the Center of History: *After/Life* and the 1967 Detroit Rebellion." They discuss the deliberate actions they took to honor the input of their community partners in creating and staging the play *After/Life*. Like Horton and Biggs, Soroya Rowley and Veronica Burgess's essay shares progressive practices for addressing ethical considerations. As the title suggests,

"No Seriously, Humor is Important," by satirizing the oppressor, they use raillery as an effective tool to address difficult topics such as domestic violence.

Part 4 explores the meaning of choice, parenthood, and lineage. Natalie Y. Moore's essay "*The Billboard* #TrustBlackWomen: Abortion as Self-Care," discusses the intersection between race and gender in her play. Inspired by the Afiya Center, a nonprofit focused on the health and well-being of the Black community in Dallas, Moore emphasizes that abortion isn't just "a white girl issue" (p. 125). Winter Phong expands the debate on who is trusted to determine what's best for their bodies in the essay "Challenging Ableist Views of Motherhood: Mind The Gap's *Daughters of Fortune*." Phong takes the reader through four works by the British company Mind the Gap, which employs various techniques from docudrama to forum theatre to reduce stigma and raise awareness regarding disability and parenthood. This section culminates with Aviva Helena Neff's personal and poignant essay, "The Maternal Ground on Which I Stand: Developing A Solo Performance within the Harris Matriarchy." Neff works intergenerationally with family members who provide the ethnography that fuels her project.

While ethical concerns pervade applied theatre, as delineated in Part 5, navigating these concerns becomes all the more pressing when engaging with young people. Practitioners often tout applied theatre's ability to illuminate the stories of people who have been misrepresented or dismissed by mainstream society. Even so, Megan Alrutz, Laura Epperson, Jasmine Games, and Faith Hillis note that visibility can result in danger, criminalization, or even death for youth of color and LGBTQIA2S+ youth. They discuss online workshops with the Performing Justice Project wherein due to their lack of privacy, students felt reluctant to openly express their gender identity. They also reflect on negotiating the restrictions of a residential treatment center for young people living in foster care. In the essay "Queering Playback Theatre," Alejandro Bastien-Olvera confronts a different challenge to visibility: a hesitancy to disclose stories amidst a society that cultivates silence, guilt, and shame around queer identity. Bastien-Olvera documents lessons he learned from workshops he facilitated in his home country of Mexico to create a process where queerness could be "a source of connection, joy, and curiosity" (p. 169). For the third essay in this section, Dana Edell is joined by youth participants Kailyn Oates and Kit Bothum to explain how a gender affinity space can foster trust and activism. During a summer program for teenage girls and gender-nonconforming teens in Wilmington, Delaware, participants devised and performed a play in which they expressed personal challenges and led discussions with audience members exploring strategies to confront them.

Just as applied theatre often relies on verbal and written skills, such as telling stories or devising scripts, the ability to build trust and gain new perspectives often happens through embodiment. The practitioners in Part 6 investigate breaking habituated notions of ourselves and others through the practices of spoken word poetry, dance, and Chinese martial arts. An Afro-Caribbean-American woman poet, Alyea Pierce shares her process of facilitating workshops in Trinidad and Tobago with survivors of violence and discrimination. Although vulnerability "is often connected to passivity and lack of agency" (p. 194), Pierce builds on the work of Judith Butler and Elsa Szatek to show how understanding and embracing vulnerability in poetic spaces can conjure hope and effect change. Like Pierce, Nicole Perry gives concrete, step-by-step techniques to foster a consent-forward space. In "Tools for Equity and Collaboration," she generously offers practices from her training in dance and intimacy coordination. DeVante Love follows these discussions with "The Art of Genderbending: Fighting Hegemonic Gender Ideology with Chinese Martial Arts," which explains the process and potential outcomes of spiritual martial arts classes and ritual performances to empower queer people of color. Focusing on movement helps decondition participants from restrictive gender norms and forge community.

In keeping with the pursuit of ongoing dialogue, we opted to end this book with a supplemental roundtable with practitioners from WorkersTEATRO and FYI (For Youth Inquiry), which reflects the anthology's overarching themes, such as the value of play and imagination and the role of the arts in collective liberatory practice. We conclude conversationally with Quenna Lené Barrett, Jasmin Cardenas, and Alyssa Vera Ramos about their work on labor rights, sexual education, parenting, Black, queer, and trans identities, and more.

Taken together, these essays and roundtables address the challenges of working in applied theatre, including confronting ethical dilemmas such as the potential for "trauma-mining." Often applied theatre seeks to amplify narratives that have been suppressed, dismissed, or misrepresented; however, by focusing on trauma, practitioners risk deficit-framing, sensationalizing, and re-traumatizing. In speaking about aestheticizing the trauma of refugees, for instance, Myriam Fotou warns that despite "a well-meaning intention behind it…to give voice and agency to the silenced and voiceless, this very often backfires when they are presented mainly as victims" (2022). Similarly, James Thompson articulates a wariness of "projects that only confront, remember, or draw on pain and suffering." He argues that "the right to silence is forgotten too often in the pressure placed on many communities to speak out. And that the place of silence – which could be full of fun and dance – is a deeply political, potentially transformative site" (2009, p. xii). While acknowledging difficult realities, the contributors to this volume offer resources to address them.

One such offering is to showcase the joy, growth, and solidarity generated through collaboration, imagination, and play. As artist-educator Judy K. Tate explains, imagination allows participants to see beyond current realities and "envision what should be" (2022, p. 204). By creating playful, prophetic spaces where the imagination can thrive and grow, we build the imaginative muscles to move seemingly fixed circumstances toward alternate futures.

A few words on terminology. This anthology acknowledges that gender identity is a fluid spectrum. As such, the authors and subjects of this book identify as male, female, non-binary, gender-expansive, and more. Certain authors have deliberately used terms such as "cis," "transgender," or "non-binary" when they felt it was important to acknowledge the broad range of gender identities that might be considered "minoritized." Additionally, some took care to use specific terminology to honor how participants self-identified. Others use "women" or "girls" to include anyone who is female-identifying, particularly when the analysis of the work is not predicated upon those distinctions. Given the global landscape of this book, as editors, we also note that gender terminology may have different meanings depending on the writer's cultural context. To that end, in addition to maintaining the format of our initial book, we upheld the same stance on the plasticity of language.

In *Pleasure Activism*, adrienne maree brown acknowledges, "Language changes so quickly these days. The right way to speak about people, about identities and about gender, about geography—everything is in motion on a regular basis. I know that in writing this book I am creating something instantly dated ... If this is being read in a future in which this language has evolved, then please know I would be evolving right along with you" (2019, pp. 16, 18). We ask the reader for the same dispensation. Given that language changes, some of the terms used in this anthology may be different from those in the past or those in the future to describe similar or even emerging concepts. In recognition of this dynamic, we have allowed for inconsistencies in spelling (e.g. "folx") and phrasing to reflect the conscious choice of the individual authors. We have also deliberately chosen not to italicize non-English common-usage words. While the *Chicago Manual of* Style section 7.49 dictates using "Italics for...unfamiliar foreign words and phrases Italics are used for isolated words and phrases in a foreign ... language" (2010), several writers have rejected this practice for its othering of those languages. As Barokka Khairani (2021) explains, it becomes "a form of linguistic gatekeeping; a demarcation between which words are 'exotic' or 'not found in the English language,' and those that have a rightful place in the text: the non-italicized." We have provided English translations in parentheses as needed.

These writings celebrate a field deserving greater recognition. We are profoundly grateful to the authors who diligently labored to bring these pages to fruition. We were honored to collaborate with contributors, who, as one author expressed, "held each other up" and inspired hope. This book would assuredly not have been possible without the brave, generous, and creative community partners.

We welcome you, the reader, to imagine, play, and move.

References and Further Reading

Biggs, L. and Ferreira, E. (2025) *Applied Theatre and Racial Justice: Radical Imaginings for Just Communities*. NY and London: Routledge.

brown, a.m. (2019) *Pleasure Activism: The Politics of Feeling Good*. Chico, CA: AK Press.

Choi, A. (2024) "Record Number of Anti-LGBTQ Bills were Introduced in 2023 | CNN politics." CNN. 22 Jan. Accessed 2 Feb. 2024. https://www.cnn.com/politics/anti-lgbtq-plus-state-bill-rights-dg/index.html.

Fotou, M. (2022) "Playing the Refugee: Aesthetics of Trauma in Mainstream Refugeehood Dramaturgy." *Critical Studies on Security*; 10(2): pp. 96–100. DOI: 10.1080/21624887.2022.2111834

Hurtes, S. (2023) "Despite Bans, Disabled Women are Still Being Sterilized in Europe." *The New York Times*. Nov. 25. Accessed 9 Jan. 2024. https://www.nytimes.com/2023/11/25/world/europe/europe-disabled-women-sterilization.html.

Khairani, B. (2021) "The Case against Italicizing 'Foreign' Words." Catapult. Nov. 23. Accessed 2 Feb. 2024. https://catapult.co/stories/column-the-case-against-italicizing-foreign-words-khairani-barokka.

Nawaz, A., Corkery, A., & Young, K. (2024). "Harris loss causes some to question what it will take to elect a woman president." PBS. Nov. 8. Accessed 11 Nov. 2024. https://www.pbs.org/newshour/show/harris-loss-causes-some-to-question-what-it-will-take-to-elect-a-woman-president

Onwuachi-Saunders, C., Dang, Q. P., & Murray, J. (2019) "Reproductive Rights, Reproductive Justice: Redefining Challenges to Create Optimal Health for all Women." *Journal of Healthcare, Science and the Humanities*; 9(1): pp. 19–31.

Prentki, T. and Preston, S. (eds) (2009) *The Applied Theatre Reader*. New York, NY: Routledge.

Reid, G. (2020) "A Global Report Card on LGBTQ+ Rights for IDAHOBIT." Human Rights Watch. 18 May. Accessed 2 Feb. 2024. https://www.hrw.org/news/2020/05/18/global-report-card-lgbtq-rights-idahobit.

Tate, J.K. (2022) "Stargate: A Theatre Company of Imagination, Hope, Life skills, and Quality Art for Justice-involved Young Men." In *Applied Theatre with Youth: Education, Engagement, Activism*. Brenner, L.S., Ceraso, C. and Diaz Cruz, E., eds. London and New York: Routledge.

Taub, A. (2023) "A Major Economic Challenge." *New York Times*, Nov. 20. Accessed 2 Dec. 2023. https://www.nytimes.com/2023/11/20/briefing/india-economy-gender-inequality.html#:~:text=But%20India%20has%20one%20of,rate%20is%20about%2060%20percent.

Thompson. J (2009) *Performance Affects: Applied Theatre and the End of Effect*. London and New York: Palgrave Macmillan.

The University of Chicago. (2010) *The Chicago Manual of Style Online* 16th Edition. Accessed 4 Feb. 2024. https://www.chicagomanualofstyle.org/search.epl?q=foreign.

UN Women. (2022) "Explainer: How Gender Inequality and Climate Change are Interconnected." UNWomen.org. 28 Feb. Accessed 27 Feb. 2024. https://www.unwomen.org/en/news-stories/explainer/2022/02/explainer-how-gender-inequality-and-climate-change-are-interconnected#:~:text=The%20climate%20crisis%20is%20not,less%20access%20to%2C%20natural%20resources.

UN Women. (2023) "International Women's Day 2024: 'Invest in Women: Accelerate Progress'." UNWomen.org. 14 Dec. Accessed 24 Feb. 2024. https://www.unwomen.org/en/news-stories/announcement/2023/12/international-womens-day-2024-invest-in-women-accelerate-progress.

Winny, A. and Bervell, R. (2023) "How Can We Solve the Black Maternal Health Crisis?" Johns Hopkins Bloomberg School of Public Health. 12 May. Accessed 28 Feb. 2023. https://publichealth.jhu.edu/2023/solving-the-black-maternal-health-crisis.

World Health Organization. (2021) "Devastatingly Pervasive: 1 in 3 Women Globally Experience Violence." WHO.org. 9 Mar. Accessed 24 Feb. 2024. https://www.who.int/news/item/09-03-2021-devastatingly-pervasive-1-in-3-women-globally-experience-violence.

Part I

Igniting Eco-Activism

1 Decolonizing the Conversation

Sustainable Development Performances in Egypt

Sarah Fahmy

"My English is awful. I can't contribute anything to sustainable development until I'm fluent, so why do you keep asking about our thoughts now? There's no use of it," exclaimed fifteen-year-old Sandy,[1] in Arabic, on the second day of the applied theatre program I facilitated in Aswan, Egypt.

Sandy had barely finished her sentence when the entire twenty-person room of young women erupted in agreement. A couple of attendees chuckled, acknowledging their limited English fluency, and others nodded in response to this seemingly well-established fact. This exchange was only one of multiple examples of internalized oppression voiced by the young women throughout the program about their belief in their ability to enact change. They assumed advocating for sustainable development was contingent upon their knowledge of English as well as belonging to a particular socio-economic class. As a bilingual Egyptian woman who spent most of my childhood in Egypt, this was a sentiment that I sadly anticipated and had once believed in myself. It became clear to me that before discussing potential contributions to sustainable development, it was important to decolonize their minds and perceptions about themselves as young Egyptian women. In both cities, several participants shared that "this program was the first experience [in which] they were taken seriously and could vocalize issues they cared about" (Fahmy, Kan, and Lewon, 2021, p. 14).

In this chapter, I reflect on the facilitation and outcomes of a 2018 applied theatre program focused on sustainable development with fifty-five young women (aged 11–17) in two contrasting cities in Egypt: Alexandria and Aswan. As the program's facilitator, I recount skits devised by the participants in each city and analyze the data that emerged from pre- and post-program assessments. I argue that by decolonizing their minds from the preconception that their participation relies on neocolonial, Eurocentric ways of knowing, this program offers an accessible avenue to support young women in the practice of voicing their opinions on sustainable development. Through community-based approaches, young women may harness the belief that they can responsibly enact positive social change within a community.

To prepare for this program, I adapted, translated, and facilitated the SPEAK Vocal Empowerment Curriculum. Initially developed by Beth Osnes

DOI: 10.4324/9781003341802-3

and Chelsea Hackett with the organization MAIA Impact in Guatemala, the curriculum uses theatre-based exercises to support young women's "physical, emotional, ethical, psychological, civic" growth (Osnes and Hackett, 2017, p. 8). In 2017, Osnes and I facilitated SPEAK workshops in Colorado, United States. Results from both Guatemala and the United States indicated that participation in this program helps young women achieve a greater sense of self-authorship and confidence in their bodies. This led me to investigate its potential to embolden young women's participation in sustainable development practices in Egypt. I previously used quantitative analysis to assess the effect of this program on the young women's voices, language characteristics, and self-perception of their authorship (Fahmy, Kan, and Lewon, 2021, p. 1). Here, I will evaluate the creative outputs and share participants' insights.

In June and July 2018, I collaborated with the Cambridge English Testing Centre at the Arab Academy for Science Technology and Maritime Transport (AASTMT) to facilitate this program. AASTMT has a long-standing commitment to community outreach and service; and the Centre, as the university's sole institute for youth summer programs with locations in both cities, was instrumental in the recruitment initiatives. The program was free and open to all young Egyptian women. Participants were expected to attend all twelve sessions and the culminating public performance. Fifty-five participants joined in total: nineteen in Alexandria (mean age = 13.5) and thirty-six in Aswan (mean age = 14.05). All were bilingual, speaking Arabic as a first language and English as a second. None of the participants had engaged in any prior theatre or performance activities. In Aswan, twenty-one participants attended public school, ten attended an experimental school,[2] and only five attended a private school with a national curriculum. In Alexandria, all attended private schools. Ten attended schools with a national curriculum, one attended an embassy school, and eight attended schools with an international curriculum, indicating a higher socio-economic status than participants in Aswan.

Alexandria and Aswan are historic, tourist cities that are opposites in geography, population density, socioeconomics, and neocolonial presence. Alexandria, on the Mediterranean, is the second most populous, and prosperous city in the country (Index Mundi, 2019), while Aswan is significantly smaller (with only 200 thousand people) (Sabbah, 2015). Located on the Nile in Sa'id Masr,[3] in the southernmost point of Egypt, Aswan has been the center of development initiatives for decades. Other Egyptians typically look down on Aswan residents, particularly those in the bigger cities in the North, like Cairo and Alexandria. While Arabic is the country's primary language, there is an increasing recognition that English is a powerful tool for social mobility, to the point that a mere British or American accent can result in a pay raise (Peterson, 2011). The socioeconomic status of a family is likely to determine the child's proficiency in English based on their access to private education (Aboulfetouh, 2014). Therefore, the aforementioned concerns of the young women in Aswan are rooted in this neocolonial expression of language dominance.

In my work, I aspire to pursue what Alrutz and Hoare describe as a "youth-allied adult," where we work as "creative partners who understand that our own (adult) liberation is bound to the liberation of youth" (2020, p. 57). I intended to elevate, celebrate, and draw upon the participants' experiences, talents, and stories, rather than focus on what they cannot access. Applied theatre could potentially be a cost-effective and sustainable way to increase gender equality and women's civic engagement in the economic and political spheres, as it only requires human willpower and guided facilitation (Osnes, 2015). I used applied theatre to help young women express their thoughts on sustainable development and explore their potential to contribute to their communities. With that in mind, the participants and I discussed systemic oppressive systems, gender-based discrimination, classism, and the impact of Westernization on their daily lives in Egypt.

This research aligns with national and international sustainable development policies. Internationally, the 2030 United Nations Agenda for Sustainable Development prioritizes gender equality and women's rights as the third out of seventeen Sustainable Development Goals (SDGs) (United Nations, 2015; Hawken, 2017). Similarly, the Egyptian government's Sustainable Development Strategy: Egypt Vision 2030 recognizes the importance of women and youth authorship (The Cabinet of Ministers, 2017; Heideman, Romano, and Kabli, 2017). Considerable applied theatre practices have been facilitated by non-governmental organizations and local independent Egyptian theatre companies nationwide. Additionally, there has been a wide range of women's creative authorship and participant-centered creations in Egypt. Describing the country as having a "real … thirst for spaces for people to discuss things," Nada Sabet, Creative Director of Noon Creative Enterprises, stresses the benefits that applied theatre may offer those in Egypt, particularly youth and women (El Shimi, 2013). Nevertheless, the art form remains relatively unfamiliar among the general public in Egypt (Fahmy, Kan, and Lewon, 2021, p. 2).

Program Facilitation

In both cities, I facilitated the entire program in Arabic. I met with each group for ninety minutes every day for twelve consecutive days. The program was split into twelve sessions, with the pre- and post-program assessments conducted on the first and last days. A public sharing took place after the eleventh session. The first six sessions centered on the scientific mechanics of the voice and how it is produced. The last six allowed participants to practice using their voices for civic engagement toward change.

Before arriving in Egypt, I translated the content and assessment materials, modifying some exercises for cultural specificity. For example, one vocal range warm-up involved making repeated sustained sounds, like AEIOU, Ta, Te, Ti, To, Tu, Pa, Pe, Pi, Po, Pu, and Ma, Me, Mi, Mo, Mu, while stretching

Figure 1.1 Participants and Fahmy practicing the daily vocal warm-ups. 2018. Photo by Olivia Attwa.

their arms above their heads to practice feeling how sounds are produced differently with the mouth palate, lips, tongue, vocal cords, diaphragm, and lungs. I added five pairs of Arabic letters that sound similar but differ in tone and sound production, such as (س، ص) (غ، خ) (ق، ك) (ض، د) (ف، ث). Using the Arabic letters, it was very clear when the participants weren't annunciating their letters properly. The participants critically identified which parts of their mouth, throat, and chest they were using to create the sounds, and laughed about needing to reengage certain parts when the sound they produced was the wrong letter in the pair.

Throughout the program, I noticed participants in Alexandria preferred speaking in English over Arabic, often code-switching between the two languages when talking and writing, which I also did. However, in Aswan, given Sandy's comment above about lacking English fluency, I consciously resisted the practice of code-switching. This meant that, at times, I paused, realizing I'd only ever said a certain word in English, like *diaphragm*, *vocal cords*, *climate change*, or *global warming*. When that happened, I took my time to think of the word rather than saying it in English. The participants viewed this as an exciting challenge to see who could say the Arabic word faster than I could. We discussed the problematic nature that our sustainable development discourse was riddled with English words and that while these words existed in Arabic, we rarely used them. By the end of the program, the participants agreed that though English as a global language may be beneficial, it is not needed for them to voice their opinions; they already possess the internal beliefs, knowledge, and expressions to enact change.

Figure 1.2 Participant writing the song lyrics on the board. 2018. Photo by author.

Given their hesitation at the beginning of the program, it was noteworthy that the participants in Aswan were more eager to lead, modify, or propose new activities. By the seventh session, they argued over who would lead an activity that day. They also mentioned teaching their siblings and parents the activities! By leading, they practiced being knowledge creators, challenging the idea that the adult facilitator is the sole educator. For example, they modified the "affirmational song" from the SPEAK program,[4] writing their own lyrics and rhythms to better represent themselves. Participants experimented with clapping rhythms and dance moves, even a Tabla drum,[5] which immediately created a more carefree atmosphere as we all showed off our dance moves.

In Alexandria, participants based their song on an existing English rhythm and had only one Arabic verse. The songs in Aswan started in Arabic, followed by an English verse, then a repeated chorus in Arabic. In both cities, devising the song enabled the participants to practice their autonomous voices and listen attentively until each person finished speaking. They respectfully critiqued others' ideas and offered collective solutions. This practice prepared them to create their skits on sustainable development.

Sustainable Development Skits

The participants devised a variety of skits to address a specific issue in their community and how they envision solving it. First, we went around the circle several times, identifying their greatest concern, then divided into groups of four to address each issue. Using Image Theatre (Boal, 1985, p. 136-140), we then created silent static human sculptures depicting the issue. The first tableau was the problem, the second portrayed the potential solution, and the third showed how they would transition from problem to solution. After performing and providing feedback, they added dialogue to create skits. Interestingly, participants in both cities (without my interference) picked similar topics. The Alexandria skits featured water pollution in the Mediterranean and its impact on the ecosystems, the impact of chlorofluorocarbons (CFCs) in the atmosphere, eradicating homelessness, and gender inequality between siblings. The Aswan skits featured water pollution in the Nile, eliminating illiteracy, gender inequality between siblings, bribery in the healthcare system that privileges wealthy patients, reliance on private tutoring and rote learning, the overconsumption of social media platforms, and gender equity in the workplace.

I will describe two examples to demonstrate how participants used applied theatre as an educational tool to raise awareness. The first, from Alexandria, is a three-minute skit about CFCs that interlaces comedy and sarcasm. The skit opens with Kenzy sitting at home and Mariam rushing in, exclaiming, "Disaster, Kenzy, it's a disaster!" Kenzy's immediate response is, "I failed, right? I know I must have," referring to her high school exams. Mariam brushes her off and proclaims, "No, worse, we're going to drown!" She goes on to explain how the sea levels are rising due to the glaciers melting in the North and South Poles and rhetorically asks, "So all the coastal cities will drown, and who lives on the coast?" while Kenzy replies, "Us!" Mariam uses her body language before responding verbally, which is characteristic of Egyptian Arabic speech patterns. They exchange several sarcastic remarks about things they will lose if Alexandria drowns, before talking about CFCs, where the gas is found, and what they can do to limit its use. They share their solutions, such as properly disposing of their refrigerators, turning off air conditioners when they leave a room, and restraining from spraying a bug when they see it. Afterward, they each proclaim how they will spread awareness to reduce the use of CFCs by specifically targeting their circle of family and friends: Kenzy commits to posting about it on Facebook, and Mariam promises to print posters to distribute at her school. After the skit, several audience members (parents and friends) asked Kenzy and Mariam further questions about CFCs, acknowledging their lack of knowledge about what contains CFCs, and noting how the young women's comical characters will help them remember the science.

The fast-paced humor in the skit is characteristic of daily Egyptian culture and communication styles, wherein jokes have been hailed "the bread and butter of the Egyptian personality" (Abdou, 2021). Jokes are powerful tools for sociocultural and political critique in Egypt; throughout the centuries, Egyptians have "resort[ed] to sarcasm and humor to express their own viewpoint or evade their problems," and as a mechanism to alleviate stress (El-Menawy, 2017).

The second example, from Aswan, is a three-minute skit about excessive social media consumption, which the participants asserted was distracting young people from paying attention to their education and their desire to actively engage in their communities. The performers place three chairs in a triangle format. At the tip of the triangle, Kermina sits dressed in a white shirt. The costume resembles her teenage innocence and susceptibility to social media, which distracts her from the real world. Nardine and Martina sit behind her, dressed in black to represent social media. We watch Kermina wake up, wash her face, and eat breakfast, while constantly checking her phone as Nardine and Martina mirror her every action. Mira, playing the role of Kermina's mother, yells from off-stage several times about dinner, family visiting, and schoolwork. Kermina brushes her off every time. Whenever Kermina tries to put her phone down, her shadows restrain her or block her, bringing her attention back to the phone. Halfway through the skit, Kermina falls to the ground from the pressure of trying to emulate the lives of influencers on social media. After a few moments of struggle, the skit ends as she pushes the shadows away from her and rises, declaring, "There is no point in just watching other people live their lives and trying to copy them. I must study and go find what I love in order to contribute to my society." After the performances, numerous parents approached me, noting how surprised they were that their daughters could address such complex societal issues, creatively. Several admitted that they never thought theatre could be an educational tool, until now; and told me they've noticed how their daughters speak and conduct themselves with more confidence in family gatherings now, as a result of their participation in this program.

In both examples, the young women creatively presented solutions to community problems they identified, envisioning a sustainable future through self-authored skits performed in Arabic. In Alexandria, the participants told me performing in Arabic allowed them to express themselves authentically and showcase their humor. Likewise, in Aswan, performing in Arabic demonstrated their ability to engage in sustainable development independently of English. This response enabled us to delve into "language as a carrier of culture" (wa Thiong'o, 1986) and explore the ways that creative authorship, sense of self, and language are all connected. We further discussed how English may be a language for communication yet emphasized the importance of continuing to explore their use of Arabic to fully envision their participation in sustainable development efforts.

Individual Pre- and Post-Program Assessments

In addition to their performances and the quantitative speech and language data (Fahmy, Kan, and Lewon, 2021), I recorded and analyzed participants' responses to the following prompts: "Hello, my name is …" "My voice is important to me because …" "My greatest community concern is …" and "One idea I have to improve my community is to …" Recorded in Arabic and English before and after the program,[6] these prompts served as a helpful self-assessment metric. I analyzed their responses using Dedoose – a computer-assistive qualitative data analysis software (SocioCultural Research Consultants, 2016).

The participants' reactions to the prompts are noteworthy, reflecting the neocolonial influence that perceives English as a sign of educational status in Egypt. In Aswan, most participants expressed hesitancy to share their thoughts, due to their limited English fluency. Whereas participants in Alexandria were more self-assured, insisting they didn't find it valuable to respond in Arabic, as it wasn't important to them. Interestingly, the Aswan participants had a lot to say in Arabic and often offered more creative responses than the Alexandrians. We spent the program dismantling their beliefs that their worthiness to contribute to sustainable development is contingent upon their bilingual fluency.

In the pre-program recordings, most participants in both cities struggled to identify how their voice and individual contribution could impact their community. Post-program, however, participants demonstrated a greater understanding of their impact, saying things like "I can deliver my message," "I express myself without fear," and "I can stand up for myself and my rights." Furthermore, they articulated their greatest community concerns in more detail, for example, going beyond "global warming" to specify and explain the "decreasing River Nile levels."

Initially, participants were uncertain about their ability to contribute due to their age and (in Aswan) location, saying they wouldn't be listened to. By the end, however, they recognized that when they practice enacting change as youths, they are better-prepared adults. Participants' reflections on how to effect change varied from self-motivation (e.g. "I can start by focusing on myself") to peer support (e.g. "I can encourage my peers to speak up") to public advocacy (e.g. "to work hard or fight for their rights"). They mentioned using social media to directly influence and model to their circles how they can partake in sustainable action. Some even mentioned, "I can help those in poverty by fundraising or volunteering with NGOs to reduce homelessness" or "I can write to the government as I believe that my actions matter." They specified their visions of how to eliminate illiteracy, increase girls' equal access to education, and reduce pollution.

Figure 1.3 Participants and Fahmy "passing the squeeze" and sharing reflections as part of their daily closing practice. 2018. Photo by Olivia Attwa.

Their pre- and post-responses reflect how theatre programming may support young women to articulate their thoughts and become more confident in stating their opinions. Analyzing the data by language and city further revealed that English proficiency is not essential for producing knowledgeable responses on sustainable development. These results surprised the participants, especially in Aswan. They mentioned feeling more assured that bilingualism is not a requirement to be agents of change.

Conclusion

The benefits of the program have also outlasted its duration. In 2018, the president of the university with which I collaborated and the governor of Aswan commended the young women's authorship and invited them to perform a few skits and a song at a locally televised public event hosted by the governor. In 2019, I was recognized by the Egyptian Minister of Expatriate Affairs for this study's contributions. I was one of the three humanities scholars out of the total thirty expat researchers invited to present at the *Egypt Can: Education Conference* to support the country's initiatives toward sustainable development and educational reform.

I have since maintained my relationships with the Ministry of Expatriate Affairs to brainstorm the revival of arts education in Egypt, including meeting with schoolteachers from middle and high schools across the Aswan governorate to discuss the incorporation of performance-based pedagogy. Most importantly, I have maintained my relationship with the university collaborators and the young women. One of the greatest benefits of the program is its success in facilitating friendships and building community. I am still in touch with most of the participants and have become more than a facilitator but also an older sister figure in many ways. Since the program ended, we have chatted on WhatsApp and Instagram, discussing ongoing program benefits, their college applications, celebrating achievements, and planning future programs – and I make sure to see them when I visit. As a facilitator, these conversations nourish and challenge me to envision new ways of listening to young women to co-develop liberatory and sustainable applied theatre programming.

Support Material

Additional images can be found under "Support Material" at www.routledge.com/9781032377636.

Notes

1 All the names used in this article are pseudonyms to protect participants' identities.
2 Experimental schools in Egypt teach their STEM subjects in either English or French.
3 A region in Upper Egypt that spans from southern Cairo to the Sudanese border.
4 The affirmational song was intended to support participants in exploring the power of their vocal range through song.
5 This drum is traditionally used in Egyptian, and Middle Eastern, North African music. In Egypt, it is common to belly dance following the rhythm of the drum.
6 I used the Voice Analyst App on my iPad. This was a free software that allowed me to easily categorize the pre- and post-program recordings in both languages (total of 440 recordings).

References

Abdou, M. (2021) "El Nokta: How Egyptians Use Jokes to Vent." *Egyptian Streets*, 28 November. Accessed 2 Nov. 2023. https://egyptianstreets.com/2021/11/28/el-nokta-how-egyptians-use-jokes-to-vent/.

Aboulfetouh, M. (2014) "Parents' Attitudes towards Their Children's Bilingualism and Cultural Identity in International Schools in Egypt." May. Accessed 2 Nov. 2023. http://dar.aucegypt.edu/handle/10526/3955.

Alrutz, M. and Hoare, L. (2020) *Devising Critically Engaged Theatre with Youth: The Performing Justice Project*. New York: Routledge. https://doi.org/10.4324/9781315102283.

Boal, A. (2002). *Games for Actors and Non-Actors*. 2nd Edition. Adrian Jackson, trans. London and New York: Routledge.

El Shimi, R. (2013) "Interactive Play on Sexual Harassment Rides Cairo's Metro (VIDEO)." *Al Ahram Online*, 16 February 2013, sec. Arts & Culture. Accessed 2 Oct. 2023. http://english.ahram.org.eg/News/64829.aspx.

El-Menawy, A. (2017) "Egyptians' Sense of Humor Is Very Telling." *Arab News*, 21 September. Accessed 2 Oct. 2023. https://www.arabnews.com/node/1165171.

Fahmy, S., Kan, P-F. and Walentas Lewon, J.W. (2021) "The Effects of Theatre-Based Vocal Empowerment on Young Egyptian Women's Vocal and Language Characteristics." *PLoS ONE* 16 (12): 1–20. https://doi.org/10.1371/journal.pone.0261294.

Hawken, P. (2017) "Women and Girls." In *Drawdown: The Most Comprehensive Plan Ever Made to Reverse Global Warming*, pp. 76–82. New York, NY: Penguin Books.

Heideman, K., Romano, J.C. and Kabli, O. eds. (2017) "Women Driving Positive Change in the Middle East." *Wilson Center: Middle East*, March. Accessed 3 Nov. 2023. https://www.wilsoncenter.org/sites/default/files/media/documents/misc/women_driving_positive_change_in_the_middle_east.pdf.

Index Mundi. (2019) "Egypt Demographics Profile 2019." Accessed 4 Oct. 2023. https://www.indexmundi.com/egypt/demographics_profile.html.

Osnes, B. (2015) *Theatre for Women's Participation in Sustainable Development*. New York, NY: Routledge.

Osnes, B. and Hackett, C. (2017) *SPEAK Vocal Empowerment Curriculum*.

Peterson, M.A. (2011) *Connected in Cairo: Growing up Cosmopolitan in the Middle East*. Bloomington, IN: Indiana University Press.

Sabbah, S.S. (2015) "Is Standard Arabic Dying?" *Arab World English Journal* 6 (2): pp. 54–65.

SocioCultural Research Consultants. (2016) *"Dedoose." Web Application for Managing, Analyzing, and Presenting Qualitative and Mixed Method Research Data*. Los Angeles, CA: SocioCultural Research Consultants. https://www.dedoose.com/.

The Cabinet of Ministers. (2017) "Sustainable Development Strategy (SDS)." *Egypt Vision 2030*. Accessed 2 Oct. http://www.cabinet.gov.eg:80/English/GovernmentStrategy/Pages/Egypt%E2%80%99sVision2030.aspx.

United Nations (2015) "Sustainable Development Goals: The 2030 Agenda for Sustainable Development." Accessed 2 Aug. 2023. https://sustainabledevelopment.un.org/?menu=1300.

wa Thiong'o, N. (1986) *Decolonising the Mind: The Politics of Language in African Literature*. Nairobi: James Currey Ltd/Heinemann.

2 Patnaik's Cyco Theatre in India

Grassroots Environmental and Gender Activism

Pranab Kumar Mandal

Introduction

Born in 1964 in Odisha in Eastern India, Subodh Patnaik is one of India's foremost contemporary theatre practitioners. His company, Natya Chetana (Theatre for Awareness), aims to educate the rural people of Odisha by exposing the policies and actions that have threatened their existence. His performance practice is rigorously field-based and workshop-oriented to "build awareness … with regard to their human right to live, express, get justice" and "to create public opinion about the strength of original Indian cultural expressions" (Patnaik 2019, p. 31). His plays dramatize the plight of the common people, especially the farmers, the Dalits, Indigenous tribes, migrant workers, daily wage-earners, and especially, women's marginalization. As this essay demonstrates, Patnaik's participatory theatre is particularly effective in its focus on the intersection between environmental justice and gender.

Background

As a graduate of drama from Utkal University in the early 1980s, Patnaik became interested in social service[1] and theatre as a tool for social awareness, which later helped him shape his artistic practice and establish Natya Chetana in 1986. Patnaik consciously rejects anything Western (e.g., theatre style, actors' training, choice of performance space) in favor of Indigenous content and forms (e.g., songs, folktales, dress, props, acting techniques, etc.). To make his theatre portable and accessible, he uses non-traditional performance spaces, live music, simple yet aesthetic stage set-ups, and handmade, environmentally friendly props.

Patnaik associates his theatre practice with the idea of loko natya (people's theatre), a concept he learned from Eugène van Erven, whose workshop on community theatre in Kolkata inspired Patnaik to "create theatre among non-artists" (Ranta-Tyrkkö 2010, p. 66). He was further inspired by the practice of the Indian People's Theatre Association (IPTA), which was active from the 1940s to 1960s and held performances on different socio-political issues in unconventional performance environments. Despite using the term "people's theatre," Patnaik disavowed the

DOI: 10.4324/9781003341802-4

party-based[2] political association of IPTA. Although thoroughly political in subject matter, his work has deliberately refrained from engaging with party politics. His notion of a people's theatre led to a core practice, which he still follows, participatory theatre-making involving "non-artists" as performers and collaborators.

This idea was reinforced during Patnaik's training in the 1980s under the Delhi-based non-government organization (NGO) Participatory Research Asia (PRIA), which fosters "development initiatives to positively impact the lives and improve the quality of living of marginalized and excluded sections of the society ... through training and educational programmes" (Ranta-Tyrkkö 2010, p. 192). Patnaik was also influenced by the notable theatre personality Badal Sircar, with whom he trained in Bhubaneswar. Although he deviated significantly from Sircar's style, he incorporated a lot of Sircar's ideology, especially the body-based acting techniques and workshop-based performances. Abandoning the expensive urban halls and proscenium theatres, Sicar brought performances to the people, free of charge: performing in the streets, marketplaces, railway stations, playgrounds, etc.

Cyco Theatre

Cyco Theatre is a site-specific form conceived by Patnaik to engage with community concerns in the rural areas of Odisha. As the name indicates, "Cyco" is a theatre modeled after bicycle expeditions. Although he originally spelled it as "Psycho," since he wanted to disturb the psyche of his spectators, he later had to change it to "Cyco," as the term "psycho theatre" created confusion among scholars and informed spectators, who mistook it as a form of the already established psycho-therapeutic theatre practice. The use of bicycles also aligns with Patnaik's commitment to environmental sustainability. His company only travels to the community by walking or cycling, never by any motor vehicle. Cycling has significantly reduced the cost of production; moreover, bicycles connect organically with the spectators for whom cycling is a major form of transportation, helping gain the villagers' trust and drawing them to the performance (Natya Chetana 2001, pp. 5–6).

The process of Cyco Theatre involves field visits to learn about the subject, collaborating with local organization/s and volunteers (some of whom also join the project as actors), developing a collaborative script, touring around the village, performing in non-traditional spaces within a three-quarter round set up, recording the reaction of the spectators, and engaging in a dialogue. Patnaik begins by partnering with a local or grassroots organization, facilitating collaborative research to develop the script and follow up on the issues after the performance. As such, Cyco Theatre projects includes extensive fieldwork to understand the community's concerns, recent incidents, Indigenous or traditional cultural forms, and other pertinent information. Volunteers from the local community join his company for intensive workshops toward a collaboratively written script. A typical Cyco Theatre project covers distances

Figure 2.1 Performers before starting their Cyco Theatre expedition. 2012. Photo by Natya Chetana.

ranging from 100 to 300 kilometers; however, with his play *Pachisi Bhuta* in 1994, the group covered 700 kilometers throughout a 100 performances. As of 2019, Patnaik's group had covered a total of 9,433 kilometers on bicycles to perform 2,774 Cyco Theatre shows (Patnaik 2019, pp. 19–21).

Figure 2.2 Performers climbing a slope of a hilly surface during a Cyco Theatre expedition. 2012. Photo by Natya Chetana.

Over the decades, Patnaik has insisted that his performances are intended to raise consciousness rather than simply entertain the audience. Therefore, he chooses not to hold the performances in the evenings when the villagers are in a relaxed mood after a day's hard labor and typically enjoy various types of entertainment, for example, Jatra,[3] the cinema, or the orchestra. Instead, Patnaik chooses an unusual time, the early mornings, before the villagers set out for work. Moreover, according to Patnaik, audiences appreciate the shows for their themes more than their production values (Natya Chetana 2000, p. 6). On the day of the performance, without giving prior notice to the community, the actors arrive at a pre-fixed village location. They invite the audience to join them by beating drums, singing songs, or circulating posters.

The company keeps the duration of the performance short, preferably within thirty to forty-five minutes to suit the spectators' morning schedule. Having been carefully scripted to evoke the audience, they then engage in a dialogue to explore potential solutions to the issues raised. If the spectators clap at the end, Patnaik feels that the performance is a failure; the performance is only considered successful when the spectators are motivated to dialogue, incited to take action, or introspectively silent.

Rather than charge for tickets, a saree is placed on the ground after the performance for the villagers to voluntarily donate whatever is possible, be it money, vegetables, rice, etc. This is what he calls natya viksha (begging

Figure 2.3 Performers draw the attention of the villagers to the time and location of the performance; usually an hour before the starting time. 2012. Photo by Natya Chetana.

Figure 2.4 Director of Natya Chetana addresses spectators before the start of a Cyco Theatre performance. 2012. Photo by Natya Chetana.

for theatre). Like Gandhi, who greatly influenced Patnaik's philosophy, Patnaik believes in living the simple, humble life to engage with the issues in rural areas. Because of the company's approach, the local people can more easily trust them and share their experiences.

Figure 2.5 Natya viksha: local spectators donating their humble offerings to the performers after the end of the performance. 2012. Photo by Natya Chetana.

Gender Justice

Patnaik focuses on five issues: "environmental exploitation, women's suffering, economic exploitation of the poor, cultural degradation, and break of unity" (Natya Chetana 2013, p. 10). The greatest number of plays, however, have been based on environmental and gender issues. More than thirty-five Cyco Theatre plays were performed between 1986 and 2018, promoting environmental and gender justice at the grassroots level in India. Most of these productions expose the systemic violence experienced by marginalized rural communities.

Some of the major environmental challenges for women in rural Odisha include poverty, water crises, river pollution, drought, deforestation, cyclones, unhygienic living conditions, malnutrition, maternal morbidity, and infant mortality. The premise of ecofeminism is comprised of "domination, exploitation, and colonization" of women, human "others" (children, poor, and marginalized communities), and nonhuman species under anthropocentric, androcentric, and capitalist agencies (Warren 2000, xiv). Environmental and gender justice movements are thus considered interconnected, as demonstrated in the Cyco Theatre plays.

As one of the poorest states in India, Odisha is known for various poverty-related issues, such as starvation, malnutrition, etc. According to the National Family Health Survey [4] Report 2023, Odisha is presently the eighth poorest state in India with a multidimensional poverty ratio of 15.68% (NITI Aayog 2023, xviii). Such abject poverty results in part from misgovernance at the state level, which has historically encompassed a "backward, conventional and stagnant agrarian economy with an extremely weak industrial base, gross unemployment and abysmally low incomes with dire distress" (Ranta-Tyrkkö 2010, p. 23). More specifically, a recent study conducted in January–February 2023 across 9,856 villages in Odisha, reported that more than "40 percent of households in at least 15 districts of Odisha have no access to safe drinking water," with 56.12% of villagers using "contaminated water in their consumption," "28.51 percent of villagers" using "muddy water," and 29.55% of villagers drinking iron-filled water (*The Statesman* 2023). Health care and multidimensional development projects have been slow to reach the population across the Indian villages, cementing the discriminating divide between the urban and the rural. As members of poverty-ridden rural households, women undergo a double layer of marginalization at the patriarchal and environmental levels.

Patnaik's play *Mathie Pani* (One Pot Water) depicts the patriarchal structure of Indian society, where women are relegated to domestic beings with the responsibility of doing household chores, including fetching water from long distances, even when they are physically unwell and vulnerable. In Odisha and many other states, such as Rajasthan, Bihar, Bundelkhand, Jharkhand, etc., the common image of women in the villages walking on a trail with heavy water-filled vessels on their heads signifies a form of gendered victimization. This situation is worsened by the refusal of state authorities to develop adequate drinking water stations in rural areas. In Maithreyi Krishnaraj's words, "[w]omen's responsibility for carrying and using water exemplify universal patriarchy, which results in certain structural and symbolic inequality between men and women" (2011, p. 38), with further restrictions imposed on Dalit women who are "debarred from using fresh water in nullas" and menstruating women who are "forbidden to fetch water from the village's fresh water source as they are seen to, 'pollute' the source" (Joshi, 2011). Reportedly, "39.1% of women living in rural India have to step out of their homes to fetch water" with 16% of them having "to walk between one kilometer and 5 [3.107 miles] (even 6 in Bundelkhand) kilometers twice a day to fetch water" (Sharda 2018; Sagar 2019). According to the *Hindustan Times*, "[e]very second woman in rural India walked an average 173 kilometers [107.497 miles] ...to fetch potable water in 2012, making her trek 25 kilometers [15.534 miles] longer than what it was in 2008–09" (2014). These treks have critically endangered the "physical and mental health" of rural women, including the "emotional stress of managing with little water and maintaining menstrual hygiene" (Chandran 2018). This is in addition to the problem of girls dropping out of school[5] due to early marriages and responsibility for household chores – all of which demonstrate how patriarchy shapes women's social, educational, political, economic, and environmental status (Pandit 2022).

Figure 2.6 Cyco Theatre performance of *Mathie Pani* in a typical open-air space. 2012 Photo by Natya Chetana.

Figure 2.7 Cyco Theatre performance of *Mathie Pani* in a typical open-air space. 2012. Photo by Natya Chetana.

Patnaik's play also highlights the adverse impact of state-centered, top-down water management in rural Odisha. The Department of Rural Water Supply and Sanitation "installed a mega water supply project at the Badi Chowk area near the village of Gobindapur in 2015, but even that water was unfit for drinking purposes" because of its high salinity (*The New Indian Express* 2023). Moreover, according to the head of Surala village in Ganjam district, "The matter was taken up with the higher authorities several times in the past, but it continues to remain unaddressed" (*The New Indian Express* 2023). The water governance in the Ganjam villages as in many other villages in India, has continued to follow a "traditional top-down, state-centered" model instead of a "decentralized and globalized multi-actor" model where local stakeholders are brought into environmental policy-making bodies (Kulkarni 2022, p. 948). Despite being the most direct victims of the water crisis in India, women have not been included in the policy-making bodies that decide on the water management in their villages, even though women's active participation has been advised by environmental scholars and activists (Shiva 1988; Krishnaraj 2011). Rather than rely on governmental action, *Mathie Pani* opens a dialogue among the villagers in hopes of finding a solution to their crisis. In particular, *Mathie Pani* engages female spectators in this dialogue.

In rural India, even in cases where men fetch water with a pot, they are looked down upon for doing women's work. *Mathie Pani* demonstrates this dynamic when Mini's husband Debraj goes to fetch water on account of Mini's ill health; people make fun of him for his shameful act of carrying water for his wife. Humiliated, ego-hurt, and angry, Debraj comes back home and throws the pot of water in disgust – compelling the pregnant Mini to go out to fetch water. As Mini falls because of her unsteadiness with a pot full of water on her head, she is rushed to the hospital in town – further highlighting the healthcare crisis in the villages in India. Mini dies at the hospital giving birth to a baby girl, and the play ends with a message that "water is a need for all, so collection and carrying the water is a responsibility of all men and women both" (Natya Chetana 2013, p. 14). By exposing the environmental and gendered oppression of women, and by promoting female leadership at the level of policymaking, the play actively participates in the ecofeminist movement at the grassroots level. Natya Chetana collaborated with a local NGO, Sikshasandhan, to conduct roughly eighty focus group interviews with local villagers and twenty interviews with government officials or representatives. The group also collaborated with Gram Vikash (Rural Development Association) of the Ganjam district for fieldwork, production, and follow-up after the performance.

Conclusion

The impact of the thirty-five-minute play *Mathie Pani* is quite extensive. The Cyco Theatre expedition happened over two phases: The first phase occurred over twelve days from April 1 to 12, 2012, and covered 239 kilometers [148 miles]; the company performed fifty-one times in different villages in the Ganjam district, attended by 9,615 villagers including 2,540 women. The second phase, from October 1 to 11, covered 237.4 kilometers [147.5 miles] by bicycle to hold fifty performances, attended by 11,587 spectators including 3,557 women. According to their project report, school-aged audiences followed the group to see performances in more than three nearby villages, as the group usually held more than four performances a day in different locations (Natya Chetana 2013, p. 19). No audience member left during any performance of the play. Audiences sat in silence at the end of the performances without any clapping or celebratory expressions; instead, they engaged in discussions on traditional gendered practices that push women into dehumanized conditions, especially in terms of health care, environmental matters, and societal norms (2013, p. 19). According to the conversation generated among the local audiences after the performances, the villagers received the play "as a precautionary announcement to take care of women's health and particularly pregnant women." Some villages "started negotiating with Gram Vikash to materialize water and sanitation projects" to increase access to drinking water (Natya Chetana 2013, p. 20).

Patnaik's activism addressing the water crisis in rural Odisha and its impact on women is central in other Cyco Theatre plays such as *Pani Pani Pani* (*Water Water Water*), 1988, dealing with the political management of water resources; *Pani Chanda* (*Collecting Money for Water Supply*), 1989, dealing with economic politics relating to water supply; *Kala Pani* (*Black Water*), 1998 and 2004, dealing with water pollution and overall destruction of river ecosystem; and *Jharana Jhariba* (*The Spring will Spring*), 2013, dealing with river-drying issues. In these plays, as well as in the case of *Mathie Pani*, Patnaik's emphasis on environmental care includes green dramaturgy – such as the use of bicycles as the primary medium of transport, daylight as the primary source of light for performances, open-air rural locations as performance spaces, live music and bare voice without artificial amplifiers, and hand-made props and hand-woven costumes/cloths that are reusable.

Through its 101 touring performances covering 476 kilometers [295.7 miles] by bicycle and reaching out to 21,202 spectators, including 6,097 women, the Cyco Theatre production of *Mathie Pani* materialized its objective of creating awareness among rural audiences toward motivating them to identify the sources of their environmental and gendered oppressions and brainstorm possible solutions from the grassroots.

Notes

1 Patnaik was formally initiated into social work when he was part of the National Social Service (NSS) unit of his college. He acknowledges that his involvement in the NSS activities in college has significantly shaped his interest in social work.

2 IPTA was conceived of as the cultural wing of the Communist Party of India (CPI), where writers, artists, and activists of leftist ideology all over the country took part to voice for liberty, equality, and social justice in colonial India. Established formally on May 25, 1943, in Bombay, this association gradually developed a theatre movement across the Indian states, where theatre practitioners held performances to protest against various forms of socio-political oppression.

3 Jatra, originating from the Sanskrit word – "yatra" (meaning "to go" and referring to its nature of touring with a performance) is a popular form of Indian performance which caters mostly to the rural audiences. Representing the social, religious, and moral issues that interest the rural India, this touring performance form includes three-side-open performance stage, music, stylized acting techniques, elaborate costumes, and often melodramatic endings.

4 National Family Health Survey is a large-scale survey conducted by the government across India.

5 According to a report published in *The Times of India* on June 14, 2022, of the "over 21,800 girls who dropped out of school before the 2019–20 school year, just over 13% girls did so as they were required for housework and almost 7% did so as they were married off" (Pandit, 2022).

References

Chandran, R. (2018) "Forced to Walk Miles, India Water Crisis Hits Rural Women Hardest." *Reuters*, July 13. Accessed 7 Nov. 2023. https://www.reuters.com/article/us-india-water-women-idUSKBN1K318B

Hindustan Times. (2014) "Rural Women go the Extra Mile in Walk for Water." August 24. Accessed 7 Nov. 2023. https://www.hindustantimes.com/india/rural-women-go-the-extra-mile-in-walk-for-water/story-KGcr9rkU62Qiw66cSifnVN.html

Joshi, D. (2011) "Caste, Gender and Rhetoric of Reform in India's Drinking Water." *Economic and Political Weekly*, 4 (18): pp. 56–63.

Krishnaraj, M. (2011) "Women and Water: Issues of Gender, Caste, Class and Institutions." *Economic and Political Weekly*, 46 (18): pp. 37–39.

Kulkarni, S. (2011) "Women and Decentralised Water Governance: Issues, Challenges, and the Way Forward." *Economic and Political Weekly*, 46 (18): pp. 64–72.

Natya Chetana. (2000) *Natya Chetana Practices: Psycho-Cyco Theatre*. Bhubaneswar: Natya Chetana.

Natya Chetana. (2001) *A Cultural Action Organisation and Resource Centre for Mass Awareness*. Bhubaneswar: Natya Chetana.

Natya Chetana. (2013) *Mathie Pani: Project Report*. Bhubaneswar: Natya Chetana.

NITI Aayog. (2023) *India—National Multidimensional Poverty Index: A Progress Review 2023*. New Delhi: NITI Aayog.

Pandit, A. (2022) "Girls Drop out of Schools Due to Early Marriage, Housework." *The Times of India*. 14 June. Accessed 26 Aug. 2023. https://timesofindia.indiatimes.com/india/girls-drop-out-of-schools-due-to-early-marriage-house-work/articleshow/92195487.cms

Patnaik, S. (2019) *In Search of Modern Indian Theatre Style vis-à-vis Theatre in Odisha with Special Reference to Theatre by Natya Chetana*. Bhubaneswar: Natya Chetana.

Ranta-Tyrkkö, S. (2010) *At the Intersection of Theatre and Social Work in Orissa, India: Natya Chetana and Its Theatre*. University of Tampere, PhD dissertation.

Sagar, D. (2019) "39.1% Women Living in Rural India Have to Step out of Their Homes to Fetch Water: Gaon Connection Survey." *Gaon Connection*, July 1. Accessed 20 Nov. 2023. https://www.gaonconnection.com/gaonconnectionsurvey/women-have-to-walk-long-distance-to-fetch-water-which-affects-their-health-gaon-connection-survey–45331

Sharda, S. (2018) "In Bundelkhand, Women Walk 6 km to Fetch Water." *The Times of India*, June 13. Accessed 20 Nov. 2023. https://timesofindia.indiatimes.com/city/lucknow/in-bundelkhand-women-walk-6km-to-fetch-water/articleshow/64565648.cms

Shiva, V. (1988) *Staying Alive: Women, Ecology, and Survival in India*. New Delhi: Kali for Women.

The New Indian Express (2023) "Water Crisis Looms Large in Ganjam village in Odisha." June 18. Accessed 20 Nov. 2023. https://www.newindianexpress.com/states/odisha/2023/jun/18/water-crisis-looms-large-in-ganjam-village-in-odisha-2586185.html

The Statesman. (2023) "40% Households in 15 Odisha Dists. Lack Access to Drinking Water." March 14. Accessed 20 Nov. 2023. https://www.thestatesman.com/india/40-households-in-15-odisha-dists-lack-access-to-drinking-water-1503162292.html

Warren, K. J. (2000) *Ecofeminist Philosophy: A Western Perspective on What It Is and Why It Matters*. Lanham, MD: Rowman and Littlefield.

3 Resisting Ecological Colonialism in the Niger Delta

Indigenous Women and the Beni Kamai Festival Theatre

Stephen Ogheneruro Okpadah

Introduction

In assessing the impact of the global scramble for natural resources, especially in the Global South, we must not simply consider the economic displacement but also the spiritual well-being of Indigenous peoples. The Niger Delta refers to the geographical enclave into which the River Niger empties its waters. According to Ikelegbe and Umukoro (2016), the region contains 33% of the Nigerian population of 220 million. The Niger Delta is comprised of oil-producing states with a population of thirty million people: Akwa Ibom, Imo, Delta, Edo, Ondo, Abia, and Bayelsa. From the nineteenth century through the first quarter of the twentieth century, the major colonial enterprise in the region was in the extraction and production of palm oil. This trade went alongside rubber extraction. The discovery of natural crude oil in 1956 in Oloibiri charted a new course in the region's socio-cultural, economic, political, and especially, geographical environment. Foreign extraction companies plundered the physical environment with impunity, while foreign and local elites and their bourgeoise consumers benefitted from the subjugation of the ecosystem.

I refer to this kind of land intrusion by foreigners and control of its people and resources as ecological power (which I abbreviate as "ecopower"). This is a political process in which non-Indigenous people dominate and determine the direction of environmental conditions of host communities, thereby advancing economic and occupational displacement of human and non-human native inhabitants. Human beings are treated as resources: utilized, managed, and controlled in the same light as their non-human counterparts to advance the capitalist agenda and process (Kerr 2008; Altman 2009). The demand for this human resource expanded from the fourteenth through the seventeenth century. At this time, Africans were transported from their continent to the Americas to work as enslaved laborers on farms owned by individuals and corporations in Europe. In fact, the colonial actors first exploited humans before advancing the exploitation of non-human resources.

Ecopower has impacted women and children in the Niger Delta more than any other group in the region. In "Sustainability from Bottom Up:

DOI: 10.4324/9781003341802-5

Women as Change Agents in the Niger Delta," Charisma Acey (2016) notes that "The impact on women's roles in society is acute in Niger Delta communities where women bear the responsibility of household survival of female-headed families or of their household unit within a polygamous household configuration" (p. 157).). For example, in the Ijaw society, the largest ethnic group in the Niger Delta, farming and fishing are exclusively female professions. In the words of Olayiwola Oluwajenyo Fasoranti and Eunice Eloghokunmo Ote (2017), "In Ijaw land, there seems to be a division of labor in the traditional economy, such that men are usually tappers of raffia palm and carvers of canoes while women engage in fishing and fish trading" (p. 573). Women thus bear the brunt of the ongoing oil spillages on rivers from oil exploration by oil companies and illegal stealing of crude oil (bunkering). As a result, they catch little or no fish and must till oil-degraded lands.

Moreover, "health risks associated with the oil industry also have severe implications for women's reproductive health" (Schobat 2014, p. 25). As an indigene of this region, an oil-producing community whose people have experienced decades of the tragedy of crude oil, I have witnessed how women have suffered immensely from the tragedy of ecopower. They return from their farms, disillusioned with the poor harvest of crops, and from the rivers, by their inability to catch a decent supply of fish. The few existing jobs that the oil companies provide only benefit the men, and it is the menfolk, who sit at the negotiation table with the oppressors to discuss the direction of environmental action. The womenfolk have realized how ineffective the men's protests against ecopower have been. In what follows, I examine how women have thus reacted to ecopower in the Niger Delta. In particular, I examine how traditional festival theatre in the Niger Delta serves as a political resistance against ecopower, with special reference to the role of women in the Beni Kamai Festival in Patani, a riverine community in the Niger Delta.

Women and Ecological Resistance in Nigeria

The discourse of resistance against ecopower has often centered on the exploits of the male gender and placed the role of women at the periphery (Shochat 2014). Names such as Isaac Boro and Ken Saro-Wiwa, the two most prominent Nigerian environmental activists of the twentieth century, continue to receive recognition in academia and globally. Furthermore, the works of scholars of petro-culture in the Niger Delta, such as Aghoghovwia and McGiffin (2023) and Iheka (2021)), continue to feature the militant advocacy of Asari Dokubo, Government Ekpemupolo, and Ateke Tom against environmental colonialism by internal and external colonialists. Such scholarship risks the assumption that women have been docile on issues that affect their environment. In fact, the Niger Delta women have been involved in the campaign against ecopower in the region.

The history of women's resistance against the unfair treatment meted on them by oil corporations and their local accomplices in the Niger Delta dates back to the 1980s. Sharon Shochat notes that:

> [T]he first documented protest took place in June 1984 in Ogharefe, a rural community in Delta State, where the community's entire womenfolk, totaling several thousand women, sieged the production station of Pan Ocean, the oil company operating on their land. The protesters refused to negotiate and eventually stripped naked, demanding compensation for land loss and pollution damage.
>
> (2014, p. 139)

Women's protest for the restoration and sustenance of the region's environment has been mostly among the Urhobo and Ogoni. In 1986, a major protest that predominantly involved women took place in Warri, Delta State. For days, the womenfolk shut down the activities of the oil company. Moreover, in the 1990s, Ogoni women joined their male counterparts to protest Shell's massive destruction of their environment and the resulting proliferation of poverty from the land grabbing by the oil companies.

The womenfolk also view environmental justice from a broader perspective than their male counterparts. Acey contends: "Women conceive environmental justice from the perspective of spirituality, food security, impact on traditional knowledge and the very structure of indigenous culture, elements related to the sowing, protection of traditional seeds and wisdom and knowledge passed on from generation to generation" (2016 p. 159). Women understand that when the lands and water bodies are degraded, they are unable to continue with their trade of farming and fishing; feeding the family, especially the children, becomes a nearly impossible task. Their focus on environmental justice encompasses environmental mitigation in the form of cutting down carbon emissions, restoration of already degraded lands and water bodies, and retrieval of the commons (lands and rivers) forcefully taken away from them by the oil companies and government. According to Acey, "in order to achieve environmental justice, indigenous women propose healing and empowerment strategies, as well as the strengthening of indigenous ancestral knowledge, to find the path for "our spirits to return to us and restore our collective dignity, our identity and our confidence in our own strength" (2016, p. 159). The environmental justice framework proposed by women in the Niger Delta is a path to building strong partnerships with non-human lives, such as animals and plants, that sustain their existence.

Protests against environmental injustice by the women of Ekakpamre, an oil-producing community from which I hail, have highlighted the economic and spiritual displacement as a result of oil spillages. In the early years of the first decade of the twenty-first century, the women of Ekakpamre raised concerns about the constant oil spills into their farms and three streams at Ekroghen, Ekenewharem, and Ekrezeghe. These three streams are connected.

Hence, whenever there is an incident of oil spillage on one, the spillage flows rapidly into the other streams. The lives of the community women revolve around the stream where they fish to eat and sell in neighboring communities. Water from the streams also serves domestic functions. Additionally, in Ekakpamre, there are certain water bodies that inhabit fish considered sacred, and as such, must be protected: they must neither be killed nor eaten. The extraction enterprise led to the depletion of the sacred rivers that inhabited these sacred fish. The injustice against women and the demystification of the cultural and supernatural essence of the people led to the women's protest against the oil companies.

Women-led resistance has also been a challenge to masculinity. The male gender plays a major role in environmental despoliation. For instance, in Ekakpamre, men often focus on the monies they get paid by the government and oil companies as compensation for the region's degradation. By contrast, in the first decade of the twenty-first century, women-led protests against the oil companies and the government's silence over the degradation of their lands and rivers. Their means of resistance against ecopower includes Indigenous festival theatre, which I investigate in what follows.

Festival Theatre as Resistance against Ecopower in Nigeria

Indigenous festivals in the Niger Delta are multi-functional. While entertainment has been a cardinal function of most festivals, they also serve to bridge the connection between the living, the dead, and the unborn: "The originality of traditional African festival, is not far-fetched from the fact that, it is an event created for the communion and reunion between the living and their ancestors and also, it is a periodic occasion, for the meeting of gods and mortals" (Okpadah 2018, p. 43). The Oloolu Masquerade Festival in Ibadan and the Ogba-Urhie in Otor-Ughievwen and Edjophe communities, all in Nigeria, are examples of sacred festivals celebrated to strengthen the cord between the living and the supernatural entities.

Most Indigenous African festivals, including those I have mentioned above, are characterized by total theatre esthetics of role-play, dance, music, and chants (Rasheed 2001; Anigala 2006; Nzekwu 2014). Costumes, makeup, and other performance esthetics are used to amplify the believability of role-play; dances are used to accompany the music and drumming. The setting for these festivals is the river, the village square, the king's palace, the market square, or the forest. Festival theatres that have the river as their setting have sacred undertones. Among the people of Urhobo and Ijaw in the Niger Delta region, there is a belief in the potency of rituals carried out at the river band and inside of the river. I have witnessed sacrifices carried out at the riverbank and the testimonies that accompany such religious practices. Indigenous aquatic festivals, such as those celebrated in the Niger Delta, are water-based "periodic celebrations of special significance in the cultural calendar of a people" (Anigala 2006, p. 7). Although in most riverine communities and cities, aquatic festivals, featuring colorful boat regattas, are performed for entertainment, some aquatic festivals in Ijaw land transcend this function. The Beni Kamai Festival Theatre in Patani, for instance, holds a religious-ritual purpose and also serves as a site of resistance against ecopower. I have observed the significant role of this Indigenous festival in environmental restoration and the role of women in this praxis.

Traditionally, women have often been relegated to the background in Indigenous African festivals. For example, the Oro Festival in Yoruba land is an all-male festival. In fact, it is forbidden for women to see the Oro Masquerade. The Oro and Egungun are all-male cult festivals, which display masculinity, the prowess of the male gender, and the frailty of their female counterpart (Isichei 1988; Akanji and Dada 2012). However, in the Beni Kamai Festival Theatre of the Patani people, women play the role of performers and "spec-actors." Patani is a riverine settlement where the indigenes are mostly fishermen, yet it is the women who sell the fish at the market as a source of livelihood and rely upon the trade to feed their family; hence, they recognize the negative implications of any change in the state of the water. Thus, women are concerned about the state of the aquatic environment and anthropogenic and capitalogenic factors that tend to dislocate it. Post-development scholars and experts argue that genuine development must emanate from the bottom. In the same way, climate justice should be created from the bottom to the top. According to Jens Hoff (2016), "Climate change researchers are now recognizing that the local level is an important component of any future solutions to the challenge of climate change" (p. 39). The Beni Kamai Festival Theatre is one medium by which women express their resistance. As a sacred festival, it becomes a space for political and socio-ecological contention.

The structure of Beni Kamai is predicated on the geography where it is celebrated: the bank of the river. The performance begins with all participants standing on the shore of the river dressed in white attire to symbolize purity and innocence. Among the Urhobo people of the Niger Delta and beyond, the white costume is also worn whenever there is a negotiation between humans and spirit entities. Adherents of the Igbe religion in the Niger Delta, Osun Festival in Western Nigeria, and other Indigenous Afro-Asian religious practitioners utilize white clothing in the process of worship (Kwakye-Opong and Adinuku 2015; Precious and Chielotam 2015). In the case of Beni Kamai, while the white costume is a symbol of purity of the human character in her appearance before the spirit co-performers, it also remains a metaphor for the need to purify this performance site. Therefore, the color is a semiotic of cleansing and an agency for the cleansing of the degraded aquatic environment. Hence, the environment for the festival performance must be freed from despoliation.

The women standing in front of the river are virgins (adhering to a traditional view of gender roles, female virginity, and the transcendental).

Most Indigenous African societies venerate virginity: There is a belief in the connection between female virginity and the spiritual realm. Therefore, certain rituals can only be carried out by virgins. The chief priest, also dressed in white, ritually cleanses the young women by applying a liquid substance to their hands. Afterward, he dances in front of them as other women clap to the drumming and song while the priest continues to dance to the rhythm of the music, which serves as the opening glee of the performance. Music and dance are used to usher in the Indigenous African narrative. Three masqueraders, dressed in white regalia, join the priest in the dance ritual. In the traditional African setting, masqueraders are believed to be the spirits of long-departed ancestors who return to the physical realm of existence to commune with the living (Amankulor 1982; Enekwe 1987; Ododo 2015). Masqueraders hold a cutlass in their left hand, in aquatic masquerades, it is usually shaped in the structure of an aquatic creature. Here, the cutlass is shaped like a crocodile with a tail to portend the ruthlessness of the masqueraders.

Women are central to the festival celebration, perhaps playing an even more active role than the men. All the women on the shoreline stage carry a bowl containing various foods, such as rice and stew, and place them in front of the virgins. Semiotics comes into play in the context of the display of cooked food in front of the river. First, the food is brought to serve the psychic entities to thank them for their provision of good health, good harvest, and fertility for the living. It is believed that a bountiful harvest is determined by the supernatural entities that reside in the river. The Beni Kamai Festival Theatre is an acknowledgment of the existence of supernatural entities in the rivers, and as such, their abode must be protected from the caprices of capitalist-induced devastation. The river is home to Edjo (the river goddess among the Urhobo people) and Olokun (the water goddess among the Yoruba people). The women also play the role of musicians. One of the women holds a microphone to sing as two men play the drums to accompany her oral rendition and that of the other women. Some of the women are also involved in the instrumentation; they play the traditional sticks that serve as gongs, emitting a melodious sound that accompanies the drumming by the two men.

The songs, dances, drumming, and chants play the role of connecting the living with the supernatural entities. These supernatural entities also act as spectators and performers. At some point, the performers, especially the women's immersion in the performance process, causes a transmogrification from the physical world into the metaphysical realm of existence, where the virgins are taken into the world of the principality of the past; they explore the present and connect with the future. At this point, they become a communication medium between the living and the spiritual water entities. Hence, the virgin characters become vessels in the hands of the supernatural entities, through which the latter convey their messages and tidings to their adherents.

The portrayal of this transmogrification comes into play when an old woman takes a basin full of food to the water and gives the spiritual entities food to eat by pouring it out into the river. Immediately after she pours the food into the water, she falls into a trance. She is held by the chief priest, who is aware of the female's transition from the realm of the living into that of the transcendental. Interaction with supernatural beings entails the creation of a dual existence, where the character has little or no consciousness of the physical realm. Her withdrawal from the metaphysical existence back into the secular realm is a gradual process. Women take hold of the old woman by both arms and pull her from the river. The young women take the plates of food from the ground as the singing, dancing, and drumming intensify. They hand the plates of food to the chief priest one after the other. The priest presents these foods to the water spirits.

The women see the festival theatre as entertainment, ritual, and agency for the aquatic environment. This environment is a conglomeration of the natural water body and the organisms and plants that live in, on, or around it. The songs sung by the women are in praise of the water that harbors the entities that live therein. The entities in the aquatic terrain sustain human life in the physical and spiritual dimensions. Fish in the river serve as food for people. If a good harvest must be made by fishermen, then they must be appeased to enable a bounteous harvest. In the same vein, some of the songs are directed at the supernatural beings who give their adherents their socio-economic wants. It is believed that these entities provide financial wealth, children, and protection against enemies. Thus, the water is seen and treated as not just a large body of liquid that flows but is viewed as a living thing. This is the reason names and genders are attributed to most water bodies in the Niger Delta region. In the aftermath of this ritual dance, the performers take basins filled with water from the river to their houses. There is a belief in the healing potency of water taken from the river.

Conclusion

Beni Kamai is an exercise against environmental colonialism. It is a theatre that explores the sacred as a space for ecological interconnectedness; the whole of the shoreline and the river itself serves as the performance space. It is in this space that the living and the supernatural entities interact. The Beni Kamai Festival Theatre is a paradigm for protest against ecopower in riverine oil-producing communities in the Niger Delta. Beyond the Beni Kamai, festival theatre can be a space where women assert their power and find a voice on issues concerning ecological degradation. Indeed, women are more impacted by environmental colonialism than any other group in the region. The celebration of the Beni Kamai Festival amplifies environmental consciousness among the people of Patani. For the supernatural deities that reside in the water to remain potent, their abode must be rid of all anthropogenic processes that degrade it.

References

Acey, C. (2016). "Sustainability From the Bottom Up: Women as Change Agents in the Niger Delta". In: Christina, S., Chris L., Jenny O., and Sachiko N., (Eds), *Women's Emancipation and Civil Society Organisations: Challenging or Maintaining the Status Quo?* (pp. 157–182). Bristol, UK: Bristol University Press.

Aghoghovwia, P. and McGiffin, E. (2023). "African Ecopoetics". In: Julia, F., Mary N., Bernard, Q., and Orchid, T., (Eds), *The Routledge Companion to Ecopoetics*. (pp. 285–294). London and New York, NY: Routledge.

Akanji, O., and Dada, O. (2012) "Oro Cult: The Traditional Way of Political Administration, Judiciary System and Religious Cleansing among the Pre-Colonial Yoruba Natives of Nigeria." *Uluslararası Sosyal Aratırmalar Dergisi: The Journal of International Social Research*. Vol. 5 (23), pp. 19–25.

Altman, Y. (2009) "From Human Resources to Human Beings: Managing People at Work." *Human Resource Management International Digest*. Vol. 17 (7), pp. 3–4. https://doi.org/10.1108/09670730910996464

Amankulor, J. (1982) "Odo: The Mass Return of the Masked Dead Among the Nsukka-Igbo." *TDR*. Vol. 26 (4), pp. 46–58.

Anigala, A. (2006) *Traditional African Festival Drama in Performance*. Ibadan: Kraft Publishers.

Enekwe, O. (1987) *Igbo Masks: The Oneness of Ritual and Theatre*. Lagos: Nigeria Magazine.

Hoff, J. (2016) "'Think Globally, Act Locally': Climate Change Mitigation and Citizen Participation," In: Hoff, J. and Gausset, Q., (Eds), *Community Governance and Citizen-Driven Initiatives in Climate Change Mitigation*. London: Routledge.

Iheka, C. (2021). *African Ecomedia: Network Forms, Planetary Politics*. Durham, NC: Duke University Press.

Ikelegbe, A., and Umukoro, N. (2016) "Exclusion and Peacebuilding in the Niger Delta of Nigeria." *Journal of Peacebuilding and Development*. Vol. 11 (2), pp. 25–26.

Isichei, E. (1988) "On Masks and Audible Ghosts: Some Secret Male Cults in Central Nigeria." *Journal of Religion in Africa*. Vol, 18, (1) pp. 42–70. https://doi.org/10.2307/1580836

Kerr, I. (2008) "Are Humans Resources?" *Career Development International*. Vol. 13 (3), pp. 270–279. http://dx.doi.org/10.1108/13620430810870511

Kwakye-Opong, R., and Adinuku, G. (2015) "Costume as Medium for Cultural Expression in Stage Performance." *Arts and Design Studies*. Vol. 8, pp. 1–20. https://core.ac.uk/download/pdf/234685822.pdf

Nzekwu, O. (2014) "Masquerade." In: Yemi, Ogunbiyi (Ed.). *Drama and Theatre in Nigeria: A Critical Source Book*. 2nd Edition. Lagos: Nigeria Magazine.

Ododo, S. E. (2015) *Facekuerade Theatre: A Performance Model from Ebira-Ekuechi*. Maiduguri: Society of Nigeria Theatre Artists.

Okpadah, S. (2018) "A Study of Festival Theatre to Flekstival Theatre: Emuodje Flekstival of Ekakpamre in Southern Nigeria as a Paradigm." *Africology: The Journal of Pan African Studies*. Vol. 12 (1), pp. 41–56.

Precious, E., and Chielotam, A. (2015) "Costume and Makeup, as a Tool for Cultural Interpretation: A Study of Egba Festival of the Kokori, Isoko Local Government Area of Delta State." *Arts and Design Studies*. Vol. 36, pp. 22–34. https://core.ac.uk/download/pdf/234686057.pdf

Rasheed, M. (2001) "'The Theatre of Healing: 'Ehoro-Iba' Masquerade Festival of Agbeyeland as a Paradigm." *The Abuja Communicator: Abuja Journal of Culture and Media Arts*. Vol. 2 (11), pp. 111–122.

Shochat, S. (2014) *Oil and Women's Political Participation: A Sub-national Assessment of the Role of Protests and NGOs in Nigeria*. PhD thesis, London School of Economics and Political Science. Accessed 26 Nov. 2023. https://etheses.lse.ac.uk/1029/

Roundtable Discussion with Lisa S. Brenner, Evelyn Diaz Cruz, Sarah Fahmy, Pranab Kumar Mandal, and Stephen Ogheneruro Okpadah

Lisa: Thank you for making time to be here. All of your essays deal with the critical topic of climate justice, notably from a Global South lens. Can you share any connections you noticed?

Stephen: When I read Sarah's discussion of sustainable development practices in Egypt, I saw similarities to the work I did recently in Nigeria with young people, ages 19–23, using creative pieces to interrogate the environmental degradation in the Niger Delta. With Pranab's essay, I realized that the core of our three chapters is how theatre can increase the agency of people in Indigenous communities who have undergone terrible situations of environmental devastation.

Sarah: I appreciate that our writing focuses on community-led and community-informed work rather than a top-down approach. It feels as if we're in community around the world.

Pranab: These things matter more when we engage with grassroots communities because it is their language and issues that we are dealing with. In this present time of climate crisis, the Indigenous communities around the world are affected the most, particularly the women. But it is also so good to see how women in Indigenous communities are staging environmental protests. We are emphasizing their experiences, their struggles, and their narratives of resilience and resistance.

Sarah: The work that we're doing demonstrates the value that can emerge when centering Global South voices on the ground rather than the Western opinions that say, "This is how you can achieve sustainable development. Now go implement it."

Evelyn: Can you talk about why you use performance as a means for activism or the efficacy of performance in your work?

Pranab: Applied theatre can break the hierarchy between the actor and the "spec-actor." Cyco Theatre targets the rural masses and presents the community's concerns before them to provoke dialogue. I don't feel any other form can generate dialogue so authentically.

DOI: 10.4324/9781003341802-6

Sarah: I view theatre as an inherently African Arab form of community development in my work. I do a lot of storytelling. I use a lot of comedy. There's conversation, singing, music, and dancing. These are all fundamental to creative expression, specifically for Egyptian women. In using the term "applied theatre," I mean doing theatre with communities and not having a pre-written script given to them. I find that it goes back into the origins of theatre, and how we can reclaim it from an African viewpoint. The Egungun is one of the oldest examples of theatre in the world. Ancient Egypt has the oldest existing script of a performance. I'm interested in going back to these histories, which have been colonized, and bringing them back as tools for education, community building, solidarity, and activism. It takes away the idea of who has value over someone else in the room. All the participants' opinions and perspectives are brought to the forefront. We're working with what people possess rather than what they don't have.

Lisa: Is there a distinction between product and process in your work?

Stephen: In the Beni Kamai Festival and other river-based festivals in the Niger Delta, the ritual act itself brings about the outcomes. The Beni Kamai integrates women performing a series of rituals on the bank and in the river. This reveals the role of women as guardians of the river. These ritual acts, which have performative elements embedded in them, create environmental consciousness in participants and people of the community.

Sarah: The product is the primary focus for funding and producing scholarship for the academy. It's for the outsiders, but the process is for the participants. The process fuels me to do this work because it's where the real magic is experienced. The distinctive moments that happen throughout the process are what create a long-lasting impact, moments the audience doesn't get to see in the final product. I've experienced this with the young women I worked with. I'm still in touch with many of them over WhatsApp or Instagram, even months after the program has ended. One of them, for example, contacted me to say, "I was really scared to speak up in class, but I actually auditioned for a play at my school, and I was cast." I would have never expected this. We did do a play, and the audience came and watched it. But they would not have known of this specific outcome that speaks to the magnitude of the influence of this work.

Pranab: Cyco Theatre has many different elements that need to fall in place in a genuine way to make the product happen: First, there are the local organizations the group collaborates with at the beginning to conduct field research. They play an important role in identifying the right questions and involving the local people who are going through that conflict. Cyco Theatre also involves "non-actors" from the community who need to understand that they're not getting any materialistic gain from being a part of this project. The live musicians and the directors are also important, as are the local spectators. The Hindu scripture, the Bhagavad Gītā, says in Chapter 2, verse 47: "Do your duty without concerning with the results." Every process should be meticulously and genuinely followed, and then the end product will be good.

Evelyn: Was there ever a time that you learned from a failure in doing this work that you can share?

Pranab: Cyco Theatre is not designed to be a "successful" aesthetic pleasure or to provide entertainment but rather to take away catharsis. The plays never end with melodramatic or happy endings. For example, with the play *Mathie Pani,* which I discuss in the chapter, the audiences are made to experience how gender discrimination in society places women in vulnerable conditions. After the performance, they questioned why the water crisis was not adequately addressed by the local government and decided they must go through the local administrative bodies.

Stephen: At the end of every applied theatre project I facilitate, I realize that there was something I failed to do. For instance, my theatre workshop on deforestation with young people in a community in the Niger Delta region in July 2023 took place under a tree. Although the workshop was a success, I realized that perhaps it would have been more successful if the site was in the bushes where trees had been cut down. I imagined how participants would have responded to the subject of deforestation in a site where they are physically attached to trees that are already cut down by loggers.

Evelyn: Can you speak to the possible ethical dilemmas inherent in this work?

Sarah: As an Egyptian woman who is also a US-based facilitator and academic, I have to check myself almost every step of the way. I unintentionally carry where I live, my education, and my positionality. For example, am I code-switching between Arabic and English when I speak? How am I recruiting ethically to ensure a variety of backgrounds, and that the programs are free of charge and don't conflict with school schedules, travel plans, or other expectations? How do I ensure that I'm continuing a decolonial praxis in the writing, the analysis, and the presentation?

Stephen: In my practice, I first consider whether participants are comfortable being part of the process and with the information being used for the research. For instance, my recent applied theatre engagement was in an environmentally devastated oil-producing community. The project used verbatim theatre to amplify the voices of women and young people. I had a series of semi-structured interviews with some fisherwomen and female farmers. Before conducting these interviews, I assured them that their identity would be concealed due to the political sensitivity of the issue being researched. During the verbatim performance, their names were pseudonymized and only recorded in audio format. I also practice what Taiwo Afolabi (2021) calls "ethical questioning." This involves posing questions that do not infringe on individual rights and cultural nuances. For example, in the Northern region of Nigeria, where religious fanaticism is prevalent, I take care to pose questions that will not intrude on the religious beliefs of the community.

Lisa: Pranab, one practice we were curious about is Natya Chetana's use of hidden cameras to record the reactions of the spectators. Can you talk about why that is integral to the work?

Pranab: The task is to listen to the community's experiences and dramatize them as it is. The reactions are silently recorded to determine whether the play successfully draws the audience's attention and whether they're feeling connected with the content. Once there was a woman who had two babies with her, one at her side, another on her lap, and she was trying to see what was being done. As the play progressed, she gave one of the babies to an elder and came closer. She silently watched the performance and started crying at the end because she felt that it was her story that this group was performing.

The reactions are important. The photographs are used for post-performance discussions and interior assessment to help the work be more authentic; although they may also be shown to the spectators. Also, maybe things are quite different in India. You don't always need somebody's permission to take photographs.

Evelyn: I appreciate this clarification. Are you saying that the company only uses it for the process? They don't publicize these photographs, or use them for commercial gain, which may be another distinction, correct?

Pranab: Yes.

Lisa: Where do you believe the work needs to go from here? What conversations do we need to be having?

Sarah: We need to develop sustainable long-term practices and programing that are not solely reliant on neoliberal funding structures and parameters of success, especially from an international perspective. And, how to work without burning out? How can we take care of our facilitators and ourselves? Given that many of us work within institutions and have other full-time jobs, how do we find that balance? Also, how might online tools fit into sustainable long-term programing?

Pranab: In India, there were many forms of grassroots performance practices in pre-colonial theatre. But today, applied theatre is hardly used as a form to communicate with and stand by the community. Applied theatre should be used more often in a country like India and taught more widely in schools and colleges.

Stephen: As applied theatre practitioners and scholars, we should engage in urgent issues, including climate injustices against women and young people in local communities. Also, we should deeply engage the marginalized communities being researched to achieve authentic participation. Applied theatre practitioners should also critically examine the positive impacts of their projects on communities.

Lisa: Thank you. To close, what are some things you're going to take away from this conversation?

Sarah: I'm excited to see more of the inclusion of environmental feminist praxis in applied theatre, especially from the Global South and a decolonial perspective. I'm looking forward to being more in community with other scholars and practitioners doing this work and connecting further.

Pranab: In India, we constantly go through these questions of colonial hangovers. I am glad to say that Cyco Theatre is a decolonized form of theatre practice. It takes so much consideration not to follow anything that is not Indian, which is not indigenous. As with Stephen's emphasis on Indigenous communities, that's what Cyco Theatre does.

Stephen: We are all decolonizing the conversation, amplifying voices in communities that are being environmentally degraded.

Pranab: This is the first time I have been a part of a roundtable because usually, we write chapters, our job is done, and we don't get to meet our colleagues or the editors. So thank you so much for giving me this opportunity to meet you all.

Evelyn: Hopefully, there will be more opportunities to connect. Thank you all for your inspiring work.

References

Afolabi, T. (2021) "From *writing* ethics to *doing* ethics: *ethical questioning* of a practitioner." *Research in Drama Education: The Journal of Applied Theatre and Performance*, 26(2), 352–357. DOI: 10.1080/13569783.2021.1880317.

For more information see:

Fahmy, S. (2023) "Performing on the Nile: young women embodying ecofeminist decolonial care." *Environmental Communication*. DOI: 10.1080/17524032.2023.2296853.

Part II

Inspiring Playful Interventions

4 Picking up the Sequins

Drag Storytime Performances, Applied Theatre, and Queer Joy

Zachary A. Dorsey

Once upon a Time …

I interviewed the former executive director of New York City chapter of Drag Story Hour (DSH), Rachel Aimee, and asked her to describe her favorite moment from any Drag Storytime performance. She laughed and quickly shared that she'll always remember the response to drag performer Harmonica Sunbeam asking her young audience if they knew what a drag queen was. One child raised their hand and theorized that a drag queen was "a cross between a dragon and a queen." Aimee found the answer and the ensuing discussion "adorable" (2019). I find the anecdote charming and also instructive. The child's response concisely figures drag performers as royalty, as fierce and powerful, as leaders to be looked up to, and as rare and wondrous creatures of fairy tales that one might wish to have more a part of our everyday lives. This moment of dialogue captures the essence of Drag Storytime writ large: the fun, surprise, meaning-making, and insight that comes from a performer dressed in drag reading books out loud. While few Drag Storytime performers would think to label their work "applied theatre," most acknowledge that their lessons about gender, positivity, friendship, and imagination happen *through* the drag performances during these Storytimes, including those call-and-response moments as the children help the drag artist read and respond to a story.

I argue that Drag Storytimes are a mode of applied theatre. Drag artists choose, rehearse, and perform scripts in libraries, bookstores, classrooms, and community spaces. They make use of theatrical elements (costume, hair, make-up, and sometimes, sets, props, and even puppets) in the creation of their fabulous personas as a way of communicating with their specific audiences. Although the songs and dances they might share and the characters they embody are different from those that the drag performers present to an exclusively adult audience at a nightclub or a boozy drag brunch, they are still intentionally deploying performance to affect the hearts, bodies, and minds of their audiences. As Jan Cohen-Cruz describes in *Local Acts: Community-Based Performance in the United States*, "the artists' craft and vision are at the service of a specific group desire" (2005, p. 91). With Drag Storytimes,

DOI: 10.4324/9781003341802-8

that desire is a celebration of stories and storytelling as a way of supporting children and their families as they continue "dreaming about what life could be" (p. 93) as a way of making a more equitable, just, and kind society.

The audience participation (singing, dancing, and most importantly, the dialogue with the performer) is vital to the event; the children and adults in the audience are co-creating the Storytime with the drag artist and their collaborators as they explore gender justice and other themes together. Certainly, as Tim Prentki and Sheila Preston suggest in their introduction to *The Applied Theatre Reader*, this is theatre for, with, and by a community (2008, p. 10), particularly when the improvisations and conversations that emerge are considered central to the endeavor. In Drag Storytimes, everyone collectively explores gender and creativity and learns from one another, be it the discovery of a new favorite story or the co-construction of a new "window" or "mirror" through the performance. Prentki and Preston articulate that "those who engage in applied theatre are motivated by the belief that theatre experienced both as participant and as audience, might make some difference to the way in which people interact with each other and with the wider world" (2008, p. 9). The goals of DSH and other Drag Storytime artists, librarians, and even the adults who bring children to these events fit within this definition. I suggest that educators, scholars, publishers, and theatre artists looking to explore the range of activities under the umbrella of applied theatre might begin to use Drag Storytimes as a particularly meaningful and memorable example of all that the field can encompass and accomplish.

In this essay, I explore the ways that drag artists apply their theatre in these events, performing as storytellers, entertainers, and educators for the children in the audience, as well as for parents or caregivers. I detail the communities and constituents that Drag Storytimes engage with, explain some of the philosophies and best practices that practitioners leverage, and examine the ways that Drag Storytime can and should be understood as an applied theatre practice. I conclude by articulating "queer joy" as both a subject and method for Drag Storytime performances. Throughout, I interweave my own experience as an organizer, collaborator, audience member, and interviewer, foregrounding the words of others (from my interviews) as often as possible. Though I am not a Drag Storytime performer myself, I unashamedly locate myself as a supporter and avid fanboy of all who participate in this vital and vibrant work.

From 2018 to 2020 I collaborated with a student of mine who performs in drag as Dreama Belle, and also with Angela Critics, the Children's Services Manager of the Jefferson-Madison Regional Library in Charlottesville, to create "Queens Who Read" events.[1] We were not a part of the Drag Queen Story Hour organization, which in 2022 changed its name to DSH for inclusivity's sake and to better represent the breadth of performers' identities. But like DSH and the other Drag Storytime groups that have been growing in popularity and renown since 2015, our work boiled down to a drag performer reading stories to children (mostly between the ages of 3–8)

Figure 4.1 Drag performer Dreama Belle brings joy to the Jefferson-Madison Regional Library in September of 2019. Photo by the author.

and their families. Sometimes there was song and dance, and occasionally a craft project. There was always discussion during and between the stories. We often themed the events with titles like "Be Who You Are" and "Love is Love." The readings centered on kindness, friendship, imagination, and laughter, and I'm endlessly proud of our achievements. At the crossroads of education, entertainment, and gender justice, Drag Storytimes like ours are a future-making project, where parents bring their children to explore gender and identity in positive, affirming ways, ideally before gender norms and gender violence are inflicted on the child from the world outside the Storytime.

Around the same time that I began working with Dreama Belle, I started researching the growing international phenomenon of Drag Storytime performances by attending these events around the United States (and once COVID began, around the world virtually via Zoom, Facebook Live, and Instagram Live). Over the last few years, I have also been interviewing the performers, organizers, and librarians who make these events. DSH suggests on its website that "DSH captures the imagination and play of the gender fluidity of childhood and gives kids glamorous, positive, and unabashedly queer role models. In spaces like this, kids are able to see people who defy rigid gender restrictions and imagine a world where everyone can be their authentic selves!" (DSH, 2023). This aptly describes what I've observed in the well over 100 performances I have attended.

"Who are the People in your Neighborhood?"

With deference to *Sesame Street*, it is important to investigate the "neighborhood" of individuals who come together to create and consume a Drag Storytime performance. Most frequently, Drag Storytime events take place in public libraries, and so drag performers work with librarians to make these performances happen. Drag Storytimes also take place in bookstores, community centers, classrooms, and even at corporate events, so the owners or managers of those spaces and establishments are involved as well. DSH performers are often accompanied by facilitators who support the drag performer and liaise with the venue staff and audience. Sometimes these facilitators have leadership roles within the organization, and sometimes they are another drag performer out of drag supporting a colleague. Drag Storytime performers may have additional collaborators – we framed my role within Queens Who Read as a dramaturg – and when events are created to record and/or broadcast, camerapersons and technology experts may be involved as well. Other people involved in a Drag Storytime performance might be in charge of publicity, security, or even funding the event. At present, DSH is the only Storytime group I know of that has an additional layer of executive directors, board members, and organizers of local chapters.

Further collaborators for these Drag Storytime performances include the audiences, of course: primarily children and their families or caregivers who accompany them. Sometimes infants, pre-teens, and teenagers are a part of the audience as well, and sometimes audience members include those who self-identify as a part of the queer community, those who want to support the library, bookstore, or center, or even just those who are curious about the Drag Storytime phenomenon.

The communities that Drag Storytime performances engage with are varied and depend on the location, design, medium, and frequency of the event. In their excellent article "Drag Pedagogy: The Playful Practice of Queer Imagination in Early Childhood," Harper Keenan and Lil Miss Hot Mess suggest that "DQSH seems to uniquely thread the needle between queer activism and broad cultural acceptance. That is, DQSH creates spaces for young children and families to immerse themselves in LGBT-themed stories, and does so in ways that seem to genuinely reflect queer ways of being and relating" (2021, p. 441). Providing a clear census of who attends Drag Storytime performances is outside the scope of this project, but suffice it to say, those who are in attendance seek out a safe and inclusive environment where they might gather with others who similarly wish to enjoy a drag performer reading stories and sharing messages of positivity, kindness, self-expression, anti-bullying, and community-making. Like many instances of applied theatre practice, while the folks who attend Drag Storytimes come from different demographics, they form a community (however briefly) by going to the event and interacting with others. Moreover, many choose to return again and again at subsequent Storytime events at that location, drag-focused and otherwise. I also understand that some audience members do what I have done – find a Drag Storytime performer whom they enjoy and then attend their readings regardless of the venue, even if it means traveling across a city, into another town, or traveling out of state.

Johnna Percell, a DC Public Library employee in the Outreach + Inclusion department, indicated to me that libraries are "supposed to support our community and help them facilitate their learning goals and community building activities that they want to do, and not to impose our own standards on them. As much as I love my field, we haven't always done a good job of being representative of our communities" (2019). Drag Storytime performances open up spaces (like libraries, bookstores, schools, and centers) to the telling of inclusive stories and the celebration of diverse ways of being in the world. This is only possible because of the range of folks who assemble and work together to make these events happen, including the individual librarians who fight for libraries to be safe and welcoming spaces for everyone, and the parents and caregivers who bring their children to the Storytimes.[2] In *Utopia in Performance: Finding Hope at the Theater*, Jill Dolan articulates that "live performance provides a place where people come together, embodied and passionate, to share experiences of meaning making and imagination that can describe or capture fleeting intimations of a better world" (2008, p. 1). Similarly, in "Royal Reading: Drag Pedagogy and the Art of Queer Literacy," Lil Miss Hot Mess and Harper Keenan suggest that DSH offers "strategies for joyfully creating community, challenging social norms, and transforming ourselves and the world around us" (2023, p. 57). Using a mode of applied theatre practiced in libraries (and similar spaces) Drag Storytime artists facilitate precisely this opportunity for community gathering and transformation by embodying more expansive notions of gender.

In separate interviews, librarians Angela Critics and Johnna Percell both offered the same analogy to explain how Drag Storytimes work best when they provide "a window and a mirror." Percell described:

> I think Drag Storytimes do a really good job showing people an option for yourself up on the stage and your little brain is expanding one more option for your future. So, it's a mirror in that way, or it's a window and you've never encountered anything like this. And now your little brain has expanded one more option for how other people can exist in the world. […] That's going to be a huge learning opportunity.
>
> (2019)

Drag Storytimes are complex performances where audiences are taught to practice empathy, to think about the lives of the characters in stories and the drag performer in front of them, and the experiences of others writ large.

Drag Storytimes' windows and mirrors, then, enable serious but playful work for all involved, artists and young and old audiences alike.

Realness and the Serious Play of Drag Storytimes

Authenticity and presence are central to the Drag Storytime experience. Children notice and tune out when performers go on autopilot, only perform for the adults in the room, or aren't invested in the story they are reading. Drag artist Clare Apparently notes that just standing in front of children isn't enough to entertain them, much less provide them with a meaningful role model. As she described in an interview with me, she approaches her work instead as "I'm not here talking at you, I'm here for you. And with you" (2019). Establishing sincere connections with the individuals in the audience is as essential to a successful Drag Storytime as a gorgeous gown, a funny wig, or glamorous makeup. DSH organizers, librarians, and other Drag Storytime collaborators teach drag performers to read dialogically, to pause mid-story, and after each story to ask questions of the children in the audience. Doing so catches and holds their attention, of course, and also pushes children to think about the themes at play, as well as helps them feel a bond with the performer. I've also witnessed countless performers complimenting children on their answers to questions, their dancing and singing, or their outfits and smiles. Even most of the online or pre-recorded Storytimes I've watched still feature moments where the potential children in the viewing audience are addressed. Being entertaining matters; but being interactive is essential to the teaching of the books' messages by these storytellers in drag, as they work to create a community that will listen to and empathize with the stories as well as one another.

Authenticity pays off in these performances. I was moved while listening to Miss Amie play the guitar for children while singing "The Rainbow Connection," which she later shared had a particular personal meaning for her. At the Storytime I attended, Miss Amie's performance was warm and genuine, and she took time to make clear eye contact with all the children, pausing to talk to a number of them. In an interview, Miss Amie described how after one performance, "A little girl wanted to get a picture with me, and her mom took the picture and then [the mother] started crying and she said: 'My daughter is incredibly autistic, and this is the first time she has ever taken a picture with someone and not started screaming'" (2020). Throughout my interviews, the majority of people I spoke with shared similar moments of meaningful connections between the performers and children. There is a common knowledge among those who participate in Drag Storytime performances that authenticity is essential to the endeavor – that the children are going to be themselves, and that they're going to notice if the performers aren't being real and present with them.

Within drag theory and the popular drag lexicon, "realness" can signal a range of things, from being able to pass (within an identity or category), to being believable, to bringing a certain degree of commitment or ferocity. The first executive director of DSH, who reads in drag as Ona Louise, explained to me in an interview that many DSH performers define drag to their young audiences simply as "when you dress up to be your favorite made-up character" (2019). Not all Drag Storytime performers actively discuss what drag is, but those who do find ways of communicating to children that even if drag and character exploration is "dress-up" or "made-up," it is also not *not* real, just like the stories that they read together. In my experience as an audience member of these performances, children seem uniquely poised to understand and accept this complexity ... or perhaps they just don't care about binaries and discrete categories in the same way that many grown-ups do.

Audiences as Active Participants

When asked about their favorite moments from Drag Storytime performances, many of the practitioners I've interviewed signaled moments where the children move from being passive audience members to active participants and authors of the Storytime themselves. Drag artist Harmonica Sunbeam shared an anecdote where children brought a story to a halt:

> So, once I was at a reading in Harlem, and I had on a black dress with these sequins all over it. And in the middle of the story, a little boy comes up and, he hands me a sequin that fell. Anything you wear with sequins or any kind of embellishment, you're always going to leave a little trail of some sort. So, it's like, we don't care. But from that point on, the rest of the kids were looking for these sequins on the ground to give to me. I had to really be like, "Oh, well thank you, well thank you." It was like everyone's mission to return them.
>
> (2019)

In picking up the sequins, these children noticed beautiful, creative, glamorous ways of being in the world, and they enacted kindness and community as they returned what Harmonica Sunbeam had shared with them. I find this story illustrative for anyone seeking to understand how Storytimes work. Drag Storytime performers (and their collaborators, including parents and caregivers) drop sequins for young audiences to find, pick up, and make use of in any way they choose, whether on that day, or weeks, months, or years into the future. Drag Storytime isn't the gateway to drag so much as a trail to kindness, community, and the appreciation of the fabulous within and all around us.

Conclusion: Queer Joy and Drag Storytimes

"Queer joy" is a loosely defined concept that has been used increasingly in recent years to gesture to stories and artworks that foreground representations of queer characters and communities in states of joy. These accounts of love, belonging, success, pride, acceptance, solidarity, and jubilation act as opposition and alternative to narratives of shame that have been told about and even by LGBTQ+ people through the years. Beyond providing replacement scripts for people to connect with and aspire to, instances of queer joy can sustain individuals, particularly in continued moments of turmoil, marginalization, oppression, phobia, and violence. The now common articulation of "queer joy" in the public sphere suggests a growing understanding that the quality and quantity of LGBTQ+ representation truly matter. In their essay in *PLOS ONE*, O. Winslow Edwards et al. note:

> [C]ertain positive emotions – such as joy, pride, and love – can broaden an individual's planning repertoire and build up enduring, beneficial psychological and social resources that can be employed to address future adversity. Indeed, research demonstrates that experiencing joy or positive emotions can decrease reactivity to stressors and support the ability to rebound from stress. Within SGM [sexual and gender minority] communities, positive SGM identity – specifically feeling pride in, appreciating, and accepting attributes associated with one's SGM identity – has also been linked to higher reported life satisfaction and lower severity of reported depressive symptoms. Thus, investigating contributors to joy and positive SGM identity can serve as a basis for conceptualizing resources that may promote resilience within SGM communities.
>
> (2023, p. 3)

While joy (queer joy, trans joy, Black Indigenous People of Color (BIPOC) joy, disabled joy, etc.) is absolutely something well worth continuing to seek out and celebrate, the term is still undertheorized by scholars and underexplored by artists and activists. What is the mechanism of joy? How is it created, circulated, captured, and harnessed? Certainly, I can imagine "joy" to be a necessary and savvy component of any number of applied theatre contexts and practices, but only if joy is talked about and explored in all its complexity, rather than merely a taxonomy of "good stories" and "bad stories."

Drag Storytimes often (but not exclusively) feature stories of queer joy wherein characters find happiness and acceptance in who they are, such as in Jessica Love's *Julián is a Mermaid*, Jessie Sima's *Not Quite Narwhal*, and Kai Cheng Thom's *From the Stars in the Sky to the Fish in the Sea*. But these events also provide stories and performances and activities that generate queer joy in their audiences. I posit that queer joy is so essential to Drag Storytime that it should be understood as its engine, the very mechanism that makes it work and that powers its forward momentum – its ability to generate more audiences and to bring about more Drag Storytime performances and audiences in the future. As a form of applied theatre, Drag Storytimes model queer joy, reflecting, and even amplifying the feeling of joy from within the stories read through drag artists to audience members young and old. This creation and sharing of joy in small and large ways fundamentally changes the world, particularly as it reinscribes who should be able to experience joy, and when, where, and how that joy should be felt, expressed, and spread.

The drag artists whom I interviewed frequently described how these Drag Storytimes also nourish and inspire them – how these performers experience joy reciprocally in their interactions with their collaborators in the audience. This reciprocity is central to many types of successful applied theatre endeavors. Dreama Belle told me that in February 2019 she became sick and couldn't appear at her regularly scheduled Queens Who Read event. Librarian Angela Critics read to the children anyway, and then the children made heart-shaped postcards for Dreama Belle, wishing her a speedy recovery toward the next Drag Storytime event (Belle, 2019). Although much has already been written about what children (and their families) gain from Storytime, it is worth noting that Drag Storytimes provide queer joy for the drag artists performing at them. They uplift drag artists and queer individuals and communities writ large, whether in attendance at a Storytime or not. Even if they never attend a Drag Storytime performance, many folks in the queer community are excited when they hear about them and buoyed by the very fact that they exist. It is no wonder, then, that Drag Storytimes have emerged as a frontline in culture wars. The battle isn't about drag, but rather about queer joy and whether it should ultimately be encouraged or eradicated. And that's why affording children the opportunity and the safe space to pick up the sequins is so deeply necessary… and why Drag Storytimes aren't likely going away anytime soon.

Notes

1 I describe this work at greater length in my article "When Fierceness and Kindness Collide: The Dramaturgy of a Drag Storytime." (Dorsey, 2020).

2 Since practically their inception, Drag Storytimes have been met with critique, protest, and threats of violence, largely in the United States, but also (though not uniformly) around the world. Most of the drag artists I've interviewed have been the recipients of threats of violence, and all of the librarians and organizers I've spoken with have talked about the need for security and safety protocols when planning these events. In tandem with book challenges and bans, and the defunding and closing of school and public libraries, this battle over Drag Storytimes is a major front in the culture wars of the early twenty-first century. Perhaps performatively in this short chapter, I banish this complex context to an endnote so as not to overshadow the work of these Drag Storytime artists and collaborators and the good feelings they engender in the world.

References

Aimee, R. (2019) Interviewed by Zachary A. Dorsey. 9 December, New York City, NY.

Amie, M. (2020) Interviewed by Zachary A. Dorsey. 11 February, Zoom.

Apparently, C. (2019) Interviewed by Zachary A. Dorsey. 18 October, Portland, OR.

Belle, D. (2019) Interviewed by Zachary A. Dorsey. 16 November, Charlottesville, VA.

Cohen-Cruz, J. (2005) *Local Acts: Community-Based Performance in the United States*. New Brunswick, NJ: Rutgers University Press.

Critics, A. (2019) Interviewed by Zachary A. Dorsey. 2 December, Charlottesville, VA.

Dolan, J. (2008) *Utopia in Performance: Finding Hope at the Theater*. Ann Arbor, MI: University of Michigan Press.
Dorsey, Z. A. (2020) "When Fierceness and Kindness Collide: The Dramaturgy of a Drag Storytime." *Review: The Journal of Dramaturgy*, 26 (1), pp. 3–11.
Edward, O. W. et. al. (2023) "Our Pride, Our Joy: An Intersectional Constructivist Grounded Theory Analysis of Resources that Promote Resilience in SGM Communities." *PLoS ONE*, 18 (2), pp. 1–23.
Hot Mess, L. M., and Keenan, H. (2023) "Royal Reading: Drag Pedagogy and the Art of Queer Literacy." *Literacy Today*, 40 (4), pp. 56–57.
Keenan, H., and Hot Mess, L. M. (2021) "Drag Pedagogy: The Playful Practice of Queer Imagination in Early Childhood." *Curriculum Inquiry*, 50 (5), pp. 1–21.
Louise, O. (2019) Interviewed by Zachary A. Dorsey. 7 December, New York City, NY.
Percell, J. (2019) Interviewed by Zachary A. Dorsey. 18 December, Washington, DC.
Prentki, T., and Preston, S. (eds.) (2008) *The Applied Theatre Reader*. New York, NY: Routledge.
Sunbeam, H. (2019) Interviewed by Zachary A. Dorsey. 8 December, New York City, NY.

5 Facilitating Gender Awareness with First Drop Theatre

Applied Theatre in Indian Workplaces

Radhika Jain

The Indian Workforce and Gender Disparity

Compared to global standards, women in India represent a significantly lower percentage of the workforce. India's female labor force participation rate (LFPR) of approximately 30% has been much lower than the universal average of 47% for several years (World Economic Forum, 2022). The World Economic Forum's gender gap report, 2022, ranked India 135th out of 146 countries. The study mentions that despite progress in several areas, such as a decrease in fertility rates and an increasing focus on women's education, India's LFPR has been declining due to conservative social norms and the need to balance competing burdens of work and family responsibilities, among other factors.

Moreover, the DivHERsity Benchmarking Report 2021 conducted by JobsForHer not only found a significant gender gap at all levels in Indian companies (a 34% participation rate) but a widening gap as it moves toward senior management levels (an 18% participation rate). The thinning of the funnel is even more pronounced in public sector undertaking (PSU) organizations: Women hold just 7.7% of management board seats and a mere 2.7% of board chairs (International Labour Organization (ILO), 2018). The study attributes this imbalance mainly to a lack of organizational strategies for identifying, promoting, and retaining skilled women at higher levels (50%) and an "organizational culture" that seems to view top management jobs more as a "man's job" (39.21%). Other reasons include a lack of positive role models or mentors (31.64%), a lack of leadership training for women (26.45%), and, albeit to a lesser extent, the differential recruitment of men and women, and sexual harassment.

We at First Drop Theatre, a Bengaluru, India-based applied theatre company, have worked with organizations of varying sizes and nature – including PSUs, which are government-owned establishments, and multinational corporations (MNCs) – to explore interventions toward better diversity and inclusion (D&I), and, specifically, gender equity. In particular, we use tools, such as Playback Theatre, Forum Theatre, and role-play. Participant and management feedback relay that these experiential methods help people go beyond

DOI: 10.4324/9781003341802-9

cognitive awareness to unearth deeper insights and increased empathy. This essay looks at how to use applied theatre tools to advance D&I while also looking at the challenges faced in the process.

Leadership through the Prism of Gender

As mentioned earlier, the gender gap widens as the hierarchical order in organizations ascends. Rather than evaluate the contributing factors of this imbalance in detail, our work seeks to understand what this imbalance means to the people involved and to facilitate dialogue and possible action in response. With this in mind, we utilize Playback Theatre (PT) as a vehicle to help organizations and, especially their leadership, understand the negative impact of the gender gap through personal experiences shared by the participants.

PT is an improvisational, interactive community-based theatre format founded by Jonathan Fox and Jo Salas in the 1970s where the actors play out real-life stories and moments shared by audience members through text, movement, images, sounds, and metaphors (Fox, 1986). With storytelling and spontaneity as the basis, PT enables a forum for shared emotions, self-reflection, dialogue, and deep connections. It also offers a space for different groups of people to be heard, especially those voices that might be silenced or left out of public discussions in their communities.

At the PSUs we worked with, we observed the disproportionate gender ratio first-hand. At one such organization, women made up only 8% of the entire workforce, and at the leadership level, the numbers were even worse in favor of men. Given that these imbalances are longstanding, we began by inviting participants to reflect on their perspective on gender dynamics before discussing their visions for the future. Hence, we asked them to share their view of both the opposite gender[1] and their own gender's strengths as leaders. This acknowledgment was important for the creation of a productive space rather than a rant session, which may have made participants feel defensive. The "conductor," a facilitator of the PT team, then elicited responses about which tasks participants felt were generally easy or difficult for them as leaders. These feelings were reflected back by the actors using quick fluid sculptures (a short form in PT). This low-stakes exercise seemed to put the group at ease and subsequently share more openly about the underlying gender dynamics.

Overwhelmingly, women expressed that their voices were often not heard, while men spoke about the anxiety of being perceived as being dominant and patriarchal if they made certain suggestions or took the lead in anything, even if it was not their intention. What also emerged was how the same situation could be perceived differently by leaders of both genders. Such gender-based differences became starkly evident when a female manager revealed an incident where she was the lone woman in a meeting. She felt that the men were insensitive, excluding her from key discussions, and making inside jokes and references, all of which made her uncomfortable. This revelation prompted a male participant to recall a similar experience in which he did not speak up because he felt it was not his place to judge if the woman was feeling uncomfortable. In this case, the actors used the format of PT called "corridors," to reflect the feelings of both sides in the situation. After both depictions were shown, the tellers relayed how the assumptions they carried had been so strongly entrenched that it stopped them from even trying to change the status quo. The enactment also represented the different tellers' inner voices; for example, the woman's inner voice about such incidents occurring, as she put it, "again and again," in her work life. After witnessing this enactment, one of the male managers said that it struck him how even one "small" act of omission (microaggression) on his part could pile up to a list of discriminatory behaviors. He mentioned how this theatricalization would make him more conscious of his actions in future contexts. PT thus helped uncover hidden biases, including interactions at the PSUs in which individuals were not aware that they were being discriminatory until they witnessed the experience from the standpoint of others.

This technique has helped address our own biases as well. As PT practitioners, we consistently train toward separating our own feelings about a shared story and try to actively and empathetically listen, so as to authentically reflect back. Nonetheless, after completing our first interaction at a PSU, our team encountered internal division. We have all witnessed patriarchy and misogyny in our own families and social spaces. However, depending on our personal experiences with gender inequality in the workplace, the male and female team members responded differently to stories about women lacking agency to vocalize their perceived biases. Some felt that with policies in place at organizations, women should be more proactive in tackling discrimination, while others argued that policies alone wouldn't suffice since there's a deeper conditioning at play.

To overcome this challenge, we shared moments in our own lives where, for different reasons, we did not have the agency to act. The other members of the team represented these stories through different formats of PT, which served as an internal tool for our own analysis. In a country as diverse as India, there is a vast difference between individuals depending on social, regional, and educational status. Sharing our personal stories, watching them being enacted, and thus understanding the multiple factors at play, helped the team members appreciate the complexity of the individual challenges in the workplace. For example, one of our team members, who comes from a very conservative family, shared her experience of the difficulty she encountered when she wanted to pursue higher education, including the judgment she faced from both extended and close family members. It dawned on the ensemble that in certain families, even in a big city today, girls did not always have the agency to opt for their own educational paths.

Different Cultures, Different Concerns

Since India opened up its economy in 1991, the country has experienced unprecedented growth and new job opportunities with multinational companies, especially in the domains of information technology (IT) and business process management (BPM). These companies have attracted a younger demographic and created a more vibrant, and, generally speaking, more diverse work culture (NASSCOM, 2016). With these organizations, we focused on how people could help mitigate discrimination by being allies. In Playback Theatre terminology, there was a "red thread" (Fox and Dauber, 1999) that emerged about feeling let down by others from whom they were expecting key support. For example, in a workshop with an MNC, a male senior leader relayed a low point in his life when he simultaneously had the pressure of a big project, the threat of job loss, and a crisis in his family: "I truly felt alone and wished someone had been there to support me." After the actors used "performative poetry" to embody his desire for an outstretched hand, the manager's eyes welled up. This display of vulnerability by a male senior leader encouraged a woman leader to talk about a situation when she did not have the support of her male colleagues when fighting for more gender-friendly policies at work. These stories revealed by leaders uncorked a deeper sharing of personal stories from others. Having women and men trust each other enough to express such moments was a live example of the spirit of allyship.

At the same time, other stories exposed how aspects of privilege, region, religion, and gender hinder allyship. For instance, one participant shared how he tried to help an "outsider," who then took advantage of him. Since then, he has not ventured to be an ally unless it's someone he knows well or who shares a common background. In some of the other sharings, people from certain lower economic backgrounds considered people in higher job positions to be privileged, and hence "unsuitable" as an ally. In this and subsequent interventions, the group observed the power of perception in influencing behavior. It was interesting to note that oftentimes the storyteller was attributing the lack of inclusiveness to the other person and was either not willing or not able to recognize their own preconceptions.

Awareness to Action

PT is an effective tool for personal reflection that hopefully creates awareness and enables multiple perspectives. With some organizations, however, we used other intervention models that offer participants the opportunity to actively change problematic narratives. For instance, at a leading IT firm, we trained employees to act out certain scenarios for managers based on common experiences, such as an HR management feedback meeting. This was done in a multi-step process. The first step was the scenarios being played out by the trained employees. Then, there was a short discussion where the participants reflected on what had they witnessed. Next, we did a "Hot Seat" exercise where the audience could now question the actors about the motivations of their characters' discriminatory behavior, to which the actors would answer while remaining in character. The exercise showed what factors conditioned that character's thinking. This led to a discussion about the characters' intentions and how each of them could have approached the situation differently. As a final step, the scenarios were played out again incorporating suggestions from the audience for alternative behaviors. The idea was not to arrive at an optimum solution but to encourage shared learning of possible different approaches.

One of the scenarios included a sensitive conversation between a woman employee and her male manager about her upcoming maternity leave. The actor playing the manager showed discomfort when the woman became emotional. We observed that this discomfort strongly resonated with the audience, especially with the men as compared to the women (who were almost in equal numbers): People shifted in their seats while others nodded their heads in resonance with the character. This response reflects a deep-rooted conditioning in Indian societies that persists to this day in which men are expected to display "strength" by not being vulnerable in public. Even today, a boy getting emotional is often chided by remarks like "Don't cry like a girl." The Hot Seat exercise showcased that it was acceptable for emotions to be involved, even in work-related interactions. The response of the women leaders in the audience helped the male leaders recognize that emotions are natural and have their place in any human interaction.

Another approach was to use PT in combination with Forum Theatre, an interactive theatre technique created by Augusto Boal in the early 1970s. Audiences watch a short play in which the protagonist is thwarted by an obstacle. Afterward, the cast repeats the scenario: however, this time, the audience members can replace the actor playing the protagonist to suggest alternative actions. PT was used to unearth which issues to address, and then Forum Theatre gave participants agency to try out alternatives (See Boal, 1985). For instance, at a leading pharmaceutical company where the overall percentage of women was about 30%, we used PT to unearth what might be discouraging women from joining the workforce. Shared stories brought to the fore issues of work-life balance, scheduling issues, unequal growth opportunities, and more. There were also stories of interactions with male peers, leaders, and managers who did not provide them with a sense of being valued. We used Forum Theatre to explore alternate approaches that would help set clear expectations and point out concerns in a win-win manner that acknowledges the value of female employees. The HR of this organization was keen to utilize the suggestions, such as creating a forum that happened frequently where women could express their concerns to HR; support groups among women employees; sensitivity and awareness workshops for men, etc.

Moving Beyond the Gender Binary

Thus far, we have only discussed gender in terms of the male-female binary and sexuality from a heteronormative perspective. This was how we, at First Drop, had initially approached our work, which reflects our own conditioning within Indian culture. However, in one of our rehearsals, a team member brought up that we had not heard any stories in our workshops that represent the LGBTQ+ community. This feedback was noteworthy as we consistently strive to be inclusive. For example, in one rehearsal a team member shared her experience as a parent of a daughter who is part of the LGBTQ+ community. Similarly, in our PT workshops, we welcome stories from all participants. We work to create a safe space by having the actors begin by introducing themselves through a personal story. Specifically, whenever the workshop topic has been inclusion or bias, we seek at least one actor to share a story pertaining to the LGBTQ+ community.

We realized, however, that we need to be more proactive in addressing gender and sexuality. To that end, we conducted a guided visualization exercise that had the participants imagine a series of events between two people. The events stop at a certain point, and the group is then asked multiple questions. The participants responded that they had assumed the genders of the two people they had visualized were a [cis] man and [cis] woman. This demonstrated an implicit bias. Afterward, we role-played scenarios showcasing the struggles of LGBTQ+ people to be able to come out in various settings. When we debriefed, the participants noted that this topic doesn't necessarily arise in the context of gender diversity training and that they need to be more conscious of it. We also realized it is imperative that the group of participants who attend workshops are themselves a wide representation of different genders. In our experience, this effort has helped different voices emerge.

Conclusion

Our experience of using applied theatre modalities to address gender sensitivity, inclusion, unconscious biases, and equity has been a journey of discovery about the gap in awareness that exists in the Indian workspace. There has been a greater intent from most of the organizations we've worked with to engage D&I programs and policies, including at the hiring level. While these efforts are laudable, a lot still remains to be done as cited in the Global Gender Gap report of 2022.

Over the last decade or so, more companies in India have been looking at experiential learning models like applied theatre for upskilling and holistic development of their workforce. Companies are using it for everything from behavioral adaptation, change management, and leadership skills to handling cultural and personal issues. One of the key advantages that experiential learning, like applied theatre, has over traditional learning methods (such as a PowerPoint presentation or a lecture) is the way it can foster deeper introspection in individuals and groups by engaging less cognitively but rather in more embodied and affective means.

PT allows us to create spaces where emotional expression can occur. With its focus on personal experiences, PT also reveals what might be informing their biases and assumptions: including the role of the family, the social milieu in which they grew up, and their education. Another benefit of PT, and other forms like Forum Theatre, is the exploration of topics from multiple viewpoints. Moreover, applied theatre techniques provide critical distance, as certain subjects (such as unconscious biases) have the potential to expose aspects of one's personality that are not easy to accept. Applied theatre's use of personal reflection, its sensorial nature, and its interactive format make it particularly impactful.

Note

1 This approach assumed a binary construction of male and female gender identity, an approach we later questioned.

References

Boal, A. (1985). *Theatre of the Oppressed,* trans. C. A. and M.O. Leal McBride. New York, NY: Theatre Communications Group.

Fox, J. (1986). *Acts of Service: Spontaneity, Commitment, Tradition in the Nonscripted Theatre*. New Paltz, NY: Tusitala.

Fox, J. & Dauber, H. (eds.) (1999). *Gathering Voices: Essays on Playback Theatre*. New Paltz, NY: Tusitala.

JobsForHer. (2021). "Understanding COVID-19's Impact on Working Women: JobsForHer DivHERsity Benchmarking Report 2020–2021," 12 May. Accessed 2 Oct. 2023. https://www.jobsforher.com/employer/blogs/understanding-covid-19-s-impact-on-working-women-jobsforher-divhersity-benchmarking-report-2020-2021/1671

NASSCOM. (2016). "Making Diversity Work. Key Trends and Practices in the Indian IT-BPM Industry." *Strictly private and confidential*, 15 March. Accessed 2 Oct. 2023. https://www.pwc.in/assets/pdfs/publications/2016/making-diversity-work-key-trends-and-practices-in-the-indian-it-bpm-industry.pdf

International Labour Organization (ILO). (2018). "Women in Leadership and Management in Public Sector Undertakings in India." March SCOPE-ILO Study. Accessed 2 Oct. 2023. https://www.ilo.org/sites/default/files/wcmsp5/groups/public/@asia/@ro-bangkok/@sro-new_delhi/documents/publication/wcms_632553.pdf

World Economic Forum. (2022). "Global Gender Gap Report." Accessed 2 Oct. 2023 https://www3.weforum.org/docs/WEF_GGCR_2022.pdf

6 Yassified Shakespeare

The Case for TikTok as Applied Theatre

Trevor Boffone and Danielle Rosvally

Who We Are: Can We Skip to the Good Part?

Nostalgically, we met online in 2020. Just like we did in 1999, we sat in front of the computer for hours on end, longing to connect. This time, however, it wasn't our parents or lack of transportation that prohibited us from meeting in person, but rather a global pandemic. We A/S/L'd[1] with other theatre scholars during Zoom writing sessions, recognizing mutual interests and shared feelings about all of this fuckery (*waves hands in the air*). We started working together because we saw the convergence of our areas: Shakespeare, TikTok, and gender expression. In 2022, we named our project *Yassified Shakespeare* to make Shakespeare accessible and to peel back the curtain on the scholarly process along the way. Leaning into the esthetic of Yassification – the process of glamifying something by making it over with a campy queer sensibility – our project leans into an over-the-top esthetic that generally queers the original object. We do this on TikTok.[2]

Figure 6.1 "What is Yassified Shakespeare?"

DOI: 10.4324/9781003341802-10

Figure 6.2 @YassifiedShakespeare TikTok.

We envisioned Yassified Shakespeare (@YassifiedShax) as a place where we could share content in relation to a book we're co-authoring, engage with the TikTok Shakespeare community (ShakesTok), and help demystify academic writing/publishing for grad students and early career academics. At the time of this writing, our videos are regularly seen by audiences of hundreds (sometimes thousands), thereby creating a digital archive of material that claims space for us in the larger ShakesTok conversation. If we look at TikTok followers as our season ticket holders and our average video view counts as our audience reach, then our performances are outpacing our subscribers. Therefore, while our account doesn't have as high a following as big ShakeTokers like @kcfox, @lungthief, and @nofearshakesqueer, we are still a notable part of the ShakesTok community.

Danielle is an assistant professor at the University at Buffalo, and Trevor is an educator in Houston, Texas. TikTok allows us to collaborate digitally, without additional overhead, and connect with an audience at almost no charge to them outside of technology they likely already own. The exchange of ideas can flow across the country between us and out to our audience with minimal cost: Our audiences don't pay to view our content, and we don't pay to play. Approaching the internet as a stage, and TikTok, especially as an applied theatre space, facilitates a broad audience of interested Shakes lovers while also making our collaboration possible despite our geographic limitations.

To us, applied theatre uses theatrical techniques to accomplish specific tasks: build community, invite collaboration (often directly from the audience), educate audiences about particular social issues, and amplify lesser-heard voices. TikTok also does these things but with greater ease. Whereas theatre typically requires audiences to (1) be made aware that a production exists, (2) be convinced to spend time and money seeking out that experience, and (3) show up in person to the theatrical space to engage with the experience, TikTok flips this on its head: Rather than a central body (be it a person or an institution) bringing people together for a common artistic project, the algorithm does this work, thereby allowing communities to find each other by doing the things they're already doing.[3] The mere act of being on TikTok and liking Shakespeare brings one closer to ShakesTok, and, given the accessibility of TikTok's creation tools, spectators have the agency and autonomy to become creators.

Moreover, the ShakesTok community centers historically underrepresented voices. As we will further detail, ShakesTok is dominated by women, non-binary, and queer folks. Our identities align with this. Danielle is a nerdy cis-female ally and Trevor is a bisexual cis-male. As theatre-makers and social media users, we have found empowerment through ShakesTok, which encourages us to embrace and publicly celebrate parts of our identities that we have had to temper in other theatrical, professional, and online spaces more strategically.

If we view ShakesTok in conversation with data such as Broadway By the Numbers, it is clear how ShakesTok represents a critical divergence from the professional stage of Broadway and other major theatre venues with its prominent representation of femme+ people (Henry et al., 2019). TikTok is an ideal site for critical work in redressing representation given how the platform encourages creators to embrace self-determination. In "TikTok is Theatre, Theatre is TikTok," Trevor claims that TikTokian "self-determination allows TikTokers to hone and retain their agency. Self-determination is marked by intrinsic motivation and the ability to control one's own life and public-facing image" (Boffone, 2022c, p. 44). On ShakesTok, content creators enter into a collective "auto-artistic directorship" in which they eschew dated identity scripts in favor of building their own artistic practice that centers what may be considered marginalized in other spaces (Boffone, 2022c, p. 44).

With this in mind, what follows is an auto-ethnographic account of our use of TikTok, as well as a call to action to treat TikTok more seriously in the realm of applied theatre because of how well it facilitates many of its goals: forming communities, connecting a group of people who might not find their stories told in mainstream spaces, and creating broad accessibility for this art (Prentki and Preston, 2009).

Community: To Thine Own Freak Flag Be True

Although TikTok has a well-defined mainstream culture – so-called "Straight TikTok" – the platform is also home to thriving sub-communities (Boffone, 2022b), which feature their own main characters, trends, norms, and esthetics. In the case of ShakesTok[4], creators overlay Shakespearean content with contemporary material: They remix the Shakespeare canon through a TikTokian lens; *Twelfth Night*, *Coriolanus*, and *Henry V* meet TikTok sound bites, effects, and dance moves to create a wholly new cultural artifact that plays to multiple audiences. While TikTokers recognize the trending piece of TikTok culture, Shakespeare lovers get the joke. ShakesTok is a space of identity expression that allows nerds the chance to play. It's a theatrical performance space; it's digital vaudeville (Boffone, 2022c). Whereas creating hyper-specific inside jokes about *Two Noble Kinsmen* or other obscure Shakespeareana might get blank stares in real life, this content has an audience on ShakesTok.

Yassified Shakespeare, in particular, helps develop an audience for the scholarship that we're working on and to reflect on that scholarship in real-time. Its creation was, in part, a way to tear down the walls of euro-centric intellectual elitism that is so strongly associated with both understanding Shakespeare and his cultural capital. As theatremakers and scholars, when we think about *Yassified Shakespeare*, our target audience is mainly young people. When we create, we are hoping to engage with not just Shakespeare scholars, but also broader swatches of theatre nerds who want to expand their knowledge base and laugh a little.

Because of the very public-facing nature of TikTok, we strive for transparency on multiple levels. We have crafted a series, for instance, that discusses the ins and outs of academic writing and publishing designed to help graduate students and early career academics with basic-level publication/writing questions. On the rare occasion that we use jargon, we explain what it means. We try to make the barrier for entry to our videos as low as possible; we don't take for granted that an interested audience has a background in Shakespeare or even theatre. In other words: With Yassified Shakespeare we are creating space for community engagement outside the traditional institutional establishments where "SHAKESPEARE" tends to live.

This transparency is an invitation to anyone with a spark of curiosity to engage with us and with the ideas that we are discussing (primarily the intersection of Shakespeare, higher education, and gender play). Inclusiveness is important to us because of the audience we are cultivating and the type of content that we are making. As noted above, ShakesTok skews toward young, queer, and femme-presenting. From our experience, ShakesTok content creators are not cis-men; our engagement has almost exclusively been with either femme-presenting persons or non-binary folks. Of course, every TikTok community includes a cohort of people who simply scroll and view content semi-anonymously. This dynamic makes it impossible for us to fully survey the ShakesTok audience, but we do know who the main characters are (the folks who comment and post thereby claiming voices in the community dialogue). These women, non-binary folks, and queer folk hold the agency to craft the community culture, set trends and esthetics, and de-center straight white men from the conversation.[5] While community members who don't post may not align with these prevalent identity markers, these silent observers only confirm how loudly the voices of content creators amplify in TikTok spaces: The voices who are being centered are those who have historically been excluded from the conversation.

Figure 6.3 @10kShakespeare describes Peter Quince's casting choices with the "Eloise" Sound.

Because the space is almost completely dominated by femme-presenting performers, gender play is part of the norm with ShakesTok content. Consider, for instance, @10kShakespeare's take on the popular "Eloise" sound. In this TikTok, @10kShakespeare gender-bends the character Peter Quince from *Midsummer* as he asks Flute to play "the woman's part" of Thisby. The TikToker plays both Peter Quince and Flute. As @10kShakespeare/Flute lip syncs to Disney's character Kronk proclaiming "I'm not a girl," she does almost nothing to alter her appearance toward stereotypical masculinity and, in fact, wears prominent red femme-presenting lipstick. While @10kShakespeare-as-Flute ironically explains that gender can't be performed, she herself performs gender as a construct of situation and action. The fact that gender play occurs on ShakesTok should not be surprising, Shakespeare has always been a critical site for gender play. Elizabethan practice involved all-male companies taking on expansive roles regardless of gender, and contemporary takes on this phenomenon similarly engage with cross-casting, drag, and everything in between.

Yassified Shakespeare videos likewise put the idea of fixed non-performative gender on blast. As the term indicates, our content skews queer: In "me as a baby" Trevor visibly transforms into an ungendered goblin-puppet-thing. In "Wednesday dance," Danielle embodies both Wednesday Addams and Hamlet, simultaneously, in one body. In both these performances, the presented gender of the performers is creatively re-mixed by the trend at hand. Trends offer performers the opportunity to strip back the necessity of gender and engage with the notion that it is both performative and unfixed. The fact that Trevor yassifies himself to become the goblin-puppet-thing is more interesting (and prevalent) than Trevor's genitals. And the fact that Danielle can be both Wednesday and Hamlet doesn't bring to light some kind of gender crisis, but rather a deep connection between Hamlet and goth culture.

Figure 6.4 "Me as a Baby" trend: Yassified.

The form of TikTok also includes audiences in the meaning-making process. Madhavi Menon (2011) asked, "If our formulations of queerness depend crucially on things being out of joint, unhinged rather than straight, then why should we not theorize our relation to time? What if we were to dispense with a model of temporal linearity that translates also into causal linearity? What if time itself were to be queered?" (p. 19). To us, these questions speak directly to the ways that TikTok interacts with time. On TikTok, time is not linear; it happens in gasps and spurts. Audiences view pieces shot weeks or even months prior, yet the direct address nature of TikTok means that these pieces reach their audiences in the "now" of the present. Time is out of joint; that is, TikTok queers time. The break from Aristotelian storytelling forces audiences

Figure 6.5 Wednesday Dance trend with some Hamlet flair.

to reimagine how stories come together without clear, straight narrative through lines. Point A to point B, in queer storytelling, is never a (pardon the pun) straight line. The zigzags are part of what makes TikTok engaging but also are clear indications of a queer storytelling heritage (Taylor Ellis, 2022, pp. 1–12). It would be one thing to hear a story told as a chapter book, with one narrative step taken logically to the next. The joy of TikTok content creation is that it's more like a choose-your-own-adventure novel; it's the same story but told from multiple points of view in multiple modalities over multiple periods of time.

In a similar way, Christine Varnado postulates that queerness is not just about genital-centered interaction, but a situation can also be rendered queer "by a twist to their shape" (Varnado, 2020, p. 3). TikTok is full of twists! TikTok's mimicry culture is part of its queerness. Trends are the use and re-use of a specific sound to create a specific type of TikTok – like users making "think goose" videos where they waddle away from the camera to do whatever is on-brand for them, mimicking two cartoon geese who did a rump-rolling walk in the 1970 Disney film *The Aristocats*. When TikTokers mimic trends, they try on TikTok's "identity blueprints" that help them fashion their identity in both online and offline spaces (Boffone, 2022a, pp. 5–6). By mimicking other content creators – essentially lip-syncing to their content – TikTokers inherently queer a space that might not necessarily be seen as queer, like a drag club, a gay bar, or a gay/straight alliance meeting might be. Of course, the act of lip-synching is a drag esthetic, meaning that this aspect of TikTok encourages Do It Yourself [DIY] drag.[6]

The use of TikTok trends points to another aspect of the platform that echoes how it can be useful as an applied theatre space. Since trends are both replicas and original creations, they are simultaneously familiar to users while also adding something new. While there is a blueprint to follow, content creators bring their own expertise, identities, and story-telling techniques to add

Figure 6.6 @YassifiedShax's take on "Think Goose."

to the conversation. Because the template is the same every time, this cast focuses on the message of the performance and the performer's quirks rather than what they are doing. In other words: It's the why, not the what that becomes the spotlight in these trends. As pieces of applied theatre, trends allow a community to build around this "why" through the "what."

While this is happening, TikTok videos play to multiple audiences, which means that they incorporate layered literacies. Because of this multitude of familiar/unfamiliar uses as well as audiences, every TikTok consists of a layered dramaturgy. Even if you're not in on the niche joke, you can inevitably engage with and enjoy a video simply by being familiar with the trend. Similar to how queer communities have historically used queer-coding as a means of forging community in a subtle way, TikTok dramaturgies facilitate a queer spectatorship in which queer and ally viewers will grasp the queerness of the video even if a casual cishet Chet (a cis, heterosexual conservative person) does not. That is, queer creators may use familiar audio from *RuPaul's Drag Race* or the Grindr notification sound to signal queerness. Although cishet Chets may view – and enjoy – these videos, the layered meanings allow cishet Chet and Bathhouse Betty to derive different understandings and pleasures from their spectatorship.[7]

Practice: All of TikTok's a Stage

TikTok subverts the demands of traditional theatre spaces that require artists and audiences to access a particular physical location. One can view TikTok on a web browser (on a standard computer) or from a phone. This base technology requirement is really the only barrier to entry. The app is free, and since most people have their phones on them at all times that makes TikTok omnipresent. TikTok can be very personal; you can put your headphones on and listen/watch in a small room by yourself without anyone being the wiser. TikTok can be part of your daily life: You can pull up the app during your workday bathroom break. TikTok is with you at your most personal moments, and because creators on TikTok tend to speak directly into the camera, it can feel intimate in a way that other theatre experiences simply do not.

Because of TikTok's accessibility, the platform represents the democratization of a theatre space: You don't need funding, you are encouraged to make content with things that are already at your fingertips. Additionally, participants are not bound to one form of interaction with TikTok; they are free and welcome to participate at the level they are willing and able to. If they simply want to view content, they can. If they want to "like" or comment, they can. They can even make responding videos or stitch videos to the front of theirs, both amplifying messages and answering in their own voices. These capabilities remove much of the hierarchy of theatre-making.

TikTok is also bite-sized. Videos on TikTok are capped at three minutes long, though often videos do best when they're under ninety seconds (and the sweet spot for most viral trends is roughly ten seconds). As such, audiences don't need much time to engage with content on TikTok. Making a ninety-second film is accessible; TikTok's format removes this access barrier for creators as well as audiences. As such, it forces us to think about how we can break down our work and messaging into bite-sized chunks. As scholars, this distillation is almost counter-intuitive to our writing training. We are more used to thinking convoluted sustained thoughts that require forty pages of articles and research to explain than we are to thinking in chunks that can be broken down into a jargon-free tight ninety seconds. This exercise has really forced us to re-examine the building blocks of our work; because, in our opinion, if we can explain what we're doing into tight jargon-free ninety-second videos, our longer, more sustained work will be clearer.

The challenge, of course, is growing an audience. TikTok's platform makes this both easier and more complicated than legacy platforms such as YouTube and Instagram. Because the TikTok user experience is more curated by technology (TikTok users are presented with a never-ending feed of content when they open the app called the "For You Page" (FYP) that is pulled by the algorithm based on the user's prior app activity), there can be an element of mystery to audience development. Also, it's a little unpredictable what is going to do well. Our "best" performing videos are not necessarily our smartest content, our most shiny content, or even our content that jives most closely with popular trends. As of May 2023, the best-performing video *Yassified Shakespeare* has put out is what we call the "thirst trap" video: a fast-paced compilation of images of Sean Teale as Dario in Hulu's 2022 film *Rosaline* smoldering at the camera (often shirtless displaying six-pack abs) while Danielle tries not-so-subtly not to leer in the corner. This video has almost 38,800 views. A not-even-close second is Danielle's take-down of critics of the Museum of Broadway (a style of video we internally reference as a "talking head"). As of May 2023, this video has over 21,300 views.

Figure 6.7 "Thirst Trap" video.

Figure 6.8 Museum of Broadway talking head.

These two examples clearly show that we've had the best success in reaching our audience when we lean into our research expertise rather than try to game the audio using trending sounds. Embracing our niche (quirky sexy Shakespeare and nerdy theatre talk) has been much better at connecting us to audiences than, say, when we tried to replicate the trend "me as a baby" (525 views as of May 2023) or the Wednesday Addams Dance (even with our Yassified Shakespeare flair) that has 309 views as of May 2023.

Another caveat is TikTok's algorithm, which has been notorious for its shady practices. Things like shadow-banning and suppressing non-hegemonic voices are made possible by the fact that the algorithm isn't public (Davis, 2022; Rauchberg, 2022). While there is a sense of how some of TikTok's proprietary algorithm works, no one has the ins and outs of it completely nailed down, and TikTok isn't telling its secrets. While we are well aware of the valid critiques of TikTok, to fully address them here would derail this train. For the here and now: Suffice it to say we acknowledge that TikTok is not necessarily a utopia for theatre even if it does address many of the historical challenges theatre faces. It doesn't replace offline practices but should be seen as something that happens in tandem with tried-and-true in-person theatre practices.

Conclusion: If These TikToks Have Offended…

TikTok – and Shakestok more specifically – has restructured our relationship with academia and theatre-making. It has forced us to re-evaluate our priorities, goals, and approaches to collaboration. It should come as no surprise that much of the outside-the-box thinking we detail in this essay has been spurred by the COVID-19 pandemic. If we, as theatremakers and scholars, have learned anything from the pandemic, it is that we need to look to digital tools to expand our reach. This is especially pertinent to communities excluded by traditional modes of theatre-making and scholarship. High ticket prices and dense scholarly writing (often behind a paywall) are just two barriers that inevitably exclude certain people from the conversation. To extend our reach, it is critical to realize that playing spaces are not just the physical synchronous stage anymore. There are more intimate spaces to engage audiences and build community.

Notes

1 A/S/L is an abbreviation for "Age/Sex/Location" and was a common opener for online conversations in the dial-up era.
2 All the QR codes in this chapter will take you to TikTok. If you'd prefer to see these videos on a webpage, please go to: https://www.yassifiedshakespeare.com/publications-and-awards/AppliedTheatre.
3 An algorithm is a computational process that does a specific task. TikTok has written a proprietary algorithm that does the task of populating a user's For You Page (FYP) and, thus, guiding their interactions with the app and the communities they build within it. For more on TikTok's algorithm, see: Zeng, Abidin, and Schäfer(2021).
4 For more on the ShakesTok community, see Boffone and Rosvally (2023).
5 Despite the radical gender play on ShakesTok, the community does have a race/ethnicity discrepancy. The most-viewed content creators are all white or white-passing, possibly reiterating how TikTok is a white space that privileges whiteness in all its meanings (Boffone, 2021, pp. 26–33).
6 For more on DIY Drag on TikTok, see Boffone 2023.
7 A "Bathhouse Betty" is a colloquial term used to describe a queer person who frequents gay bathhouses. The term was ushered in by Bette Midler's infamous concerts at the Continental Baths.

References

Boffone, T. (2021) *Renegades: Digital Dance Cultures from Dubsmash to TikTok*. New York: Oxford University Press.

Boffone, T. (2022a) "The Rise of TikTok in the US Culture" in Boffone, T. (ed.) *TikTok Cultures in the United States*. London: Routledge, pp. 1–12.

Boffone, T. (ed.) (2022b) *TikTok Cultures in the United States*. London: Routledge.

Boffone, T. (2022c) "TikTok is theatre, theatre is TikTok," *Theatre History Studies* 4, pp. 41–48.

Boffone, T. (2023) *TikTok Broadway: Musical Theatre Fandom in the Digital Age*. New York: Oxford University Press.

Boffone, T. and Rosvally, D. (2023) "'Everyone in Illyria is Bi You Absolute Cowards': Shakespeare TikTok, *Twelfth Night*, and the Search for a Queer Utopia," *Shakespeare Bulletin* 40(4), pp. 481–507.

Davis, C. (2022) "Digital Blackface and the Troubling Intimacies of TikTok Dance Challenges" in Boffone, T. (ed.) *TikTok Cultures in the United States*. London: Routledge, pp. 28–38.

Henry, S.P., Ameijeiras, I.J, Libby, A., Sotomayer, B., Bouju, F. and Lim, S. (producer). "Broadway by the Numbers." 2019. https://production.pro/broadway-by-the-numbers

Menon, M. (ed.) (2011) *Shakesqueer: A Queer Companion to the Complete Works of Shakespeare*. Durham: Duke University Press.

Prentki, T. and Preston, S. (2009) *The Applied Theatre Reader*. New York: Routledge.

Rauchberg, J. S. (2022) "#SHADOWBANNED: Queer, Trans, and Disabled Creator Responses to Algorithmic Oppression on TikTok" in Pain, P. (ed.) *LGBTQ Digital Cultures: A Global Perspective*. London: Routledge, pp. 196–209.

Taylor Ellis, S. (2022) *Doing the Time Warp: Strange Temporalities and Musical Theatre*. London: Bloomsbury Academic.

Varnado, C. (2020) *The Shapes of Fancy: Reading for Queer Desire in Early Modern Literature*. Minneapolis: University of Minnesota Press.

Zeng, Jing & Abidin, Chrystal & Schäfer, Mike. (2021). "Research perspectives on TikTok and its legacy apps: introduction." *International Journal of Communication*. 15. pp. 3161–3172.

Roundtable Discussion with Trevor Boffone, Lisa S. Brenner, Zachary A. Dorsey, Radhika Jain, and Danielle Rosvally

Lisa: Thank you for joining this conversation. One resonance we see in your essays is that your work explores the stories we tell and how we might retell them. Any thoughts about that?

Radhika: I agree with the idea of stories being the cornerstone. TikTok is right now banned in India. This is something that I would want to see: how something can be so accessible. And taking stories to libraries, to kids, and how those narratives become so important.

Danielle: On TikTok, we're using this digital platform to engage with people in quick, microbursts; from thirty seconds to three-minute segments that go directly to their phones. So, we're trying to increase access to storytelling in new ways.

Zachary: I'm thinking about the ways that we open up the space of storytelling but don't over-determine who the target audience is or how they're going to interact with it. For instance, with the TikTok community, I love that line about the cohort of people who simply scroll and view content semi-anonymously. I mean frankly, that's me. But with all of our projects, we can't 100% predict how these stories will land on everyone or trace where they go afterward. But there's an excitement to not knowing what kind of wonderful queer combinations or juxtapositions come out of Shakespeare in the digital world, or how an intervention that happens at your job might open up a new perspective.

Lisa: Participants come into these spaces because they already have a connection to it: You go to the library presumably because you love books, or it's a place to gather in your community. You go to TikTok because you already have an interest in the subject, or you're in the workplace because that's your place of employment. Rather than expect an audience to come to a theatre space, you are going out into public spaces in hopes that audiences will gain both new ways of interacting with these spaces and new perspectives on identity.

Zachary: In addition to opening up spaces, I see an opening up of the term "applied theatre." When trying to translate this term to my students,

DOI: 10.4324/9781003341802-11

I fall back on Shakespearean productions in prisons or facilitating workshops in high schools. But we are coming up with new examples of what counts as applied theatre, expanding the concept and reconsidering its possibilities. I think all of us get there through play. All of these projects are based upon the ability to step into a role that is joyful, exciting, and accessible.

Lisa: That makes me think about what success looks like. How do we assess play?

Trevor: What we find exciting is when we share a new book in Shakespeare studies or theatre studies, and we have comments from people who are eager to learn that such a thing exists. For instance, in one video, I discuss Carla Della Gatta's book *Latinx Shakespeares.* We had tons of comments from people like, "I am a Latino actor in Utah, and I didn't know that Latinos did Shakespeare for my entire life. I didn't feel like I was reflected in this space, and knowing this book exists solidified me as a Shakespearean actor." We see this from all sorts of marginalized groups, especially women and nonbinary folks who are engaging with our content.

Danielle: Which helps demystify and democratize theatre, making it available to a wider community, including grad students and early career folks.

Zachary: I think "success" has something to do with care for our partnering communities. With Drag Storytimes, we think about how to ensure that everyone present has a good time but has also gotten the resources and the respect they need.

Radhika: I resonate with what you said about care because there's a vulnerability to sharing your stories. Success for us could mean people lingering after the performance, just to talk, or that after a few months, people still want to converse. These are qualitative things; you can't really measure them.

Lisa: If we value care in doing this work, then what are the ethical concerns to consider?

Zachary: For several years, I worked as the dramaturg for Queens Who Read, a Storytime endeavor over in Charlottesville, Virginia. When Covid hit, our drag performer moved to New York and started a graduate program. The librarian that we were partnering with moved on to other projects. Within my university teaching life, everything got tremendously upended as we moved online, and all the rest. So, we never connected back to the community to resume Drag Storytime. One question implicit in care and applied theatre is the sustainability of the project.

Trevor: Sustainability is something that Danielle and I talk about a lot in terms of our collaboration. We try to balance the care and the workload: who is doing more, who is doing less, and sometimes we pick up the slack for each other.

Danielle: I'm on a tenure-line, and Trevor isn't, so I need to make sure that, ethically, the resources that I have available are available to us as a team. And also for me, specifically with this project, I am very aware that I am a staunch ally, but I'm not a member of the queer community, and therefore I try to make sure that I'm not speaking for the community or taking advantage of it – both of which cis-het people have historically done to the queer community.

Radhika: There's a risk in our work that we could impose our point of view or enter a space with a certain attitude. I feel it's ethically important to sit with these concerns: What's coming up from the participants rather than us pushing our agenda? Also, asking for consent is important. We enter their space and leave, but they are going to stay and continue to work with each other afterward. So, we must be cognizant of the consequences of sharing stories. If we are doing an intervention with the employees where the management is not there, they need to feel their confidentiality will be respected, especially since our workshop is sanctioned by the management.

Lisa: That makes me think of another common theme: collaboration. Whether it's the collaboration between Trevor and Daniel; First Drop Theatre and its partnering companies; or, in Drag Story Hour, there's a collaboration between the performer, the librarian, and all the folks who are involved in making the event happen. And then, of course, there are the people who interact with these performances. So, what emphasis do we need to put on the process versus the product?

Trevor: For Yassified Shakespeare, we have two aims: On the one hand, we work collaboratively to educate theatre and Shakespearean communities on TikTok. Our artistic practice also helps us to work through our writing. It's sort of a brainstorming space. We might be working on a chapter, and we have an idea, and we will task each other to create a TikTok to explain that concept. So, we do our homework. Then we share it. We talk about it, and it helps us to get the words on the page and to make it accessible to whoever might be reading the writing and to people who are watching the video. The process gives us real-time feedback from the community. Every video is a finished product to a certain extent, and in the last twelve months, we've posted about 200 videos. Some of them are great; some of them are bad, but a lot of them just do what they need to do. They start a conversation, they reach the target audience, and they further move the needle of what our project is trying to do.

Danielle: One of the great things about creating on TikTok is that the aesthetic does not encourage mastery. It's very like scrappy, DIY [Do It Yourself]. Things aren't perfect. You need to make do with what you have. So, for us, process is the name of the game. And even though we do have a product to show for the thing that we made, it's the process that is the important part.

Zachary: With Queens Who Read in Charlottesville, and I imagine with folks at Drag Story Hour, is that while the process matters, the product matters very much. Everyone wants a joyful world-making, "aha!" kind of a performance! At the same time, these performances lead to other Drag Storytimes. It's iterative, which also leads parents and educators to seek out other, more positive representations of gender play and queer role models. So, the product matters, but also how can it enter into an ecosystem that sustains itself and also goes further to cultivate a world where there are more of these positive representations?

Radhika: For us, there is no clear beginning of the process, and there is no clear end because it's always ongoing, specifically, when we are looking at gender. It starts with our own stories. It starts with how we are working with ourselves because that shows in the way we come across to participants. We have to consider our implicit biases; we keep challenging our notions. And the product does not end with that one performance or one workshop. The product shows every time we work on ourselves and bring our own stories out in rehearsals, which in turn affects how we bring out stories for others in the performance space.

Lisa: There are micro-products along the way, one thing leads to the next, and there's a bit of a dance, if you will, between process and product.

Zachary: It's not a linear process. Other things that we listen to or watch, come back to inform the work.

Lisa: Speaking of a nonlinear process, I want to come back to a thread from the beginning, which was this notion of play. What's the value of play, especially given what you talked about earlier, opening up new ways of thinking, new resources, and new ways of seeing ourselves and others?

Trevor: Danielle and I love to play, and, at the end of the day, we're both PhDs. The way we've been trained to do research is very serious and dry. What we've tried to do is show off our personalities in our research, and our artistic practice. We try not to be afraid of the criticisms we have heard: people who don't "get what we're doing," or why we're using TikTok as a space to do it. Or that it's less than or not serious. I think it's been freeing for both of us to do this experiment, which has untethered us, and allowed us to write and create and do things offline with more freedom and more creative liberties and agency, and play.

Danielle: You have to keep playing or first: You're going to get bored, and second: You will dry out of ideas. Let's not forget that play is the birthplace of creativity. You have to sort of shake off the shackles of "should" to think laterally, which will get you the brilliant connections and sort of the juicy parts of writing, not to mention joy. I am honored to be working closely with grad students for the first time, and they are so excited to engage with our work because it's just so different from the other things that they're reading. That's partly because we made the decision early on that we were going to write the way we wanted to write and not the way was prescribed to us by the form of academia. One of the pillars of our partnership is that if we're not having fun, it's not worthwhile.

Trevor: A writing retreat is a few hours of writing a day, and then we're exercising together. We're doing puzzles. We're making stupid TikTok dances. That might not necessarily be a traditional way of writing, but at the end of the day brings us closer and makes our relationship stronger. And then that energy goes into the work.

Zachary: Of course, play is central to Drag Storytime performances, giving children a place to see drag performers themselves play with gender and identity, and play with these stories. But we're only able to do what we do because the audience is there to authorize the play and to co-create the joy. Many Drag Storytime performers I've talked to say they aren't teaching joy so much as having it renewed in them by being in front of these children, who always are playing and understand dressing up and putting on different identities.

Radhika: I'm in applied theatre because it involves play, and I'm sustained by it for this reason. Generally, we're working with adults, and play often becomes a new concept. It breaks the monotony of what they're doing, and that itself makes them open to new ideas. It helps break learning patterns. Play is also essential for me as a facilitator, playing with what's coming up in the structure.

Zachary: This conversation makes me feel the need to continue finding my people: folks willing to collaborate and push me on what I think of as art-making practices, reconsidering "the who, the where, and the what" of best practices. This conversation is also making me think about how to get better at applied theatre, how to sustain it, and how to productively stretch the form.

Lisa: One of the projects of this anthology is documentation because if this work is not recorded, then people won't know about it or study it. So, I love that we are documenting work happening in spaces that people might not be considering.

Part III

Affecting Responses to Violence

7 Facilitating Afecto in Resistance to Violence

Patricia Ariza's Work with Female Victims of Colombia's Armed Conflict

Sarah Ashford Hart

In this essay, I consider how socially engaged practitioner Patricia Ariza's theatre work with displaced and victimized communities, especially women, contributes to Colombia's peace process.[1] Human rights discourse has positioned applied theatre as an intervention, yet this framework has often ignored how applied theatre moves us *somatically*. Ariza's approach offers an alternative perspective to Global-North-centric applied theatre conversations, as it emerges from a past-present history of colonization, dispossession, and extraction shared with other Latin American countries where women's bodies are the territory of violence and resistance. It reveals how women's embodied practices of re/co-existence offer a path to peace "from below," transforming normalized violent relations into life-affirming relations based on an ethics of radical care.[2]

Drawing on my experience witnessing her projects in 2022 with the Corporación Colombiana de Teatro in Bogotá, as well as interviews with Ariza during my dissertation fieldwork in 2019, I consider how the collective creations she directs allow all those present to feel more connected as part of both the problem and the solution. This indicates how applied theatre facilitators can renegotiate the neoliberal notion of theatre as a tool for "fixing" others' problems. For instance, promoting the use of testimonial narratives to "heal" trauma espouses an individualistic, Western approach that does not acknowledge community healing practices and requires victims/survivors to retell their stories in discursive terms that can be re-victimizing, while artists and institutions profit from the suffering of so-called others. Ariza's work involves narrative representations of traumatic experiences, but it centers on somatic expression/witnessing, which, I argue, potentiates afecto – a felt connection of care and solidarity (Hart, 2019).

Applied theatre scholars and practitioners often overlook affective transformations; instead, we focus on visibility or reintegration as indicators of social change, instrumentalized in neoliberal institutional agendas. For this reason, certain scholars have questioned the term *applied theatre*, arguing that it "traps the work 'through a primary focus on usefulness'" and "in neoliberal times, 'usefulness' is not necessarily a value-free or ideologically suitable focus" (Freebody et al., 2018, p. 4). Alongside measurable results (such as

DOI: 10.4324/9781003341802-13

the performance product or participant/audience statistics), Ariza's approach offers counter-hegemonic ways of being together. In discussing her projects, I argue that an affective mobilization is necessary for discursive intervention to have any real hold. The impact of this work is not only the effect on ideas and actions but also a widened sense of possibilities in terms of becoming with our world.

I am present in this research as an implicated, active listener; I must remain aware of my positionality and be careful not to impose a Global North perspective. Having witnessed Ariza's work live, I approach it through my body, paying attention to the affective impact it has on me as an audience member sharing an experience. Recognizing I am not a neutral presence, I undertake this project, in part, because, as a "reverse" migrant (or ex-pat), with roots in both North and South America, I find myself in a position to facilitate dialogues, connections, and (ex)changes between contexts, languages, and countries. My status as a PhD candidate from a US university played a part in how warmly I was received during my fieldwork in Colombia, and the fact that I live in Bogotá and have a Colombian family adds a sense of familiarity to my interactions. Still, I am seen as a "gringa," which means not only "from North America" but also white-presenting (my Venezuelan heritage makes no great difference in that perception). This makes me a strategic ally to local artists yet still an outsider.

Engaging "Female Victims" in Theatre for Peace

What does reimagining Colombia entre mujeres (between women) look like? According to Ariza, it means a felt sense of cuerpo entero (wholeness of body): "We are a very fragmented country, the people cannot see their whole body reflected, so art and storytelling can help to reunite the nation" (Sept 17, 2019b, Interview). The ongoing armed conflict and its articulation within civil society and institutions have made it impossible to consolidate a common vision of the country among Colombians (Chaparro Amaya, 2018). Accordingly, Ariza's work stems from a desire for a more cohesive, inclusive national imaginary. Moreover, the normalization of violence has meant a "moral indifference to violent death and suffering according to place of residence, age, colour, [gender] and poverty of the victims which disqualifies them for having rights" or deserving care (Humphrey, 2018, p. 468). One of Ariza's main aims is to raise awareness of society's responsibility to include and care about victims/survivors, particularly women.

Widespread fear of the "other" within the nation is at the heart of actions that "obliterate the other" and reproduce a culture of violence (Rotker, 2002; Chaparro Amaya, 2018). This othering is predicated on feminization. Diana Taylor argues that in Latin America women's bodies have been constructed as the national "territory" to be fought over and dominated by patriarchal movements, left and right, that have gained power by feminizing and subjugating the "other" (1997). Of course, patriarchal violence is not biologically male, just as a feminine relationality is not biologically female. Victimizers are not only men, and victims are not only women. However, the point at hand is that patriarchal scripts are so deeply ingrained that they impact people's lives in very real ways. As Rita Segato has noted, there is a new kind of warfare playing out in regions like Colombia that centers on violence against women in unprecedented forms; rather than solely a geographical territory, the primary battleground has become women's bodies, inscribing them with signs of loyalty or antagonism to armed groups (2016). Intertwined matrices of oppression (i.e. modernity, coloniality, and capitalism) based on patriarchy attempt to dispossess women of their bodies and their life force (Paredes Carvajal, 2014; Cabnal, 2020), yet relaciones afectivas (care networks) remain key to survival, and women are their axis.

Ariza's work (re)enacts the ways women repair relations damaged by violence, practicing an alternative relationality based on the capacity to care for life in the face of death (a relational possibility for *all* bodies). She explains why this creative work necessarily begins with women:

> Women are the ones who mourn, while men kill each other in war. More than 70% of the displaced population is made up of women. They are the ones who take care of the children, the sick, and the elderly. They are the ones who, with few assets and often without being able to bury their dead, must face being uprooted, which means losing everything and starting from scratch.
>
> (Viceversa Magazine, 2015, *my translation*)

In the collective creations Ariza directs, the care labor performed by female victims is embodied as a form of resistance to long-standing patriarchal practices of dominance. The female body is reclaimed as a collective life force, setting an example of radical care for others to follow – *radical* in the sense of going to the root of the problem: the devaluing of life.

While men are the majority of the dead and disappeared, women are most affected as survivors of the armed conflict, often losing their family members, homes, livelihoods, and physical safety. Because Colombia is in the midst of a peace and reparations process, there is a need to recognize and heal these scars of violence; Ariza's practice, therefore, prioritizes reappropriating the "female victim" identity.[3] This is not the same as pathologizing victims' trauma as the problem to be fixed; rather, it is about including those who have been most harmed in the peace process to build a better future for all, in which violence is not the common denominator of relations. The focus on "female victims" runs the risk of essentializing women as "helpless" and "in need." Ariza stresses, "Your life cannot only be about being a victim. It's important to value everything that a person brings, not only the pain they feel because of something that's happened to them. We must provide the opportunity for them to express themselves as full beings" (Sept 14, 2019a, Interview). Her testimonial theatre does not represent fixed subjects;

it is a process of becoming more than. Rather than approach the work from a deficit perspective,[4] Ariza's approach is deeply participatory; everyone who is present can redefine their relationships with one another and the world (Preston, 2016).

While Ariza is arguably the most renowned, other Colombian theatre facilitators (like Alejandra Borrero and Luz Marina Beccera) also center female "victims" experiences as a common standpoint from which to denounce the violations of rights. Ariza, like others, takes a "strategic" approach to essentialism that makes use of universalizing gender discourses in the fight for rights (Spivak in Nicolás Lazo, 2009) – specifically, the right to live free from violence – by recognizing how women across diverse positionalities have experienced violence, subjugation, and dispossession in different, intersecting, and related ways (Cabrera & Vargas Monroy, 2014). The decolonial communitarian feminist perspective is particularly helpful in understanding this work. It cultivates "affection for alterity as a community value," reframing community in terms of Pachamama (reciprocal relations among humans, the earth, animals, and plants, forming an organic whole) in order to construct a world that celebrates and cares for life, refusing to perpetuate a paradigm of death (Guzmán & Triana, 2019, p. 38, *my translation*).

In a recent piece that Ariza devised with the Escuela de Mujeres en Escena (School for Women on Stage), twelve participating women from a range of economic backgrounds, generations, and localities created characters based on "personal and group research into the stories of women who have marked history" (Corporación Colombiana de Teatro, 2022, *my translation*).[5] The Escuela is housed in the Corporación Colombiana de Teatro, which Ariza directs. Situated in the historic city center, the location is accessible from all sides of Bogotá, offering a space where women can unite across differences. In their piece titled *Venga le cuento: Historias de mujeres* (*Come I'll Tell You: Stories of Women*), the performers honor the legacies of women they do not want to be forgotten. The theatre is converted into a kind of salon with multiple tables, each a small set in and of itself, which contains a character and her universe of objects. Audience members move from table to table to listen to each monologue for a few minutes, before moving on to another table of their choice. Each person experiences a unique version of the show, as it is impossible to visit every table during the one-hour duration. The result is an intimate, itinerant experience of witnessing narratives that are individual yet co-present.

Venga le cuento centers on listening, care, and non-violence, offering a way of co/re-existing entre mujeres; this feminine relationality is not instrumental nor hierarchical, but creative – in the sense of women striving to recreate themselves, building community, giving life, and valuing embodied knowledge (Gutiérrez Aguilar et al., 2020). The performers bring to life characters whose legacies connect to their own stories, family histories, personal values, and shared struggles. Some of the memorable characters include Debora Arango, a censored Colombian artist who was the first to paint female nudes in the mid-1900s; La Gaitana, a young Indigenous woman who led the resistance against the Spanish invasion in the mid-1500s; and La "Loca" Margarita, a vehement supporter of the liberal party whose husband and son were killed by the conservatives, driving her to roam the streets of Bogotá throughout the early 1900s. The performers embody these women while remaining present themselves, revealing the reasons for their role choices and asking the audience pointed questions.

Another piece, devised to commemorate the third anniversary of the Truth Commission (and five years since the 2016 Peace Accord), *Salida al sol, Camino a la paz* (*Sunrise, Path to Peace*), interweaves the causes and effects of violence in a collage of music, movement, poetry, and dramatic vignettes. The show highlights the need to make a stand for peace across differences and create a new social contract based on radical care. While it includes some male performers, playing victimizers as well as victims – such as soldiers, landholders, workers, and protesters – it is driven by the majority female cast (both trained actresses and victims-turned-artists) embodying a range of women's experiences. There are two mothers whose sons were forcibly disappeared by the state as falsos positivos ("falsely accused" as guerillas or narcos and extrajudicially murdered by the military), and an ex-guerilla who signed the peace agreement. They each play themselves. There are also a dozen actresses/dancers, each playing multiple roles, including displaced campesinas (female peasants); sisters and mothers of men killed by armed groups; the ruling class; and the souls of the dead. The piece critiques the ways that violence is perpetuated by the self-love of supposedly autonomous individuals who misguidedly believe themselves free from responsibility to others. It calls for a more conscious kind of love that affirms all life as interdependent, via an expressly feminine relationality.

In an early scene, the chorus of women become displaced campesinas, "dancing in the night to defend life with their own," as a campesina character states (Ariza, 2021). Accompanied by a traditional Afro-Colombian bullerengue song (that provokes goosebumps), the women clutch their belongings in burlap sacks as they run from gunfire, helping each other escape. In tableaux, they express their love for their stolen land and the animals that form part of their relaciones afectivas. In a dance of endurance and protest, they zapateo (stomp in rhythm) as a group, waving a Colombian flag in the center. Later in the piece, the mothers of the "falsely accused" speak of their heartbreak upon losing their sons, their endless search for the bodies, and how despite being ignored, silenced, and persecuted by authorities, they've kept their sons' memories alive. They affirm, "I am not alone," and the chorus of women echoes, "We are all with them." As a recurring motif, white dove puppets are held up on rods above the performers' heads, at first appearing one at a time, and then taking the stage as a flock: a shared life force that extends beyond the individual, elevating toward truth and peace as a collective body with the capacity for change-making. This theme resonates with an earlier scene when the ex-guerilla shows how she transformed herself to serve the collective good.

She describes how she and her comrades gave up their arms willingly, exchanging her fatigues for a red dress, like the dresses the other women in the cast wear, and runs to join the chorus of women with her arms extended behind her like a bird, becoming part of their persistent, hopeful dance of unity.

As evidenced in these scenes, Ariza's work revolves around women finding new expressions of their creative power as a collective pathway toward living free from violence. She explains: "Among the vulnerable population – women, all of them – there is something difficult. The body is to be exhibited, to look beautiful, or to do housework, to clean, to wash. It is a body that is permanently under attack. So, changing the codes of the body is very important…seeing the body and using the body in a different way is a very interesting liberation" (Sept 14, 2019a, Interview). Ariza thus redefines women's role in society as more than "victim" or caretaker, reaffirming their humanity, and valuing their strengths – particularly, their capacity to mobilize afecto.

Geographically, Colombia is a patchwork territory of diverse regions that have traditionally been difficult to unify and moreover have been cut up by processes of colonization, dispossession, and extraction. For this reason, Ariza's work often incorporates performers' embodied practices (i.e. dance and music) from different regions and ethnicities, such as the piercing bullerengue in *Salida al sol*. She explains, "It is a way of showing lost territories. And when I say territory, I refer to the body, the culture, and the land itself. With actions and with shared presence, a place is made in afecto" (Satizábal & Marín, 2015, p. 70, *my translation*). In her productions, the afecto generated among bodies in the performance space establishes a feminist territory for peace, cultivating a feeling of being-with that facilitates listening, to (re)constitute the collective body-territory.

Narrative and Affect Enmeshed

Ariza's method broadens the scope of testimonial theatre to include non-verbal (physical and musical) vocabularies. Her approach is one of heightened "realness," where performers express their lived experience in an intentionally raw yet theatrical manner – as in the case of the ex-guerilla, who wipes away her tears with her uniform jacket after removing it, in a real-life Brechtian gestus. It is clear to the audience when performers are telling their own stories versus playing characters. However, through the collective creation process, the material becomes shared, and the division between "community participant" and "professional performer" is blurred. When performers take on character roles, there is an added level of poetic abstraction (verbal, physical, and/or musical), positioning "character" as a synecdoche for a community, while remaining linked to a situation of real injustice; this fictional approach to testimony can intensify the connection with reality (Puga in Sotomayor-Botham, 2016). For instance, in *Venga le cuento*, the actress who plays the artist Debora Arango begins by speaking as herself, saying that she has been learning to play the flute. She gives a small demonstration and points out that being an artist makes you vulnerable but adds that we should not give up on our dreams, drawing a connection between her quivering notes and Arango's struggle to gain visibility as a painter.

While many readings of testimonial performances privilege verbal language and symbolism, such an approach would miss the nuance of Ariza's work, as it ignores how afecto impacts audiences somatically. As Ariza says, momentary feelings of connection can potentiate an alternative, nonviolent way of relating that affirms life (Satizábal & Marín Eds., 2015). In the audience of *Salida al sol*, I felt afecto emerge from the moments that focused on the performers' embodied co-presence. This in turn initiated a deep kind of listening, calling on witnesses to *feel* as well as understand how our lives affect and are affected by others.[6] When the chorus takes the stage, they move and speak as a collective, identifying themselves as murdered lideresas (female community leaders), orphans, mothers, and sisters of the 6,402 people assassinated. Abstract movements by the group punctuate the speech of each performer as she addresses the audience face-on, generating a visceral sense of implication, interdependence, and vulnerability that we must take responsibility for in order to ethically cohabit in a shared territory.

Because the female body is a site of both discursive and physical violence, Ariza's productions combine social critique and embodied co-presence to change how we feel and understand our capacity to care. The attuning of bodies in the space to listen somatically allows us to hear words and what's between them more fully. This is why the many vocabularies at work – physical, visual, musical, and verbal – are all important. Ariza describes her productions as *polyphonic actions*, expressing in multiple vocabularies the voices of many people, each containing numerous voices. I would add that it is not just what is said or symbolized when expressing someone's story but what cannot be said and still resonates between bodies that allows the self to feel interconnected with others. In this way, recounted suffering does not lead to separateness but collective bodying – an experience akin to pleasure, a celebration of life.

What made *Venga le cuento* moving, for me, was being physically surrounded by other audience members, listening not only to the actors' narratives but to the energies circulating among bodies in proximity. The imperative *Venga* (come) in the title elicits physical movement toward the speaker as a prerequisite for them telling us something important (*le cuento*). This addresses the problem of separation – the fragmentation of the national body and the distancing of the privileged from the pain of "others."

Some ethical questions remain around representational politics: Can female "victims" be placed center stage without their suffering being sensationalized? Why include trained performers in a cast with "victims" who can speak for themselves? When facilitators build careers working with vulnerable populations, can we be sure we are not using them for our own gain? As a survivor of forced displacement (as a child) and the genocide against the Patriotic Union Party (as an adult), Ariza can teach other facilitators, like me, a great deal about ethics and esthetics. In a recent interview, she explained, "The narrative of the nation is broken by desafecto (disaffection) and violence. Reconstructing it is a collective task…we women have to recount years of violence and patriarchal exclusion … victims have to express their accounts in multiple vocabularies" (Guzmán, 2023, *my translation*). It is implicit here that these accounts must then be widely seen and heard.

While I agree it is crucial for society to witness testimonies of victimization and be held accountable, I wonder about the impact on the narrators. Ariza told me in an interview that participants find freedom in theatrical expression. I imagine, though, that for some of the women in the Escuela de Mujeres, the liberatory experience is more about being part of the group's creative process than it is about being onstage. While some take the stage with captivating presence and confidence, others seem more unsure of their place in the spotlight and less confident in their performance; however, it is clear they feel it is vital to be there. When I asked Ariza if it is essential for the participants to always have a public performance, she replied: "There always has to be a showing. It can be for a small audience. Some people are shy." Referring to testimonial performance, she added: "When someone is in a lot of pain, it's difficult for them to talk … Forcing someone to talk would be another kind of violence. You have to change the pain" (Sept 14, 2019a, Interview). To this end, she aims to find what it is people are able and willing to express and in what way – for instance, a dance or a song they know. This can then be interwoven with the stories of others in a way that builds strength and connection.

The collective creation process is thus key in cultivating afecto. When the time comes for public performance, this connection of care and solidarity endures, touching the audience and challenging desafecto. Another emergent question, then, is how large-scale this work can become without losing its intimate imperative (*Venga*) or its raw realness (female victims literally dancing and singing in the night to defend life).

Conclusion

Applied theatre is not only about making experiences legible nor forming "good" citizens; it is also about expressing and witnessing all kinds of affects, thus facilitating a felt connection to the complex webs of relations that shape our world. In addition to its discursive impacts, Ariza's work creates spaces where female victims' embodied practices demonstrate counterhegemonic ways of being together: where pain can be expressed, witnessed, and transformed into rage, strength, and love – healing the collective body-territory. In resistance to normalized, misogynist violence that destroys communities, the performers in *Salida al sol* and *Venga le cuento* assert themselves as inseparable from one another, their territories, and their differences. Bodies of all kinds take the stage for peace as one, finding strength in polyphonic action that incites a feminine relationality based on radical care, calling upon audiences to follow their lead, and recognize our own part in this story.

Notes

1 Throughout this essay, the term "women" is used inclusively for all people who are women-identified.
2 Radical care is a praxis of coalition building, mutual aid, and solidarity (Hobart & Kneese, 2020) that offers an alternative to the neoliberal/(neo)colonial model of morally obligated care as charity and self-care as individualistic self-preservation.
3 While the "victim" label implies powerlessness and passivity, not strength and survival, the term is used *strategically* to advocate for dignity, reparations, and rights, by activist groups.
4 Taking a deficit perspective is problematic because it reduces participants to the perceived "failure and/or lack of ability of that group of persons to be empowered or productive in their current circumstances" (Freebody et al., 2018, p. 6).
5 This production was co-directed by Nohra González and Ángela Triana. In terms of diversity, the cast is mainly white-mestiza, with one afro-Colombian performer.
6 I refer here to an audience made up of the Corporación Colombiana de Teatro community and a general public attracted by the piece's content matter – all likely left-leaning but representing a range of backgrounds. However, Ariza's large-scale productions like *Salida al sol* tour nationally, reaching much wider audiences.

References

Ariza, P. (2019a) Interview and translation by Sarah Hart, Sept 14, 2019, Interview.

Ariza, P. (2019b) Interview and translation by Sarah Hart, Sept 17, 2019, Interview.

Ariza, P. (2021) *Salida al sol, Camino a la paz*. Bogotá: Coproduced by Comisión de la Verdad and Corporación Colombian de Teatro. Video of theatre performance. https://www.comisiondelaverdad.co/salida-al-sol-camino-la-paz

Cabnal, L. (2020) "Acercamiento a la construcción de la propuesta de pensamiento epistémico de las mujeres indígenas feministas comunitarias de Abya Yala." In *Momento de paro, tiempo para rebelión: Miradas feministas para reinventar la lucha*, 116–134. Buenos Aires: Minervas Ediciones.

Cabrera, M. & Vargas Monroy, L. (2014) "Transfeminismo, decolonialidad y el asunto del conocimiento: algunas inflexiones de los feminismos disidentes contemporáneos." *Universitas Humanística*, 78: 19–37. DOI: 10.11144/Javeriana.UH78.tdac

Chaparro Amaya, A. (2018) *La cuestión del ser enemigo: El contexto insoluble de la justicia transicional en Colombia*. Bogotá: Universidad del Rosario.

Corporación Colombiana de Teatro. (2022) "Venga le cuento 'Historias de mujeres'." Accessed Jan 12, 2023. https://corporacioncolombianadeteatro.com/eventos/venga-le-cuento-historias-de-mujeres-2/

Freebody, K. Balfour, M. Finneran, M. & Anderson, M., eds. (2018) *Applied Theatre: Understanding Change*. Cham: Springer. https://link.springer.com/book/10.1007/978-3-319-78178-5

Gutiérrez Aguilar, R. Sosa, M. N. & Reyes, I. (2020) "El entre mujeres como negación de las formas de interdependencia impuestas por el patriarcado capitalista y colonial. Reflexiones en torno a la violencia y la mediación patriarcal." In *Momento de paro, tiempo para rebelión: Miradas feministas para reinventar la lucha*. Buenos Aires: Minervas Ediciones.

Guzmán, J. C. (2023) "'La cultura es el combustible para la vida': ministra Patricia Ariza." *El Tiempo*, Jan 4. https://www.eltiempo.com/cultura/arte-y-teatro/ministra-de-explica-por-que-cambiar-el-nombre-del-ministerio-731096?fbclid=IwAR3YBVZfeGPCLXjLkvT-Uk5oYaBEbibk2I5mIYt7WLzAGVnSylGpdp1d6VA

Guzmán, N. & Triana, D. (2019) "Julieta Paredes: hilando el feminismo comunitario." *Ciencia Política*, 14 (28): 23–49. DOI: 10.15446/cp.v14n28.79125

Hart, S. A. (2019) "Movilidad y encierro 'Sur-Sur': reflexiones sobre la práctica de performance participativa como investigación en la penitenciaria femenina de Santiago, Chile." *Revista corpo-grafías: Estudios críticos de y desde los cuerpos,* 6 (6): 214–226. https://revistas.udistrital.edu.co/ojs/index.php/CORPO/article/view/14242

Hobart, H. J. K. & Kneese, T. (2020) "Radical Care: Survival Strategies for Uncertain Times." *Social Text,* 38 (1): 1–16. DOI: 10.1215/01642472-7971067

Humphrey, M. (2018) "The Political Lives of the 'Disappeared' in the Transition from Conflict to Peace in Colombia." *Politics, Religion & Ideology,* 19 (4): 452–470. DOI: 10.1080/21567689.2018.1538671

Nicolás Lazo, G. (2009) "Debates en epistemología feminista: del empiricismo y el standpoint a las críticas postmodernas sobre el sujeto y el punto de vista." In *Genero y dominación: críticas feministas del derecho y el poder,* coordinated by Gemma Nicolás Lazo, Encarna Bodelón González, Roberto Bergalli, & Iñaki Rivera Beiras. Barcelona: Anthropos.

Paredes Carvajal, J. (2014) "Dissidence and Communitarian Feminism." *Emisférica,* 11 (1). Accessed Oct 2, 2023. https://hemisphericinstitute.org/en/emisferica-11-1-decolonial-gesture/11-1-dossier/e111-dossier-dissidence-and-communitarian-feminism.html

Preston, S. (2016) *Applied Theatre Facilitation: Pedagogies, Practices, Resilience.* London: Bloomsbury. Kindle Edition.

Rotker, S. (2002) "Cities Written by Violence: An Introduction." In *Citizens of Fear: Urban Violence in Latin America,* edited by Susana Rotker. New Brunswick: Rutgers University Press. Kindle Edition.

Satizábal, C. & Marín, A., eds. (2015) *Performances: habitar la calle, habitar los cuerpos: Patricia Ariza.* Bogotá: Ideartes & Mincultura.

Segato, R. L. (2016) *La Guerra Contra Las Mujeres.* Madrid: Traficantes de Sueños.

Sotomayor-Botham, P. (2016) "Teatro testimonial contemporáneo en Chile: Dilemas éticos y estéticos." *Revista Nuestra América,* (10), Jan–July: 193–203. Accessed Oct 2, 2023. https://bdigital.ufp.pt/bitstream/10284/6766/1/Nuestra%20america_nr10_13.pdf

Taylor, D. (1997) *Disappearing Acts: Spectacles of Gender and Nationalism in Argentina's "Dirty War."* Durham: Duke University Press.

Viceversa Magazine. (2015) "Vuelve el Teatro de Patricia Ariza." March 16. https://www.viceversa-mag.com/vuelve-el-teatro-de-patricia-ariza/

8 Moving Women from the Margins to the Center of History

After/Life and the 1967 Detroit Rebellion

Kristin Horton and Lisa Biggs

By all accounts, Sunday, July 23, 1967, was a scorcher. In Detroit, the temperature had climbed into the 90s. It would soon become clear to those who witnessed the events that day that the sun was no match for the protests burning across the city. At about three o'clock that morning, the Detroit Police Department (DPD) raided an unlicensed, after-hours party on 12th Street, one of the city's most established Black communities. The eighty or so patrons partying at Bill Scott's "Blind Pig" did not go easy. To their surprise, the DPD was met by righteous, organized resistance that had accumulated after decades of peaceful attempts to end police brutality. Rumors that the police sexually assaulted at least one woman at the party compounded their outrage. Using cue balls, bottles, bricks, and anything else they could grab, they soon drove the police from the scene. Next, they turned their frustration onto the nearby businesses, slumlords, and predatory developers who maintained and profited from anti-Black racism. By dawn, fire alarms rang across the city. One of the twentieth century's largest civil uprisings in the United States had begun.

In 2014, as a new assistant professor of performance studies at Michigan State University (MSU), Lisa Biggs began researching the history of the 1967 Detroit Rebellion. She quickly discovered that most accounts focused on the experiences of men and that popular myths attributed the unrest to the work of a small cadre of militant, Black male criminals rather than structural inequality. Women and girls, who constitute over fifty-two percent of Detroit's population today, are largely omitted from histories of the city's life, including the history of the 1967 rebellion, in which they played a pivotal role. Biggs writes,

> In photo after photo, women and girls appear alongside men and boys. Of the over seven thousand people arrested from July 23 to July 28, 1967, 10–12% were women or girls (the youngest was ten years old). Forty-three people were killed including two white women and one little girl, Tanya Lynn Blanding, shot and killed by the National Guardsmen who opened fire on her building.
>
> (2017c)

DOI: 10.4324/9781003341802-14

Questions concerning who these women were, their roles, and their responsibilities during the unrest, the subsequent military occupation, and its aftermath inspired Biggs to research their stories. Working with students enrolled in her MSU theatre and performance studies courses, Biggs began to collect alternative oral histories and archival materials about female experiences in the city. Sifting through the material, she recognized that the stories offered a compelling counter-narrative to the declensionist published histories and popular fallacies that position Detroit as the poster child for the "failures" of Black civil rights leadership (Hamera, 2017, pp 1–18). The archive demanded a critical re-reading of what counter-revolutionaries have called "riots" and revolutionaries, the "rebellion." Soon, Biggs began to envision *After/Life*, a one-act play designed to reveal the psychological motivations behind the unrest and the determination of Detroit's women to rebuild their city and their lives in its wake. In the spirit of the stories she and her students uncovered, Biggs focused *After/Life* on the history of police brutality and activism in the years leading up to the rebellion, such as the 1963 police murder of Cynthia Scott, a Detroit-based, Black, sex worker (2017c). Biggs used that event and other stories about crime, policing, and community organizing to pose questions about how popular narratives concerning Detroit attribute or deny dignity and value to human lives, and how those perspectives shape cultural practices and public policies that impact people's lives today. Unlike other dramatic portrayals of the unrest, such as Dominique Morisseau's *Detroit '67*, *After/Life* braids together oral histories with archival materials, poetry, song, and dance. The script is intended to catalyze community engagement by connecting the historical narratives of the past with the present.

After two years of script development at MSU, in 2016, Biggs invited me to serve as director, given our shared ethos in the centrality of audience-centered work. Early on, it became clear that any kind of community-engaged work around the rebellion in Detroit would mean entering a space not only of resilience and great determination but also a site of trauma. In this essay, we reflect upon our process of developing and staging *After/Life* in Detroit, a few blocks from where the rebellion began, in conjunction with city-wide commemoration events marking its fiftieth anniversary.

Development of *After/Life's* Core Values

The events of 1967 comprise a difficult, complicated, and ongoing history, a "50-year rebellion" that historian Scott Kurashige argues never ended, with the revolution still to come (2017, p. 7). Community-engaged practice and research have their own problematic history and legacy, during which aggrieved communities have been exploited by researchers perpetuating an array of epistemic injustices. Additionally, as non-Detroiters, we risked inadvertently reproducing the same kinds of oppressions we sought to critique, such as extractive and exploitative research practices. To that end, the methodology of the project would become just as important as the project itself.

I'm a cisgender woman of Anglo-Scottish ancestry raced as "white" within the framework of racialization in the United States. I grew up in a military family in multiple locations throughout the United States and abroad. Lisa Biggs is an African-American cisgender woman originally from the Southside of Chicago. Our journeys intersected in the mid-90s at the Living Stage Theater Company, the radical social outreach arm of Arena Stage in Washington, DC where we both served as members of its interracial acting ensemble.

Living Stage's focus on participatory theatre and social change brought together our shared interests in liberation and performance through rehearsal and process. Located at 14th and T Street, once considered the home of DC's "Black Broadway," Living Stage served its surrounding community, particularly students and teachers in the DC public school system, unsheltered families, teen mothers, as well as the incarcerated. The company's process combined performances that focused on issues relevant to its audiences with workshops based on improvisational theatre techniques. Living Stage's work was premised on the idea that by participating in the act of creation, audiences would "see themselves differently in relation to their community and come to know it is within their power to transform themselves and their world" (1995, p. 1).

While we were there, the late Rebecca Rice, an African-American theatre artist and former company member, returned as an associate artist to train the acting ensemble. Rice brought years of experience as an anti-racist/anti-oppression trainer as well as a critical Black feminist lens to the improvisational storytelling process that formed the basis of her work. Rice's direction and mentorship made an indelible impression on us, challenging us to confront ourselves along with our audiences. It was there that Biggs and I developed a shared set of artistic and philosophical values grounded in Rice's teachings, as well as an abiding respect for audience-centered work that would continue through artistic collaborations in the decades that followed.

Despite this shared history, given our positions as non-Detroiters, we needed to expand our frameworks to help us think through and critique our practice. According to many of our interlocutors, non-Detroiters have often misconstrued the story of the rebellion, with devastating effects on city residents. To create an equitable relationship with the community, we undertook a "review of the practice." Our goal was to find like-minded organizations with expertise in navigating these concerns. Ultimately, we drew on the work of Cornerstone Theater, a company based in Los Angeles that has made theatre by and with communities for more than thirty-five years, and the University of California Center for Collaborative Research for an Equitable California (CCREC), an initiative that links interdisciplinary researchers and community organizations, in equity-oriented, collaborative, community-engaged projects.

Cornerstone's work provided a model for building partnerships with the goal of developing beneficial relationships between the project and the community. Cornerstone's examples of how to ensure "the community's voice is heard throughout the production process" and to eliminate "the hierarchy between artists and community" were foundational (2006, p. 5). Their approach enabled us to ask important, new questions: What, for example, did the community want to learn about 1967? Additionally, Cornerstone's strategies for community participation in script development reminded us that Detroiters were not a singular or monolithic entity. In preparation for rehearsals in the city to begin in June 2017, we strategized how to invite more perspectives into the project, including points of view that would "challenge some of the community's assumptions about itself" (2006, p. 57).

We were also influenced by CCREC's approach to justice-oriented research and critical analysis of the complex ethical questions that arise in community engagement, especially regarding knowledge production and "democratic possibilities of collaborative research" (CCREC, 2023). Particularly inspiring was CCREC's focus on reciprocity, which encouraged us to find ways for project resources to flow back into the community.

Through our "review of the practice," Biggs and I identified *After/Life's* four core values: foregrounding the community (in its multiple definitions); de-centering our roles as writer and director in each aspect of the process; providing platforms for a multitude of perspectives; and finally, re-directing project resources back to the community. This resulted in developing an expansive network of partners that included local grassroots organizations and state institutions, as well as an ensemble-based rehearsal process emphasizing collaborative devising techniques.

Project Resources and Partnerships

With support from the Michigan Humanities Council, in the spring of 2016, we assembled an advisory committee of scholars, artists, and activists who worked on the rebellion in Detroit. This helped us build a network that included: the Joseph Walker Williams Community Center (JWWCC), MSU's Detroit Center, Grace Episcopal Church, the Detroit Historical Society, Detroit Repertory Theater, Wayne State University, and the Ruth Ellis Center. This network was vital to our work in multiple ways: It connected us to other artists and organizations working on '67; introduced us to community members interested in collaborating; raised awareness about the project; and provided us with an invaluable resource for critical reflection and accountability.

That summer, Biggs and I continued reviewing the narratives of the rebellion across disciplines. Questions emerged: Who tells these stories? What assumptions inform each narrative? Where are the gaps and contradictions? How do the narratives differ when told by grass-roots organizations versus state or federal institutions? What might we learn if the voices of women moved from the margins of history to the center? How might we ethically engage Detroiters in the research and artistic process?

After/Life's **Rehearsal Process**

The choice to foreground the community determined where we would audition, rehearse, and perform the play. Early on, Detroit Repertory Theater, one of the oldest and most established companies in the city, offered its space to us; but, it didn't feel right to perform the piece at a location where a large portion of the intended audience would have to travel to see it. Alternatively, Andrea Robinson, director of the JWWCC located two blocks from where the rebellion began, expressed a need to reaffirm the center's role in the community, precisely at a time when city-wide budget cuts were further marginalizing it. She invited us to present the play on-site, and together, we developed a production plan that would allow for a portion of *After/Life*'s rehearsal process to take place without disrupting their ongoing activities and to direct project resources toward the center.

That spring, we conducted auditions for local community members in the JWWCC with the goal of creating an intergenerational ensemble interested in the histories of '67 and social justice. Ultimately, the ensemble and creative team for *After/Life* featured members of the Virginia Park (12th Street) community alongside students from MSU and Wayne State's Masters of Fine Arts MFA acting program. For her audition, Deborah Chenault-Green, a lifelong Detroiter, provided a first-hand account of the night the rebellion began. Aged twelve at the time, Chenault-Green was at her aunt's home at the corner of Hazelwood and 14th Street, preparing for her mother's birthday party. Because of the heat, she and her cousin had pulled mattresses out on the porch to sleep. They awoke to the noise and light of the fires just blocks away. Stories like these created a vibrant rehearsal environment infused with lived experiences and memories.

Recognizing that stories about the rebellion might be difficult for community members to share and for other cast members to hear, we also worked with Chelsea Gregory, a restorative justice practitioner who consults with individuals and organizations on community-engaged practices. While Gregory was based in New York at the time, her network included Detroit-based artists and activists such as adrienne maree brown, whose work became pivotal in imagining the project's future. Gregory encouraged us to use a range of strategies, such as establishing rehearsal room agreements to provide frameworks for navigating the process and for holding one another, and ourselves, accountable. One of our favorite agreements was for us to "stay on our growing edge and be willing to be changed by the process." For us, it was a powerful reminder to listen deeply to what was happening in the room and be changed by it, continually.

Biggs and I tried to create a non-hierarchical rehearsal process by decentralizing roles that are often perceived as authoritarian (e.g., the director) and emphasizing collaborative, ensemble-based approaches. To ensure that community members participated in leadership positions, we hired a local costume designer, stage manager, and house manager. Similarly, we drew from other forms of expertise among the ensemble. For example, a company member was invited to create choreography for the production, and Deborah

Chenault-Green gave us permission to use poems she wrote about her memories of 12th Street before, during, and after the rebellion.

The content was generated in several ways, including creative exercises utilizing materials from the research and improvised scenes inspired by group discussion, with Biggs as the playwright shaping both the form and content. In many ways, this mirrored our experiences at the Living Stage. Rice taught us to work from joy even as we engaged with difficult or traumatic content. As Rice reminded us, "Black culture consists of more than just pain" (Biggs 2017b, p. 78). To tell the full story of the rebellion and of the Black community that ignited it, it was incumbent on us to make space for joy as well as laughter. Often, our rehearsal process would begin in the spirit of "coming as we are," a frequent refrain of Rice's that encapsulated our fundamental belief that everyone had something valuable and important to contribute. As a result, despite the grief and anger within many of the '67 stories we shared, our rehearsals were often joyful celebrations centering on hope and possibility.

One of the most impactful yet simple things we did was hire one of the JWWCC's regular patrons, who bakes out of her home, to bake for a free lemonade and cake party we hosted for JWWCC members on the first day of our on-site rehearsal. This provided an opportunity for us to introduce ourselves and encourage the JWWCC patrons to ask us questions, watch rehearsals, and give us feedback. It worked. In the common area of the JWWCC, rehearsals took place surrounded by the center's daily life. Amid weightlifting, card

Figure 8.1 After/Life opens with a dance party. Joseph Walker Williams Community Center. 2017. Photo by Katie Wittenauer.

games, and bake sales, the show emerged. As we rehearsed, people gathered, asked questions, shared their stories, and conversations started and continued. Biggs recalls,

> The senior patrons really supported the show. They shared their memories during the rehearsals and the piece itself and expressed their appreciation for the project again and again. By the end of the run, whenever I pulled into the parking lot, the elders sitting outside would smile, wave, and call my name, if they knew it. Sometimes, they just called "You-With-The-Play," which was fine with me. They appreciated what we were about, and I'm proud we earned their respect.
>
> (Biggs and Horton 2017)

Performances and Reception

After/Life was created over an eight-week period and performed during the last two weeks of July 2017, with the audience sitting in a large 1970s-style conversational pit. While there is much to say about the esthetics of the piece, I will share a few examples here that best illustrate *After/Life*. Several sources inspired us: civic events, church services, and social dance programs from the late 1960s and 1970s, including a Detroit television dance show *The Scene,* on which one of our ensemble member's parents had been regular dancers. To support frequent transitions and allow for actors to play a multitude of characters, actors remained on stage with minimal costume changes happening in full view. To create esthetic distance for a community that experiences police brutality, we utilized imaginary objects for props, such as guns, and symbolized violence. Throughout the performance, we encouraged Call and Response, and the piece ended with a ritual candle lighting and naming of the women who died during the rebellion. The audience was invited to join in singing "Ella's Song," by Sweet Honey in the Rock, which celebrates the words of civil rights activist Ella Baker in its refrain: "We who believe in freedom cannot rest until it comes."

The story of *After/Life* foregrounds the experiences of women and girls in its telling of the rebellion. A poem written and performed by Chenault-Green opened the play, introducing audiences to the neighborhood from a young girl's perspective:

> Hopscotch, tag, hide and go-get-it
> Baseball in the alley, nowhere to hit it
> Boys wearin' holsters and guns
> Learnin' to shoot
> Riding the Popsicle bikes
> Pockets full of loot
> Hot days, steamy nights…

Music heard all night long from the Calumet Bar
The innocence and beauty of 12th Street
Before the Riot
Before the Community died

(Biggs 2017a, p. 2)

The poem reminded audiences that 12th Street was more than the ignition point of the unrest: It was a home. *After/Life* reintroduced and represented the community before the aftermath of '67. To those who grew up there like Chenault-Green, 12th Street raised them, and it overflowed with wonder. By day, it bustled with locally owned stores where their mothers and grandmothers shopped. By night, it transformed into "the Strip," one of the few areas where working Black people could relax and socialize.

Like any community, 12th Street was filled with complexity, which the play illuminated by including a scene in which three neighborhood women – a Black beautician, a white (preferably Jewish) butcher, and a Black sex worker – intervene to protect a young girl from street sexual harassment. The sex worker, St. Cynthia Scott, ends the encounter by chastising the men:

> You betta leave that child alone. You ain't got no business bothering her. You heard what I said. That about the oldest damn penny in the goddamn world. You think she want that? Don't nobody want none of what you got.
>
> (Biggs 2017a, p. 8)

This scene underscores the myriad of critical roles women and girls played in their community.

After establishing the neighborhood from their perspectives, *After/Life* expanded into other stories about their lives in the years leading up to the rebellion. The play used the story of St. Cynthia Scott's murder by DPD to illustrate women's experiences of crime, safety, and justice, drilling down on the racialized and gendered nature of policing. Scott, a twenty-four-year-old Black woman, was stopped by two Detroit police for allegedly engaging in prostitution in the early morning hours of July 5, 1963. Scott denied their accusations, as did the man she was with that Independence Day weekend. When Scott refused to get into the squad car, the police shot her dead. Local activists, including members of the clergy and women who knew Scott, rallied for the police to be held accountable. Biggs transformed an archived interview with one sex worker into a monologue that encapsulated many low-income working women's perspectives on Scott's murder, safety, and justice in the city:

> That officer had been harassing Cynthia for weeks. For weeks and weeks and weeks, and she didn't want to pay no more. This is what was supposed to go down. Police arrest a girl for streetwalking, and turn her loose if she pay. Cynthia had paid and paid, and she didn't want to pay no

more. She wasn't the only one. The dope man, barber shop, grocery store, pharmacy, gas station, picture man – all of them, all of them, dealing with this. She knew if you don't kick in, you'd suffer the consequences. Things was really, really bad, but I didn't think they'd kill her. Not like this. This could blow the lid off police headquarters, 1300 Beaubien.

(Biggs 2017a, p. 21)

After/Life demonstrated that women understood the conditions under which they lived and the possible consequences of defying harmful norms and expectations. In response to this monologue, the actor playing St. Cynthia turned to the audience and asked them, "Who gonna arrest the man that's collecting money for the police?" That line communicated many women's exasperation with the status quo.

The story of Louise and Danny Thomas, a married Black couple, who were chased out of a historically white public park by a white mob, expanded the conversation about anti-Black racism into the broader community. The River Rouge Park incident (as it came to be called) ended Danny's life and caused the loss of Louise's first child when she miscarried days later. It also spurred a broad coalition to demand action from local Black leaders and white lawmakers:

ST. CYNTHIA

They treat us worse than dogs. Somebody ought to go down to police headquarters.

NARRATOR 8

They won't listen to anybody, especially not to a group of Negro women.

NARRATOR 1

They gonna listen. Where's that preacher husband of mine?

(Biggs 2017a, p. 25)

Through these scenes and others, *After/Life* represented the challenges and the precarity of women's lives in Detroit. Moreover, it revealed how women organized to defend themselves and how they struggled together to transform the conditions of their city.

When Chenault-Green, who played Wilma, the daughter of the proprietor of the "Blind Pig," got slapped by a white Detroit cop during our staging of the raid, audience members audibly gasped. It was the sound of people collectively recoiling in horror and recognition. It was the same sound that party-goers uttered on July 23, 1967, the night of the rebellion. It was the sound that launched the first bricks thrown at the police in our production, and like those thrown in July 1967, it carried the weight of history.

To continue our goal of centering the community, the audience was invited to share their memories of '67 and comment on the play in the middle of the performance. This created opportunities for elders to relay their experiences, and in some cases, for their children or grandchildren to hear these stories in a new light. Furthermore, these sharing painted a fuller picture of the role of women in the rebellion and how they risked their lives while helping families and neighbors. Biggs shares,

> One man recalled that his mother piled her children into a car to evacuate them out of the city. Another woman told us that her mother faced down a National Guardsman's rifle and bayonet to get her children home. Teaching their children to load weapons, to hit the floor and duck for cover to avoid getting shot by the police, and to be forever wary of men in uniform – all these things became a necessary part of mothering during the rebellion.
>
> (2017c)

The project was met with a supportive response from the community, as well as from members of the advisory committee who came to see it, including Dr. Geneva Smitherman, a Detroit native and Black studies scholar. She believes *After/Life* may be the first accounting of the rebellion from a Black feminist perspective.

Figure 8.2 Actor Kristy Allen speaks with audience members about their memories of the '67 rebellion. Joseph Walker Williams Community Center. 2017. Photo by Katie Wittenauer.

After the play concluded, Biggs made several visits back to Detroit the following year. Williams Center director Andrea Robinson relayed she was regularly asked if the play would return. Likewise, several community elders said they were proud of the work and encouraged the project to continue, not only to know the history but to see a play that portrays the neighborhood with dignity and respect. According to Robinson, the play also brought renewed interest in the Williams Center, bringing back hundreds who hadn't been in years, as well as others making their inaugural visit. In the year following the performance, it became the second-most patronized parks and recreation center in Detroit. Robinson also attributed immediate structural improvements to the interior of the building due to the interest generated by the show.

The Future

In the spirit of adrienne maree brown's *Emergent Strategy (2017)*, the *After/Life* project continues to iterate. Its work is far from over. Since its debut, Biggs added a second act featuring a series of prompts with the objective of providing space for communities to reflect on the play together with their own stories, experiences, and hopes for the future. Some of these prompts include hosting a panel or workshop with local Black Liberation Movement and LGTBQ+ organizers to connect their community histories with '67. In February 2023, Drew University's Department of Theatre and Dance produced a staged reading of the play featuring original company member Deborah Chenault Green. Drew's producer Kimani Fowlin dynamically responded to the second act prompt by including a post-performance discussion featuring historians and survivors of the Newark '67 uprising. For Biggs and me, it was

Figure 8.3 The Ensemble of *After/Life* at Drew University. Directed by Judy Tate. 2023. Photo by Lisa S. Brenner.

a dream come true as we witnessed new connections forged between Detroit and Newark with powerful lessons unearthed about racism, gender, violence, exploitation, policing, public safety, as well as justice and joy.

References

Biggs, L. (2017a). *After/Life*, unpublished.

Biggs, L. (2017b) "Art saves lives: Rebecca Rice and the Performance of Black Feminist Improv for social change," in Luckett, S.D. and Shaffer, T.M. (eds), *Black Acting Methods: Critical Approaches*. New York: Routledge, pp. 72–86.

Biggs, L. (2017c) "The Untold Stories of Women in the 1967 Detroit Rebellion and its Aftermath." *The Conversation*, 9 August.

Biggs, L. and Horton, K. (2017) "After/Life Tells Untold Stories of the '67 Rebellion," *Howl round*, 16 October. Accessed 6 Aug. 2023. https://howlround.com/afterlife-tells-untold-stories-67-detroit-rebellion.

Brown, A.M. (2017) Emergent Strategy: Shaping Change, Changing Worlds. Chico, CA: AK Press. [note her name is in lower case on purpose).

Center for Collaborative Research for an Equitable California (CCREC). (2023) *Summer Institutes*. Accessed 15 Jan. 2023. https://ccrec.ucsc.edu/summer-institutes.

Cornerstone Theater Company. (2006) *Cornerstone Theater Company Community Handbook*. Los Angeles: Cornerstone Theater Company.

Hamera, J. (2017) *Unfinished Business: Michael Jackson, Detroit, & the Figural Economy of American Deindustrialization*. New York: Oxford University Press.

Kurashige, S. (2017) *The Fifty-Year Rebellion: How the U.S. Political Crisis Began in Detroit*. Oakland: University of California Press.

Living Stage Theatre Company. (1995) *Living Stage and the Creative Process*. Washington: Living Stage Theatre Company.

9 No Seriously, Humor Is Important

Soroya Rowley and Veronica Burgess

We are community-based theatre artists who have been working together for over a decade with numerous organizations across San Diego, CA. We first met in 2009 through our work with The Playwrights Project, a non-profit organization that primarily teaches playwriting in K-12 schools. Through our company *Circle Circle dot dot*, we collaborated from 2012 to 2020, and today, we work as teaching artists for San Diego's *Old Globe Theatre*.

Building upon those years of experience, we are committed to telling stories that educate, engage, and provoke activism through a satirical lens and a pleasure activist perspective. Author and facilitator adrienne maree brown describes *pleasure activism* as "learning to make justice and liberation the most pleasurable experiences we can have on this planet" (2019, p. 13). Although we often engage with disturbing content, such as domestic violence, if our storytelling only elicits negative feelings (e.g. fear, disgust, guilt, sadness, or hopelessness), people might resist engaging with the material and thus miss an opportunity to learn from it. Simply put, difficult topics are easier to digest if presented in a funny way. Moreover, focusing only on trauma can result in "deficit framing" (Palma et al., 2023), whereas using laughter as a tool for processing pain helps humans cope and move forward.

Our work springs from the rasquache esthetic born in the 1960s with the Chicano/a/e power movement's tradition of combining theatre, activism, and humor (Anderson, 2017). Veronica's training comes from her extensive history with Teatro Izcalli, a company featured in the first book of this series on applied theatre (Artega and Chavez-Artega, 2022). Teatro Izcalli (Theatre of the House of Reawakening) is part of the creative lineage of Luis Valdez, who founded Teatro Campesino (Theatre of the Farmworker) in 1965. Teatro Campesino was an important part of El Movimiento, the movement led by Cesar Chavez to unionize the exploited and disenfranchised people working on farms in California's Central Valley. They wrote and performed a style of theatre called Actos, which they defined as short dramatic scenes that utilize satire to expose social problems (Valdez, 1994, p. 12). The emphasis was on "communication to the oppressed, not about them" (Bagby and Valdez, 1967, p. 70). For Teatro Campesino, the purpose of performing the Actos was to

DOI: 10.4324/9781003341802-15

disseminate information among the people, who were then able to improve their working conditions through unionization.

For Teatro Izcalli "Humor serves as a communal form of introspection and empowerment" (Artega and Chavez-Artega, 2022, p. 147). It is also an important form of building community because "by laughing at a situation, the audience acknowledges a shared recognition of what is being depicted. When we all laugh together at something that may be painful, individuals realize that they are not alone; the situation thereby becomes less personal and easier to cope with" (p. 148).

Soroya was first introduced to Chicano/a/e theatre during their first year of college in a course that featured the work of Culture Clash, a comedic theatre troupe founded in San Francisco in 1984. This collective was drawn together by a shared sense that humor was lacking in the performing arts and activism scene at the time. As stated by founding member Richard Montoya in a 2016 interview, "Even in Chicano literature, there is a humor that goes back to a very Mexican sensibility of life and death and irony" (Qtd. in Leonard, 2016, p. 16). Soroya also learned about Teatro de las Chicanas, which was founded in 1971 by a group of women confronting the sexism and misogyny that were rampant within El Movimiento and the male-dominated teatros of that era.

Despite the many potential benefits of using humor in applied theatre, artists will often avoid this approach, given the real danger of insulting,

Figure 9.1 Soroya as Ms. Simmons, Veronica as Miss Hobbs, and Andrew Steel as Mr. Fleming pose for a photo before their performance of *La Sirena* at The Merrow in Hillcrest, San Diego. February 2020. Photo by Dennis Shinpaugh.

offending, or even retraumatizing folks (Zgoda et al., 2016). We approach this ethical dilemma in the same way we approach every creative project: as an ongoing process of learning and refining our methods. As a case study to frame our discussion, we examine our 2018 production of *La Sirena,* a ten-minute, musical-dramedy based on an interview with a client of the Access VAWA (Violence Against Women Act) Program,[1] produced as part of a community-based theatre class at the University of San Diego. *La Sirena* depicts a story at the intersection of race, gender, and citizenship, in which an abuser used his wife's undocumented status as a cruel means of control. Our goal was to bring awareness to this issue, which is particularly relevant in the border region between San Diego and Tijuana, and to provide knowledge of a specific organization that could be of critical importance to someone in the audience or a loved one of theirs. Below, we offer three of our best practices to create comedic, activist theatre.

First, if the basis of the humor relies on a "shared recognition of what is being depicted," the piece must be created with the consent and collaboration of the group members it seeks to represent. With *La Sirena,* we had established trust with Anne Bautista, the attorney for the VAWA program at that time, through workshops at the center. Anne asked one of her clients if she would be willing to meet with us for an interview. The interviewee was an active and passionate volunteer and advocate for the organization; however, she wanted to remain anonymous to protect herself and her family. She consented to this project, believing that her experience could serve as inspiration without the risk of being identified.

Although *La Sirena* was based on one particular woman, we were conscious of the fact that we were representing an experience that has been shared by many. Unfortunately, there are countless immigrant women in the United States and all around the world who find themselves in situations where their immigration status is used as leverage by an abuser (Moynihan et al., 2008). In some cases, the abuser is a partner or family member; in other cases, the abuser is part of the human trafficking market; and in some cases, they are both. Through our work with Access, we learned this community exists right under our noses; the problem is prevalent but well hidden. Survivors of domestic abuse remain silent for many and varied reasons. Most often, a person will stay with an abuser for fear of losing their home and financial resources. Referred to as *economic abuse,* abusers achieve control over their victims by controlling their finances. Another reason to stay silent is the stigma and shame associated with their situation (Raj and Silverman, 2002).

Our understanding of domestic violence is ever-evolving. In the United States, "wife-beating" was perfectly legal until 1920. And it wasn't until 1970 that the criminal justice system began to treat domestic violence as a serious crime rather than a private family matter. Today, we define domestic violence as "any physical, sexual, or psychological abuse that people use against a former or current intimate partner" (Hanna, 2018). Psychological abuse is arguably the most insidious form of domestic violence because it is often invisible, sometimes even to the victim.

In the case of the woman on whom our piece *La Sirena* is based, she didn't realize she was experiencing domestic violence until the police informed her that she was. Her husband did not physically harm her; he would destroy her property, yell, verbally abuse her and their children, and threaten to have her deported. In addition to controlling all of their finances, he forbade her from leaving the home. The final straw for her was when she discovered that her husband had tricked her into signing paperwork that gave him sole custody of their son. She called the National Domestic Violence Hotline. The operator notified her that a space had just opened up at the San Diego YWCA [Women's Young Men's Christian Association], but it would not stay vacant long. She quickly packed her children and very little else into their family SUV and bravely left her abuser. The YWCA connected her with *Access* for legal assistance. She was able to gain documented legal status in the United States under *VAWA* and regain legal custody of her son.

Our approach to interview-based theatre is founded primarily on the work of Katherine Harroff, the former artistic director of *Circle Circle dot dot* and currently the interim director of Arts Engagement at the Old Globe Theatre. Before an interview, we communicate with the interviewee about expectations for the process and the production. We jokingly refer to this as the *fine print*. The topics for the *fine print* fall into three categories: *content, artistic license*, and *feedback*. In the *content* section, we explain that everything said in the interview is considered "on the record" or "fair game to be used in the play" unless specified otherwise. We encourage interviewees not to share anything they would not want included in the play; but if and when they accidentally do, all they have to do is let us know, and we won't use it. This is also the moment where it is best to ask permission to record the interview and/or to take notes.

On the flip side of "everything is on the record" is the reality that we cannot include in the play everything the interviewee will share. Much of our work is in short form. True to the tradition of the Acto, *La Sirena* focused on just four particular moments. Each segment was a phone call between our main character, Sirena, and another person: her husband, her mother, an operator for the domestic violence hotline, and an immigration attorney.

Artistic license is the next topic in the *fine print*. We are not doing documentary theatre. We write fictionalized stories inspired by actual human experiences. This helps us to protect the interviewee but also serves the story by opening up creative possibilities. We also change the names of the people in the story. We often combine characters, or we might change their gender or other identity markers, timelines may shift, and the order of events may change. And whenever it serves the story, we love to utilize surrealism, music, poetry, and dance to make the play more theatrical and compelling.

Finally, in the third section of the *fine print,* which is *feedback,* we make a commitment to our interviewee that they will have the power to approve,

Figure 9.2 Soroya, Veronica, and Andrew during their performance of *La Sirena* at The Merrow in Hillcrest, San Diego. February 2020. Photo by Dennis Shinpaugh.

veto, or change any aspect of the play at any time in the process. We will send them the script and invite them to readings and rehearsals. Even if it's the dress rehearsal before the opening of the show, if they ask us to make a change, we do it. Their approval is key.

In addition to the importance of consent, there should be members of the creative team who reflect the background of the interviewee. After conducting the interview and setting out to write a rough draft of the script, Soroya realized another writer was needed. As a white person, not fluent in Spanish, with no personal experiences of immigration, Soroya knew they could not fully honor the story that was gifted to them and therefore asked Veronica to collaborate. As someone who immigrated to the United States from Mexico, Veronica shares some of the lived experiences represented in the play. Veronica was also instrumental in writing the Spanglish sections of the script, particularly the first song, which is a Spanglish version of "Part of Your World" from Disney's *Little Mermaid*. With advances in technology, language translation is easier than ever before; however, it does not capture cultural references shared by the community and could even possibly be offensive.

The second practice when using humor to deal with difficult content is to target those with power. In *La Sirena*, the character who had the most power was the abusive husband Michael, and therefore was the most caricatured. In the first scene of the play, Sirena is on her way to visit her sister when she gets a call from Michael. He is irate because he came home from work during his lunch break and expected her to be at their house. The satire highlights the unreasonable expectations of the abuser. Sirena responds calmly and rationally to Michael, who is presented as overly emotional, dramatic, and even childish. He throws a tantrum and says things like, "Oh, so your sister is more important than me, huh?!" The performance of the character Michael always elicits laughter from the audience, which effectively diminishes his power.

And the third best practice is to base the humor on actions, behaviors, and situations rather than appearances or identities. For the character of Michael, it is his childish behavior and actions that elicit laughter. In this case, the audience is laughing *at* the character, not *with* him. Later in the play, when Sirena calls the domestic violence hotline, the phone operator has a series of charming and disarming colloquialisms that make both Sirena and the audience chuckle. She says things like, "Honey, this hotline is like a wedding chapel in Vegas, we're open 24/7!" and, "Oh no, sounds like you are just a hen in a fox house. You watch your tail out there!" In this case, the audience is laughing *with* the characters on stage instead of *at* them. The actions and choices of the characters are at the center of the humor because we are telling a story about a person striving to achieve their objectives.

We have observed through our many years of doing this work that people may care about an issue and want to do something to help. However, they oftentimes have limited resources and are unsure how best to utilize them. We therefore use theatre to shine a light on social problems and specific organizations that work to address them. Audiences can then directly interact with those organizations or refer someone who may need these resources. In order for audiences to connect with organizations like Access, however, they must first be willing to engage with the subject matter. Our entertaining and humorous pieces offer a means to witness these stories without feeling threatened or overwhelmed. This ability to soften the edges of difficult conversations makes the work of theatrical comedy a potent tool for confronting gender-based violence. We hope that through sharing our discoveries of best practices for using humor in applied theatre, more artists will feel empowered to experiment with this critical tool.

Note

1 The Access VAWA Program was hosted by the community-based non-profit organization Access Inc. and it provided pro-bono legal services to immigrant women regardless of legal status, who were survivors of domestic violence and/or trafficking. Unfortunately, the program closed in 2021. Today Access Inc focuses on their youth education and pathway to jobs programing. https://www.access2jobs.org/.

References

Anderson, M. (2017) "A Lesson in 'Rasquachismo' Art: Chicano Aesthetics and the 'Sensibilities of the Barrio.'" *Smithsonian*. Accessed 2 Aug. 2023 https://www.si.edu/stories/lesson-rasquachismo-art.

Artega, M., & Chavez-Artega, A. (2022) "Laughter, Healing, and Belonging." *Applied Theatre With Youth: Education, Engagement, Activism*. New York: Routledge. pp. 145–153.

Bagby, B., & Valdez, L. (1967) "El Teatro Campesino: Interviews With Luis Valdez." *Tulane Drama Review*, 11 (4), pp. 70–80. DOI: 10.2307/1125139

brown, a. m. (2019). *Pleasure Activism*. AK Press.

Hanna, C. (2018) "Domestic Violence." *Encyclopedia of Crime and Justice*. Encyclopedia.com. Accessed 2 Aug. 2023. https://www.encyclopedia.com.

Leonard, S. R. (2016) "Equal-opportunity offenders: Getting to know Culture Clash." *Berkeley Rep: Culture Clash (Still) in America*. Berkeley Repertory Theatre. Accessed 2023 <https://issuu.com/berkeleyrep/docs/program-cc/s/10235078>.

Moynihan, B., Gaboury, M. T., & Onken, K. J. (2008) "Undocumented and Unprotected Immigrant Women and Children in harm's Way." *Journal of Forensic Nursing*, 4 (3), pp. 123–129.

Palma, C., Annmary, S. A., Danforth, S., & Griffiths, A. J. (2023) "Are Deficit Perspectives Thriving in Trauma-Informed Schools? A Historical and Anti-Racist *Reflection, Equity & Excellence in Education*, 57(1), pp. 76–92. DOI: 10.1080/10665684.2023.2192983

Raj, A., & Silverman, J. (2002) "Violence Against Immigrant Women: The Roles of Culture, Context, and Legal Immigrant Status on Intimate Partner Violence." *Violence Against Women*, 8 (3), SAGE journals. pp. 367–398. DOI: 10.1177/10778010222183107

Valdez, L. (1994/1990/1971) *Early Works: Actos, Bernabe, and Pensamiento Serpentino*. San Juan Bautista: Arte Publico.

Zgoda, K., Shelley, P., & Hitzel, S. (2016) "Preventing Retraumatization: A Macro Social Work Approach to Trauma-Informed Practices & Policies." *The New Social Worker*. Accessed 2 Aug. 2023. https://www.socialworker.com/feature-articles/practice/preventing-retraumatization-a-macro-social-work-approach-to-trauma-informed-practices-policies/

Roundtable Discussion with Lisa Biggs, Lisa S. Brenner, Veronica Burgess, Sarah Ashford Hart, Kristin Horton, and Soroya Rowley

Brenner: Thank you for being here. To start our conversation, a thematic thread we saw connecting your work is the relationship between gender and violence and theatre as a means of healing, coping, and affecting the world. Would anyone like to speak to that?

Soroya: I appreciated Sarah's use of the term "afecto" [a felt connection of care] It feels like a feminine way of knowing, being in tune with your body, and listening.

Sarah: I think all of the projects could be a space of afecto. With Soroya and Veronica's work, voices and bodies laughing in the same space can soften perceived separateness. With Kristin's and Lisa's work, I love that moment of collective gasp mentioned in their essay. There was also a space for an alternative kind of relationality to patriarchal racist violence and "official" histories.

Kristin: Sarah, I loved how you characterized the creative process and rehearsal as ways to practice change and imagine future possibilities. And also, how Veronica and Soroya's essay evoked adrienne maree brown's pleasure activism, which gives me hope.

Veronica: Hearing everyone talk reminds me of those feelings you get when you have those collective gasps and heightened emotions connecting you. One way that we all connect is through laughter. As a lifelong jokester, or payasa, I believe laughter is the best medicine. I consider myself a healer by using that gift to make people laugh. Soroya and I work through that lens of ridiculousness which permits people to laugh at something horrible and/or uncomfortable, thereby lessening its power.

Brenner: All of your essays talk about your process as a way to change how theatre is created and produced, particularly in connection with community. What elements of the process do you feel were valuable?

Biggs: We seem to be a group that collectively wants to interrupt how narratives are made by recentering people who are often ignored, overlooked, and violently put down by the dominant storytelling practices. That practice of choice was important for my Michigan State students.

DOI: 10.4324/9781003341802-16

It was certainly important when we went to Detroit with the play because we were not only stepping on sacred ground but a bloody battlefield. I mean, the bodies are not there, but the burnt-out infrastructure is a reminder to everybody about how little the city, state, and nation cares about them. The community center that we were in is their space. We were the guests, and we had to demonstrate to people that we were not there to colonize it or intrude. So the process has a different heart to it. We're not selling anything.

Soroya: The process is not the product, but it is the purpose. And I loved how in Lisa and Kristin's project, they really took their time. It's about this journey and the relationships that you build with the community. With community-based theatre, which is my preference for the term "applied theatre," you need to hang out. And that's the joy of this work, the time we get to spend together is our most precious resource.

Sarah: I want to jump in on the term "applied theatre." That term is not used in Colombia. It's "theatre in community." And I like that a lot. There's a push for this work to be seen as professional, so it's not seen as somehow alternative or less-than. Rather, this work has the intention of being part of the community where it's based.

Brenner: You raise an important point. The course I teach is actually called "Theatre in the Community." But, when working with a community, things can go wrong. So, what are some of the ethical concerns that you've faced in doing your work, and how did you navigate those concerns?

Veronica: With the project Soroya and I worked on, steps were taken to respect the woman whose story the piece was based on, who wanted anonymity. Even though we used humor, we wanted to maintain respect and not distract or diminish what she was experiencing, which was not humorous. Therefore, she was always involved every step of the way and invited to view the project as well.

Soroya: Sometimes people want to be heavily involved, and sometimes they prefer not to. The woman whose story we told wanted us to take the reins. I would send her drafts, and she would give me small edits. By contrast, most people want to be more involved, and they become co-writers, which is also a fun and wonderful way to do it. Either way, it is about always keeping them updated every time there's a draft, sending it to them for approval, and inviting them to rehearsals and the final performance.

Brenner: Another theme in your pieces is that people involved in the performances have experienced violence firsthand. You're careful not to position them as the problem while acknowledging that their stories still need to be heard as a means of moving forward.

Sarah: Ironically, one of Ariza's pieces was commissioned by Colombia's Truth Commission, which is a part of the state. Here, the victims of state violence are part of a project that is commissioned by the state. But survivors have a lot of information and ways of healing, communal healing that others can learn from. Given that Ariza's work helps audiences learn from the victims or survivors about how to overcome trauma and violence as a society. Ariza also strategically utilizes the institution. Rather than blindly serving institutionally imposed aims. We have to consistently ask ourselves, at what point does our work become institutionalized? I see this work bravely and creatively surviving in a place where just doing this work is very precarious.

Brenner: Soroya, you mentioned that it's about the process, not the product, yet at the end of the day, there is a product. How can we measure success in doing this work? Is there a particular moment that stands out for you?

Soroya: When the thing you create can continue to grow and have life, that is a success. Another one is when the community grows to trust you and wants to have you back; that is a big sign of success.

Kristin: For Lisa Biggs and me, success is measured by *After/Life's* capacity to live on without us. This has meant examining what it means to responsibly disengage from being at the center. It was therefore exciting to see a new community such as Drew University take on this project without my directing the production as well as see it outside of Detroit. At Drew, the theatre and dance department brought into conversation individuals with lived experiences of the Newark and Detroit '67 uprisings by bringing a member from the Detroit community to participate in the production. Witnessing the discussion and the new relationships that formed realized a core value of the project. Success is seeing the project enter into a support system that isn't reliant on Lisa and me so that it can live on its own and be reimagined by other communities.

Veronica: To that point, I see success when the work doesn't end there. When it continues to give life and inspiration to something more. Obviously, when the audience responds, and you're getting positive communal feedback that shows your success, but specifically for our show, I felt great success with our product because it catapulted another project. It left us with inspiration, hope, and a moment of "Wow, if we could do it with this story, let's do it with other stories."

Sarah: The pieces also do a good job of acknowledging conflict as something that's not always bad. Of course, violence is obviously problematic, but conflict isn't necessarily violent. In Colombia, they want the peace process and the reconciliation process to recognize that there are many worlds within Colombia, not just one. The work documented here is an acknowledgment of those different worlds and even the differences within each different world. Not by looking for unison or consensus or sameness, but by the idea of multiple communities that are part of a shared territory and that don't have to cause fear. It's important to develop these relationships, and to have collective resilience.

Brenner: Where do you feel we need to move forward as a field?

Soroya: Theatre as a whole needs to change, to bring in more and different folks than they've been bringing in from the donor and subscriber class. The only way to do that is by making theatre relevant to the community and by going to the community spaces to meet folks where they're at. I want to give credit to the Old Globe, where Vero and I work, for launching a rebrand of their *Theatre Beyond the Stage* programing that highlights our work in community engagement.

Sarah: I think all of this work responds to the need to understand facilitation from a Global South perspective. I say that because the Global South exists within the United States as well. Reframing applied theatre from a Global South perspective can be decolonial and help us appreciate practices that are often not included in the traditional canon, work that hasn't received large-scale visibility. I would dare to say that a Global South way of looking at this work values the affective changes, which is a change in how bodies feel, how bodies relate to changes in the energy or the feelings moving in space, especially the afecto toward something potentially less harmful and that makes living more possible.

Veronica: I keep thinking about the word "representation." The voices of the people who don't get to be heard. So that's where I think this work needs to keep growing.

Kristin: I think capitalism is an intersecting problem with what's been mentioned. A colleague of mine, who's a legal scholar, wrote about how we live in a culture that largely defines democracy as a form of government, when in fact, it's a way of life. It's about participation. The theatre industrial complex similarly emphasizes product over process. Everybody in this conversation has been talking about the centrality of the process of healing and forming new relationships. That's what I would love to see keep happening.

Biggs: Unfortunately, I feel like the field of applied theatre (I prefer the term "engaged theatre") is sometimes more interested in going into other people's communities and "fixing them." I would encourage the field to go home, wherever or whatever home is. Thinking about theatre as a process that everyone needs; this work needs to happen with the subscription-holders of the dominant theatres, the people at our church groups, the people in our community centers, and the people at the corner grocery store. In the United States, we're seeing a time in which there's a dangerous narrative circulating about the disenfranchised and aggrieved white majority being a victim of state violence. Although based on bad information, they feel that way, and they also do not have arts programs. I'm not going to do that work personally, but I hope that people will.

Sarah: Yes, this work has to happen at all levels of a structurally unequal, oppressive society. I think, in Ariza's work with female survivors, who have lived through the loss of loved ones and state violence, they've had to rebuild their worlds and their communities and transform that anger into something else. That's something everybody can learn a lot from. I teach at a university with students who are very privileged within Colombia, and who have not been directly affected by the armed conflict. So, when we work on listening to the oral history of female victims, there's an important shift that happens. They start to feel more connected to the whole peace and reconciliation process as well as the violence.

Brenner: In closing, what are you taking away from this conversation?

Veronica: We're not done. That's it. Let's keep going. We're not done.

Soroya: I'm thinking about how we need to find a way to reframe theatre and understand that it's not a product to be bought. It's part of our oral tradition as humans.

Biggs: It's good to know that people are out here doing this work, which can feel very isolating at times. But it's lovely to have this dedicated space together.

Kristin: I'm inspired to know about everybody's work here. These are tough times, and it's easy to feel hopeless. But what I might take away here is that I actually do have hope. And that's because of the way each of you has framed the capacity of relationality that exists in process and rehearsal.

Sarah: I agree that we're not done. and I agree that there is hope. I want to think more about women in this field and what that has to do with collaborative nonhierarchical ways of working. We live in a hyper-productive reality where money makes everything hierarchical, which relates to gender, race, and everything else. So, I am going to think about that continual discovery of different kinds of relationality or ways of working.

Brenner: Thank you. I'm moved by everything that everyone's saying. And just to hear out loud, somebody saying, "I have hope." We have to nurture and protect and be deliberate in doing this work.

Part IV

Reclaiming Bodily Autonomy

10 *The Billboard* #TrustBlackWomen

Abortion as Self-Care

Natalie Y. Moore

We gathered on a Zoom call to hash out a scenario that quickly emerged into art imitating life. My first play, *The Billboard*, was set to be produced by the 16th Street Theater in the summer of 2022. This spring call included the director, the acting artistic director, the managing director, and me to button up production details for the world premiere. Security came up: *The Billboard* is about abortion. Specifically, it portrays a fictional Black women's clinic in Chicago's South Side Englewood neighborhood and its fight with a local gadfly running for city council who had put up a provocative billboard: "Abortion is genocide. The most dangerous place for a Black child is his mother's womb." This action spurs the clinic to fight back with its own provocative sign: "Black women take care of their families by taking care of themselves. Abortion is self-care. #TrustBlackWomen."

At this point, the law still protected abortion in all fifty states. The US Supreme Court had yet to roll back a fifty-year protection and the leak of Justice Samuel Alito's opinion hadn't happened yet. But I knew Roe sat on the brink of elimination when the conservative court added abortion to its docket via the Dobbs v. Jackson Women's Health Organization case in December 2021. As a reporter, I also knew that the court typically releases its controversial decisions at the end of the term, and, by my calculation, that meant the late June premiere of *The Billboard* and the overturning of Roe would collide like two Mack trucks.

Abortion rights advocates needn't be soothsayers. For years, states chipped away at legal protections, and former President Donald Trump appointed Supreme Court justices hostile to Roe. Even as I expressed to the 16th Street Theater team the imminent fall of Roe, I felt some incredulity. Stripping away rights is not typical of the court. As one prominent activist told me, it's hard to get people to fight for rights they think they already have. Abortion in this country is politicized and not treated as a healthcare issue. In this polarizing environment, we had to at least pose questions to ourselves for *The Billboard* production: Would protestors bum-rush the theatre? Would they heckle from the audience? Disrupt community talkbacks? Should we even host post-show discussions? How should we prepare?

DOI: 10.4324/9781003341802-18

I thought of a scene from the play in which clinic board chair Dawn and founder Tanya debate whether to hire security when the political pressure ramps up. I found myself almost parroting Tanya about not backing down.

***

I started writing *The Billboard* at my kitchen table in October 2018, the weekend Ntozake Shange died and a few years before I thought Roe would ever be overturned. In the opening scene, I drop an homage to Shange, whose play *For Colored Girls Who Have Considered Suicide/When the Rainbow is Enuf* hit Broadway in 1976. The poster still hangs in my home and is one of the first monologues I memorized as a student at eta Theater on Chicago's South Side.

Journalism is my day job. I cover urban affairs in my hometown Chicago with race as the lens for WBEZ, the National Public Radio (NPR) member station. Journalism informs my book writing, and I have written books I wanted to read that didn't exist. Daily reporting affords me the privilege of interviewing people, distilling information, and informing the public. I hold public officials accountable. I tell nuanced stories from Black communities – beyond the narratives of violence that tend to dominate. From block club presidents to scholars, to public housing residents to activists, I do my best to choose assignments rooted in community and sometimes bolstered by data. Reporting projects include open prisons in Finland, racist housing appraisals, public school dropout rates, and racial disparities regarding COVID-19.

Playwriting isn't a genre I envisioned. But audio script writing and writing plays share a commonality – both require writing for the ear. I hear the cadence and rhythm in voices when I'm out with my recording equipment. In fact, an NPR training book points this out, and some editors even say to think of your feature scripts like a three-act play. Another similarity between audio and plays is intimacy. When you're in the theatre, it's live. The actors are close. And with audio, if you're listening to me on the radio, you feel as if I'm speaking directly to you. Listeners are not thinking of thousands of others in the audience who are also tuned in. Playwriting spoke to me, and the 16th Street Theater gave me a chance. I wasn't arrogant enough to think I could magically master the genre. I took a class at Chicago Dramatists, and a weekend homework assignment evolved into *The Billboard*.

The backstory is a group of Black women in Dallas who challenged and ultimately inspired me. In 2018, a Black man representing the National Black Pro-Life Coalition put up a billboard in the city with a picture of a Black woman cooing at a Black baby: "Abortion is not healthcare. It hurts women and murders their babies." These types of anti-abortion billboards targeting Black women had popped up in Black communities all over the country in the past decade. At a press conference, Congressional candidate Stephen Broden said, "The scourge of abortion has hidden behind political correctness in the Black community for too long. The heinous practice is devastating and decimating our community across this nation" (Moore, 2011). His thirty billboards featured Barack Obama's face in a colorful mosaic: "Every 21 minutes, our next possible leader is aborted." The Chicago City Council passed an ordinance condemning the billboards, and the issue gained as much traction as Republicans received in votes on the South Side.

The Afiya Center, a Dallas-based nonprofit focused on Black women's health, crafted a more exacting response in 2018: "Putting a billboard like this, one in an area full of Black women is a gesture that will not go unchecked," co-founder and executive director Marsha Jones told the press (see Young, 2018). The Afiya Center put up its own billboard in response to Broden's with a picture of three relaxed Black women smiling: "Abortion is self-care. #TrustBlackWomen." The social media response accused the Afiya Center of eugenics, genocide, and glorifying abortion. And these reactions were from Black folk, many of whom identified as pro-choice.

While I didn't join the indigent outrage on Twitter (now known as X), I had never considered abortion as a form of self-care. The Afiya Center billboard shocked me, and I didn't like why I cringed at the message. The intrigue lingered. After all, I was not against abortion rights. So, I talked to friends in reproductive justice circles who explained to me why self-care is a necessary descriptor for abortion because it strips away stigma and allows women to do what they need to do for their own peace of mind or health.

Then I read scholarship by Black women such as Toni Bond, Loretta Ross, and Dorothy Roberts. The journey taught me about a group of Black women who attended a 1994 pro-choice conference in Chicago. Seeing the lack of an intersectional lens on the issue of abortion rights, they caucused in a hotel room until the wee hours of the morning. "Reproductive justice" was born, grounded in Black feminist thought and a human rights framework. The four pillars are: the right to have or not have a child; the right to parent the child with support to thrive; to live free from community-based or state-based violence; and the right to sexual pleasure the way one desires (see Sistersong, 2023). A reproductive justice framework is about movement building and centers the voices of those who have been disenfranchised. A gulf often exists between the "right" to have an abortion and "access" to abortion. As I've heard numerous times, Roe was the floor and justice is the ceiling.

Upon reflecting on the self-care billboard and my uncomfortability, I realized that I was a product of the 1990s Clinton-era tagline: Keep abortion safe, legal, and rare. Even pro-choice circles stigmatize abortion or cloak it in "a decision between a woman and her doctor" secrecy. Today, I realize the Afiya Center billboard pushed discourse even if the public wasn't quite ready. Now I shrug at "self-care," slightly embarrassed by my taken-aback initial reaction.

Abortion, in fact, is a form of self-care. Art can challenge and expand minds. Therefore, I decided to pen *The Billboard* in an intra-racial setting on the South Side of Chicago. By swapping Dallas for Chicago, I signaled that the play was not a historical reenactment of the 2018 events. I was determined to tease out conversations around abortion, patriarchy, politics, and power. Another throughline for the audience to ponder is who gets to speak for the community. Honest conversations about abortion were needed in Black spaces beyond so-called "pro-choice" and "pro-life." Whenever I'm asked what I want the audience to think after experiencing *The Billboard*, I say I want them to leave with more questions than they had when they came in. A good friend told me her mother told her abortion is a "white girl issue." It's not. On the flip side, Black women have abortions at a higher rate because of health disparities. Black women have less access to health care, less access to birth control, and less access to information (Chinn et al., 2021; Hill et al., 2023; Thompson et al., 2022; Watson, 2022).

When a friend told her mother and an older Black female mentor about *The Billboard*, their response was the same: "That's a white girl issue." This confirmed for me that the play is a vehicle to springboard community discussion and awareness around intra-racial issues. Abortion may be the main theme of *The Billboard*, but I wanted to create a space in which Black women pummeled patriarchy and pushed back on the hackneyed idea that feminism only belongs to white women. I firmly believe that art is a means to change hearts and minds. The play gives the audience multiple ideas to chew on.

***

Five characters comprise *The Billboard*. Tanya is the executive director of the Black Women's Health Initiative (BWHI). She's a doctor who has delivered babies and performed abortions. Dawn is the BWHI board chair. Both are in

Figure 10.1 The cast of *The Billboard* as displayed in the lobby during the production. 16th Street Theater, Northwestern University's downtown campus theater, Chicago. 2022. Photo provided by the author.

their mid-40s. Kayla is a BWHI program assistant who is an alum of its teen program Brilliant Black Girls. She is nineteen or early twenties and runs the social media accounts for the clinic. I wrote Kayla as a tribute to Black Girl Magic, which I feel typically leans toward middle-class sensibilities with a college education and a natural hair esthetic. Kayla is a young woman from around the way who has a lot to contribute. Demetrius is the aforementioned gadfly running for the Chicago city council. He's a pro-Black misogynist who puts up a billboard that says: "Abortion is genocide. The most dangerous place for a Black child is his mother's womb. Keep Englewood Black. Vote Demetrius Drew for City Council." Demetrius is less of an ideologue and more of an opportunist. Rounding out the cast is Cheryl, the incumbent Demetrius is trying to best. She's been in office for twenty years, savvy and stagnant.

The intergenerational lens in *The Billboard* is intentional. Most of the women share their own abortion stories and work together in ways that belie ageist stereotypes. Tanya boldly responds to Demetirus' billboard with one across the street arguing that Black women have the right to make decisions for their families and their bodies. And thus, the dueling billboards clash as do the characters and various responses to the messages. The play is a multimedia production requiring sound, video, and projection design during montage and social media scenes.

Figure 10.2 LaQuis Harkins, Margo Harper, and Milan Falls in *The Billboard*. 16th Street Theater, Northwestern University's downtown campus theater, Chicago. 2022. Photo provided by the author.

The sixth character, if you will, is Chicago, a city of rough and tumble politics where people "vote early and often." BWHI and the city council race are set in the Englewood neighborhood. The Black South Side community is known for violence and poverty but is much more than that shorthand. It's also contested space and the fear of gentrification looms over the neighborhood, but decades of economic disinvestment is the real culprit. *The Billboard* is an abortion story set in a particular place, but I believe there's universality in specificity.

Haymarket Books agreed that *The Billboard* carried a cultural impact and published the script in March 2022. I added extra content: an intro, a Q&A with Toni Bond (one of the foremothers of reproductive justice), a foreword by scholar Imani Perry, and an afterword by Jane Saks. Again, this was before the Justice Alito leak and before the country reckoned with the fall of Roe. I did local book events and a little bit of travel. I spent time with a friend, and we did an event together in Tennessee. Her clinic (for births and abortions) was preparing to open an office in southern Illinois. The clinic knew abortion would soon be illegal in Tennessee because of what's known as a "trigger law," a law established so that when Roe was overturned, abortion would automatically be banned in the state.

***

Tanya is unapologetic. She doesn't care if society is ready for her abortion message that takes on capitalistic interpretations of what constitutes self-care. To her, the time is right. Although she and Dawn are on the same side, they disagree on how important "changing the narrative" is. Back on the March call with the theatre team I mentioned at the top of this essay, I was unequivocal about public engagement. Tough conversations and public encounters are part of journalistic obligations. We joked that I sounded like Tanya, but since *The Billboard* was going to be performed at a new Northwestern theatre, we did agree to check in with Northwestern University's downtown Chicago campus security.

Previews were set for June 23 and June 24, which is the day Roe fell. That same week positive COVID-19 tests from a couple of cast members delayed the opening by a week. But the public found the timing uncanny. Here we were in the throes of a major upheaval on the news daily and giving audiences a place to process the court gutting the legal right to have an abortion. Meanwhile, Illinois passed measures to protect abortion in case Roe fell. Abortion is legal in the state and has become a haven for people to cross state lines for reproductive care.

I didn't write the play to incite immediate action. My journalism training means I draw the line at activism. I can't say that *The Billboard* spurred legislative or grassroots activism. And frankly, I had no expectations. The place where I am most comfortable is in post-show discussions.

The Billboard enjoyed several talkbacks: YWCA Chicago, Planned Parenthood of Illinois, and the Chicago Foundation for Women each sponsored a night, filling the theatre. After every performance, I joined the female chief executive officer on stage to take questions from them and the audience (see Moore and Patton, 2022). My WBEZ colleague Sasha-Ann Simons did two talkbacks. One was dubbed "Englewood Night" in which female community activists from the neighborhood discussed what it is like to do work in the community. One young executive director emailed me afterward and said she felt seen in the play, and, just like the character Tanya, once had to track down a city council member at a meeting to inquire about funding.

The surprise talkback was with Marsha Jones and Michelle Anderson from the Afiya Center in Dallas. They flew to Chicago to see the play. Marsha said Demetrius was triggering because he was so familiar. I watched Marsha and Michelle nod their heads during the play. Hearing them say how I captured the emotion in *The Billboard* filled me up. Hearing them talk about the fallout that continues welled me up. It was an honor to spend time with them.

By the production's end, we didn't face any protests or pushback. Definitely no violence or threats. I'm happy we forged ahead with public engagement. The only piece of negativity was this Facebook post when *The Billboard* was published as a book: "Southsiders southsiding, laughing and playing about aborting Black fetuses just like Margaret Sanger told the women auxiliary of the KKK she would. Now a BW from the south side of chicago play about it [sic]." Facepalm and eyeroll emojis next to the text.

I prevented myself from replying with the same emojis. But I took a screenshot to remind me that people aren't always ready for new messages.

References

Chinn, J. J., Martin, I. K and Redmond, N. (2021) "Health Equity Among Black Women in the United States." *Journal of Women's Health* (Larchmt), Feb. 30 (2), 212–219. Accessed 15 Aug. 2023. https://www.liebertpub.com/doi/10.1089/jwh.2020.8868

Hill, L., Artiga, S. and Ranji, U. (2023) "Racial Disparities in Maternal and Infant Health: Current Status and Efforts to Address Them." KFF. 14 March. Accessed 24 Apr. 2023. https://www.kff.org/racial-equity-and-health-policy/issue-brief/racial-disparities-in-maternal-and-infant-health-current-status-and-efforts-to-address-them/

Moore, N. Y. (2011) "Anti-Abortion Campaign Targets Black Chicagoans." WBEZ, Chicago. NPR News, March 29. Accessed 23 Oct. 2023. https://www.wbez.org/stories/anti-abortion-campaign-targets-black-chicagoans/35be0e2f-73e7-472a-8828-828cea49f864

Moore, N. Y. (2022) *The Billboard*. Chicago, IL: Haymarket Books.

Moore, N. Y. and Patton, T. (2022) "The Billboard: A Play About Abortion Book Launch and Discussion." Haymarket Books. YouTube. March 14. https://www.haymarketbooks.org/blogs/425-the-billboard-a-play-about-abortion-book-launch-and-discussion

SisterSong, Inc. (2023) "Reproductive Justice." Sister Song. Accessed 15 Aug. 2023. https://www.sistersong.net/reproductive-justice

Thompson, T.-A. M., et al. (2022) "Racism Runs Through It: Examining the Sexual and Reproductive Health Experience of Black Women in the South." *Health Affairs*. Feb. Accessed 24 Apr. 2023. https://www.healthaffairs.org/doi/10.1377/hlthaff.2021.01422

Watson, K. (2022) "The Ethics of Access: Reframing the Need for Abortion Care as a Health Disparity." *The American Journal of Bioethics*, 22 (8), pp. 22–30, DOI: 10.1080/15265161.2022.2075976.

Young, S. (2018) "The Truth Behind Pleasant Grove's New Anti-Abortion Billboard." Dallas Observer. July 29. Accessed 23 Oct. 2023. https://www.dallasobserver.com/news/new-dallas-anti-abortion-billboard-10957671.

11 Challenging Ableist Views of Motherhood

Mind the Gap's *Daughters of Fortune*

Winter Phong

In 2015, I began working with a small theatre start-up, BurkTech Players, which strives to build a neurodiverse inclusive space for artists. The organization was founded by adult students from the Burkhart Center for Autism Research and Education and graduate students from the School of Theatre and Dance at Texas Tech University. I served as the inaugural managing director, offering leadership while helping to produce biannual performances including short plays, new works, devised theatre, and original dance choreography. As a queer disabled person, I understand the unique challenges with how others see you and pass judgment on your ability and the perceived limitations of your identity. For this reason, I sought out other companies to inform our work.

On a research trip to the United Kingdom, I was introduced to Mind the Gap, based in Bradford, England. Started in 1988, Mind the Gap emphasizes the development of disabled artists, specifically autistic individuals and those with learning disabilities to create "work that is artistically fresh, pioneering, authentic and accessible" (Mind the Gap, 2024). In fostering dialogue and taking a nuanced activist approach, Mind the Gap has been able to collaborate with researchers, practitioners, and community members to promote social justice – such as issues of gender, disability, and civil rights – through applied theatre. Mind the Gap takes what I identify as a multiple-audience approach, employing various techniques to amplify underrepresented voices and emphasize authentic storytelling: In addition to interactive theatre, they devise shows by sharing personal accounts in workshops and by thoughtfully and systematically conducting interviews with people from the disabled community. Their productions challenge audiences to rethink ableist perspectives that inform social, cultural, economic, and medical opinions of disability. The opportunity to engage with and research this theatre has been pivotal in shaping my career, my subsequent work with the BurkTech Players, and my time at Texas Tech University.

Since 2015, Mind the Gap has developed a performance and live arts series, *Daughters of Fortune*, culminating in four works. Each project in the series uses a different performance method, including a play (*Mia*), a Forum Theatre piece (*Anna*), an outdoor spectacle (*Zara*), and a film/photo documentary

DOI: 10.4324/9781003341802-19

exhibition (*Paige*). These works included research partners at the Royal Holloway University of London, led by Dr. Kate Theodore and Laura Franklin. Together, this series represents a whole-community approach to examining the rights of motherhood for those with learning disabilities. While *Daughters of Fortune* included all genders, the productions skewed to persons who experience pregnancy and give birth, more specifically, the roles and experiences of mothers with disabilities.[1] Mind the Gap's desire to challenge audiences by addressing ableist perspectives was central to the development of each project. The series questions the status and expectations surrounding Westernized motherhood, asking their target audiences – from family, caregivers, medical practitioners, and social service providers – to community members, to unpack their notions of "fit" and "unfit" mothers.

Historically, and even in instances today, persons with disabilities have been sterilized to prevent those considered "unfit" from being parents. Hysterectomies, tubal ligation, or the more current practice of implanting permanent contraception devices have often been conducted without knowledge or consent. Forced sterilization is an unfortunate and ongoing side effect of the eugenics movement. In a recent study to assess sterilization among women with cognitive disabilities, a review of data concluded, "females with cognitive disabilities had significantly higher odds of female sterilization (adjusted odds ratio [OR] 1.54, 95% CI 1.19–1.98, $P < .01$) and hysterectomy (adjusted OR 2.64, 95% CI 1.53–4.56, $P < .001$) than those without cognitive disabilities," and those sterilized were also younger on average (Li et al., 2018, pp. 559–564). Some laws have been enacted to prevent sterilization and others to dismantle segregation systems for those with disabilities (Rowlands and Jean-Jacques, 2019, pp. 233–249). In response to a request and execution of nearly forty sterilizations (rulings upheld by the United Kingdom's High Court in the 1990s), activists sought to redress assumptions of ability to care and the notion of "unbridled fertility" among those with cognitive disabilities (pp. 233–249). The United Kingdom subsequently enacted the Mental Capacity Act 2005. However, this Act, and similar legislation enacted since, is often criticized for its paternalistic nature, wherein those who might be potentially sterilized are offered further protections against sterilization, yet the disabled party is rarely consulted (pp. 233–249). This law continues a pattern of assumptions about persons with disabilities, that those with disabilities, especially learning or cognitive disabilities, are genderless or are infantilized. They are cared for as child-like figures with little attention to sexual maturity and their perceived or desired gender roles. The lack of "gender perspective" also means that sex crimes committed against women and other "women's issues remain underrepresented in research and policy" and "Neither of the recent significant policy initiatives in England – Valuing People (Department of Health and Social Care, 2001) or Valuing People Now (Department of Health, 2009) – make reference to gender issues" (Tilley et al., 2012, pp. 413–426). Mind the Gap's work pushes against these outdated notions of gender and reproduction for those with disabilities.

During my first visit in 2016, Mind the Gap Artistic Director Joyce Lee shared the impetus for their production cycle, *Daughters of Fortune*, which stemmed from the experiences of their members. In a devising session, a new mother's rights and abilities were called into question because of her learning disability. The real-life mother who inspired the story, a relative of a company member, was given advice from a medical professional that was against her best interest as a mother. The mother assumed that she could trust the advice but was ultimately deceived, a common experience with parents interviewed by the Royal Holloway team (Theodore and Franklin, 2020, pp. 39–40). While this experience was the impetus for creating *Daughters of Fortune*, the organization sought out personal narratives beyond the company to learn more about the complexities of the issue. Their witnessing and listening give space for personal narratives, and collective sharing provided context and nuance for building impactful performances that might speak for the disabled community at large, in essence, building on the notion of "for us, by us, about us."

Mind the Gap partnered with Dr. Kate Theodore, faculty, and Laura Franklin, researcher, of Royal Holloway University to collect additional narratives and investigate lived experiences for mothers (and some fathers) with learning and/or cognitive disabilities. Researchers found across all twenty-two interviews that 95% of interviewees had felt "positions of powerlessness," with around 60% experiencing "early experiences of powerlessness" and/or "feeling betrayed by powerful others," and over 70% reported being "denied a voice" (p. 37). One interviewee shared, "I still believed what the social worker said that once I'd done all the assessments, I could have my son home. But she lied to get what she wanted." Another noted, "I was honest with them … it was like it was used against us," and a third interviewee provided, "Social Services talked to them [other professionals] more than they talked to me…when they did talk, they treat[ed] us like a two-year-old, talking down to us…" (pp. 40–41). As Lee continued to investigate this issue further, she uncovered an extensive and dense manual that essentially provided a checklist of required competencies for which caseworkers would test parents, predominantly mothers, to measure success and a right to parenthood. The interviews and shared stories would go on to inform all the performance work done across *Daughters of Fortune*.

The practice of story-sharing and interviewing is a common applied theatre technique for disability theatre because it helps to center the disability experience and "crip reality." Crip reality extends beyond the mere notion of disability to consider factors like additional time, money, and care needed to manage the complexities of having a disability. The artists, who experience similar disabilities and crip realities as the mothers (and fathers) interviewed, share political and social concerns. The company engages with real stories from the community in hopes of better serving them through their theatrical practice. Accessibility starts before an actor steps on stage; once the consideration of disability is integrated into the production process, patrons will embrace a cultural shift as artists with disabilities share their stories (Johnston, 2016, pp. 154–160).

Because theatre is highly social and engages communities, it serves a unique function in the procession toward equality. As artists with disabilities attempt to gain footing within their fields, community engagement as it pertains to artists with disabilities can take on a prominent role (Johnston, 2016, p. 13). Organizations can shift policies to consider a "social model of disability as an evolving concept," and communicate directly with patrons and community members to understand "the interaction between persons with disabilities and the attitudinal and environmental barriers existing in society" (Halder and Assaf, 2017, xi). Stein and Faigin assert that the representation of disability in the arts has the power to effect social change and can serve as a way to "educate and entertain." Theatre carries the potential to share ideas that scientific definitions cannot capture (2015, p. 148). Sandahl (2018) contends that by representing disability as a social identity within a larger community and acknowledging the power of disabled characters and artists, theatre can more productively include persons with disabilities in text and on stage.

Mind the Gap's work is thus best defined as "disability theatre." This practice and aim are different than theatre inclusive of disability. Theatre has generally moved toward inclusivity in productions, like the recent Broadway run of Martyna Majok's 2018 Pulitzer Prize-winning play, *Cost of Living*. Majok's work examines two relationships between disabled characters and their caregivers. While Majok's work offers incredible insights into crip realities, the play is at its core a play about relationships. Another play inclusive of disability, *Teenage Dick* by Mike Lew, provides a critique of William Shakespeare's *Richard III*. Given the myopic view of Shakespeare's Richard, companies have also begun to rethink the staging of the classical piece. In 2022, the Public Theatre's Free Shakespeare in the Park produced *Richard III* featuring a racially diverse cast inclusive of gender and disability. This inclusion of disability highlights a necessary change in casting and may impact perceptions of disability, but these works are not strictly about advocacy or activism.

While we see some shift, like in the plays noted above, all too often narratives continue to repeat theatre's contentious history with disability. Historically and even today, disability is something to be put on by an actor, either signifying a character flaw or some challenge to overcome. Victoria Ann Lewis notes that "the seductive plot possibilities…with its emphasis on a bodily transformation accomplished by an isolated effort of will, are irresistible in creating conventional dramatic structure" (2005, p. 94). In multiple recent articles, disabled artists respond and journalists reflect on the realities of "cripping up," which gives a false portrayal of disability; one author suggests this is tantamount to appropriation. Many artists critique the authenticity of work by able-bodied actors and espouse disabled artists should play disabled characters (Atkins, 2019; Bahr, 2021; Considine, 2015; Harris, 2020; Lepley,

2022; Nielsen and RespetAbility, 2021; Prooker, 2022; Rowe, 2017; Soloski, 2016). It is necessary then, that theatres take on practices and productions that center on advocacy and activism around persons with disabilities. Mind the Gap's work and their approach toward audiences stems from Western culture's evolving definition of disability: In response to first, the moral model (touched by an angel/devil), as well as a medical one (diagnosis and deficit centered – *dis*-ability), disability communities are attempting to assert the power to not only define what disability means but also establish civil rights (Snyder and Mitchell, 2006, pp. 35–43).

Disability advocacy is not about creating avenues for "normalcy," but instead recognizing the complexities of crip realities. Petra Kuppers, a feminist disabled performance artist and theorist, argues that centralizing cultural creation around singular scientific truths creates fallacies, like "the psychological stereotype that says that disabled people want to be 'normal,'" which leads to false representation on stage (2004, p. 51). She argues that "debates surrounding race, gender and class have had to face the problems of the *natural*, this common-sense logic that fixes people in their relative positions and into clear narratives" (p. 50). Snyder and Mitchell note that "each investigative field sought a passage into the intangible interior of human personality through the body as its signifying medium" (2006, pp. 37–38). The depiction of disability became a plot device, yet those with disabilities could not participate or perform depictions of themselves. Lewis asserts that emerging playwrights, drawing from personal experience "will add to this indictment of the medical model [and] is a construction of disability that places the tragedy of disability not within the individual but within a society that makes participation impossible due to the architectural and attitudinal barriers" (2005, p. 95).

Mind the Gap's dedication to developing socially conscious theatre has led them to establish a training academy to support the development of their artists. Artists build capacity to support applied theatre practices in multi-year and multi-production processes like *Daughters of Fortune*. The multiple genres of the four productions that comprise *Daughters of Fortune*, work in unique ways to build audiences around awareness, care practices, cultural understanding, and community experiences. My familiarity started with *Mia*, a play that challenges societal perceptions and assumptions of cognitive and learning disabilities. The production asks audiences to consider parenthood as a right and social justice concern. Here, Mind the Gap confronts the long-held theatrical practice of making disability a costume (something for an actor to put on or take off) by centering the disability experience, showcasing barriers that disabled parents face as they navigate roles forbidden to them: mother, father, actor/artist. Throughout the play, disabled parents act out typical parental tasks, like feeding, changing a diaper, and calming an infant. This approach critically examines parenthood, asking audiences to consider "fitness" against the common tasks of raising a child.

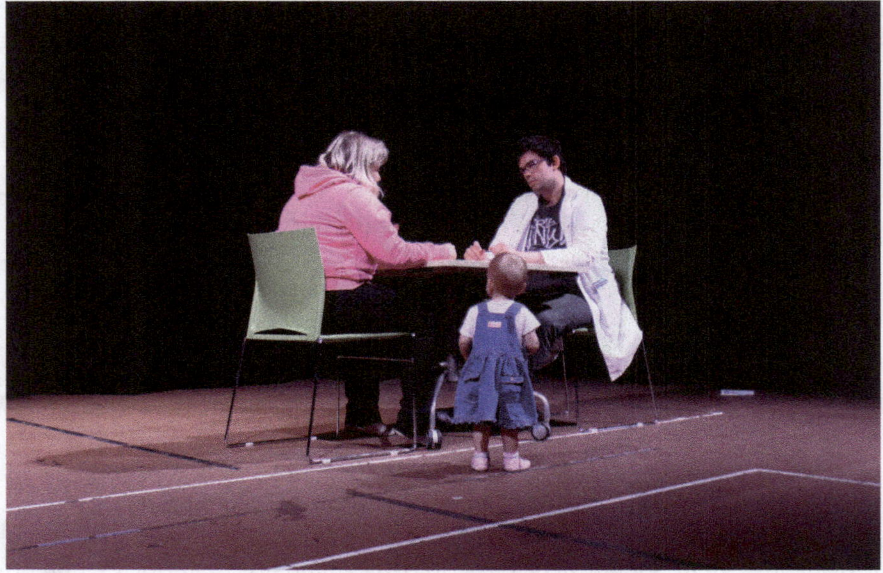

Figure 11.1 A medical professional (Daniel Foulds) and Anna (Zara Mallinson), discuss her pregnancy and Anna's ability to care for a baby. Mind the Gap Studios, Bradford, United Kingdom 2016. Photo by Maria Spadafora.

The next work in their quartet, *Anna*, a Forum Theatre piece, targets healthcare providers, psychologists, and social service organizations. The work explores the challenges Anna faces as she reveals her pregnancy to loved ones, visits her healthcare provider, and is assessed by social services. Royal Holloway's Department of Psychology website not only allows users to book a performance of *Anna*, but it also shares the report of the project and a series of short training films produced by Mind the Gap (Mindthegap.org).

Anna was also adapted into an online format to continue the workshops during the COVID-19 pandemic. I was able to join a couple of the online sessions in 2021. In keeping with a Forum Theatre format (see Boal, 1985), audiences watched a rehearsed scene depicting a protagonist who is discriminated against because of her disability. The scene was then repeated; however, this time, the audience could provide verbal suggestions for the character of Anna to play as she began her appointment. After a suggestion was enacted, there was time for reflection before the scene started again. In the hour-long virtual sessions, the actors were able to address multiple suggestions from audience members. By using this process, caregivers were better able to understand the complex motivations, fears, and concerns that might impact a disabled mother's choice. Care providers prescribing solutions often did not result in an improved outcome. The process revealed the complex reality of disabled mothers to a targeted audience of care providers.

Figure 11.2 Parental Figure (Daniel Gould) and partner (Paul Bates) discuss Anna's pregnancy and parenthood with support from workshop participant, as Anna (Zara Mallinson) looks on in astonishment. Mind the Gap Studios, Bradford, United Kingdom 2016. Photo by Maria Spadafora.

Figure 11.3 A parental figure (Daniel Foulds) and Anna (Zara Mallinson), a soon-to-be mother, discuss pregnancy and motherhood with interaction from an audience member. Mind the Gap Studios, Bradford, United Kingdom 2016. Photo by Maria Spadafora.

As someone who visits hospitals and clinics regularly, *Anna* aptly represented the registration and sign-in process, which can be intimidating and might benefit from evolving strategies for care. As the audience offered suggestions to the character of Anna, they revealed assumptions about disabled adults' investment in their wellness and care, presuming that motherhood is something not desired by disabled patients. The actor playing Anna played out their suggestions, including waiting for her caregiver before heading to registration. This proposal, however, exacerbated her already abbreviated appointment time being further cut short. The audience ultimately suggested lengthened check-in times to address care needs and adequate time spent listening to the patient and building trust.

Paige, a documentary project, consists of a short film, a photo book, and an exhibition. The film and photobook complement the training films produced by Mind the Gap. Installed as a traveling and virtual exhibit, the work allows audiences to engage in the stories that inspired *Daughters of Fortune*. The piece offers an immersive experience. Audiences are welcomed into spaces and community centers supporting disabled persons to better understand the people whose lives are impacted by notions of "fitness." The virtual exhibit and film showcase footage of the original storytellers entering and walking through community spaces, homes, and neighborhoods as they narrate their

Figure 11.4 Actor (Daniel Foulds) with participant reviewing scenarios as the production team helps the audience explore strategies to support families as they navigate motherhood for learning-disabled mothers. Mind the Gap Studios, Bradford, United Kingdom 2016. Photo by Maria Spadafora.

challenges and rights as mothers, fathers, and disabled people. Audiences can then privately consider their own response to the issue of motherhood.

Zara rounds out *Daughters of Fortune*, a collaboration with Walk the Plank and Emergency Exit Arts, both from the United Kingdom. An outdoor spectacle, featuring "a soaring musical score, a cast of over 100, cherry pickers, tanks, 3D projections, and a mechanical moving 'baby' that's bigger than a double-decker bus" who comes to life through multiple puppeteers (Mindthegap.org, 2021b). The baby, Eva, symbolizes the elephant that is so big it cannot fit in a room: motherhood.

Throughout the play, Zara fights to keep her baby at home. Before Zara gives birth to Eva, a reporter interviews the crowd to gauge their perceptions of parenthood and disability, specifically those with learning and cognitive disabilities. Audience members are encouraged by actors and a planted cast of sign-carrying activists to accept Zara becoming a mother. The live news anchor then cuts to recorded footage of Mind the Gap artists interviewing people on the street in the community days before the live spectacle. The interviewers' inquiries pertain to the rights of parents and social justice concerns, with reporters offering open-ended rather than leading questions, revealing a real mix of community perceptions – some in support of Zara and women like her, and others showing their general ignorance of the issue of "fitness."

Figure 11.5 Zara (JoAnne Haines), a new mother, is lifted into the air to interact with Eva, her larger-than-life baby (operated by puppeteers). Piece Hall, Halifax, United Kingdom April 2019. Photo by Chris Payne.

The newscast also takes commercial breaks between interviews. Two satirical standouts are an ad for *Lust Island*, a spoof of *Love Island*, a popular reality television series that gathers scantily clad singles together to find love, and a game show called *Don't Drop the Baby*, complete with a catchy theme song and contestants experiencing the challenges of early parenthood, from diaper changing to feeding. *Lust Island* confronts the notion of sexuality, or in this case the desire for sex. This narrative of lust is counter to depictions and popular notions of people with disabilities. The game show, on the other hand, draws on assumptions of "fitness" and maturity, addressing the same assumptions as *Mia* but as a comical farce of child-rearing to a catchy tune.

The significance of these issues soon comes to life, though, once baby Eva is revealed. Zara tries to balance family, legal, and social challenges while being a mother for the first time. For Zara, there is an added layer of pressure: social services. The audience is directly engaged in the conversation and encouraged to become allies as they cheer on Zara and baby Eva. The show concludes with massive projections showcasing the real voices behind

Figure 11.6 Protester (ensemble member) holding a sign in support of Zara, a learning-disabled mother battling for her parental rights. Piece Hall, Halifax, United Kingdom April 2019. Photo by Ant Robling.

the project, as captured in interviews. The work directly calls on the audience to become advocates and activists for disabled mothers like Zara, who, much like any new mother, needs a good support system and compassion.

In conclusion, Mind the Gap's multi-style approach allows them to reach various audiences, who may or may not be aware of disability justice. While *Mia* takes a more traditional esthetic, it portrays the very real and complex issue of parental rights in a way that centers the realities of disabled parents and artists. *Anna*, *Paige*, and *Zara* represent three different approaches to applied theatre that serve distinct audiences. Using an interactive audience method, *Anna* targets caregivers and providers to consider the barriers faced by disabled mothers. Participants must confront assumptions about learning and cognitive disabilities while developing solutions that might positively impact real-world care, like improved patient processing and enhanced listening skills. *Paige* offers a chance to witness the experiences of parents with disabilities while providing a quiet chance to reflect and identify one's own biases and assumptions about disabled parents. The outdoor spectacle, *Zara*, takes place in the community (in addition to the open-air Piece Hall, it was performed at the Geraldine Mary Harmsworth Public Park). As with a company like the San Francisco Mime Troupe, rather than expecting audiences to trek to a traditional venue, this show brings theatre to the public, perhaps even attracting the attention of onlookers.

Mind the Gap's work has been translated into practices with the BurkTech Players. We introduced a "Welcome Week," where we offer company members and guest artists a chance to learn together about each other, theatre, and autism. Additionally, guest artists have expanded our training, like Luc Vanier and Elizabeth Johnson who taught the Alexander Technique. As we advocate for inclusivity, we have conducted two major projects and research to support our partner's activities (Burkhart Center for Autism Education and Research and the School of Theatre and Dance at Texas Tech University). These projects emphasized learning in theatre and dance for youth, pre-kindergarten through high school, and provided specialized training to support working with diverse student populations.

In meeting audiences where they are, we create a space to converse about gender, disability, socio-economic realities, and various other social justice concerns. If we continue to ignore or merely use disabled stories as plot devices, we lose perspectives, realities, and desires that are central to disabled identities. Instead, applied theatre allows artists, organizations, researchers, and community members to be partners in effecting change.

Note

1 Fathers with disabilities were still included in their narratives and in the community feedback collected by the Royal Holloway team; however, the father's role was often linked to dual parental rights and less individually examined.

References

Atkins, I. (2019) "Giving Up 'Cripping Up'." [online] theboar.org. Accessed 11 Nov. 2023 https://theboar.org/2019/03/disabled-access-arts/.

Bahr, S. (2021) "Study Shows More Disability Stories Onscreen, but Few Disabled Actors." *The New York Times*. [online] 28 Jul. Accessed 11 Nov. 2023. https://www.nytimes.com/2021/07/28/arts/television/disability-representation-study-film-television.html.

Boal, A. (1985) *The Theatre of the Oppressed*. Trans. McBride, C. and McBride, M. O. L. New York: Theatre Communications Group.

Considine, A. (2015) "Ready, Willing, and, Yes, Able." *American Theatre*, 32 (9), pp. 32–76.

Department of Health and Social Care. (2001) *Valuing People: A New Strategy for Learning Disability in the 21st Century*. [online] GOV.UK, United Kingdom: Assets Publishing Service, pp. i–142. Accessed 11 Nov. 2023. https://www.gov.uk/government/publications/valuing-people-a-new-strategy-for-learning-disability-for-the-21st-century

Department of Health. (2009) *Valuing People Now: Summary Report March 2009 – September 2010*. [online] United Kingdom: Assets Publishing Service, pp. 1–64. Accessed 11 Nov. 2023. https://assets.publishing.service.gov.uk/media/5a7cc35340f0b6629523ba98/dh_122387.pdf.

Halder, S. and Assaf, L.C. (2017) *Inclusion, Disability and Culture: An Ethnographic Perspective Traversing Abilities and Challenges*. 1st Edition. Cham, Switzerland: Springer International Publishing. DOI: 10.1007/978-3-319-55224-8

Harris, M. (2020) "The Actors with Disabilities Redefining Representation." The New York Times. [online] 25 Aug. Accessed 11 Nov. 2023. https://www.nytimes.com/2020/08/25/t-magazine/actors-disability-theater-film-tv.html.

Johnston, K. (2016) *Disability Theatre and Modern Drama: Recasting Modernism*. New York, NY: Bloomsbury Publishing Inc.

Kuppers, P. (2004) *Disability and Contemporary Performance: Bodies on Edge*. Abington, Oxon and New York, NY: Routledge.

Lepley, T. (2022) "How Performers with Disabilities are Changing Theatre and Hollywood." [online] www.accessibility.com. Accessed 11 Nov. 2023. https://www.accessibility.com/blog/how-performers-with-disabilities-are-changing-theatre-and-hollywood.

Lewis, V.A. (2005) *Beyond Victims and Villains: Contemporary Plays by Disabled Playwrights*. New York: Theatre Communications Group.

Li, H., et al. (2018) "Female Sterilization and Cognitive Disability in the United States, 2011–2015," *Obstetrics & Gynecology*, 132 (3, September), pp. 559–564.

Mindthegap.org (2021a) "Anna: Daughters of Fortune – Online Exploring Learning Disability and Parenthood." Mind The Gap. Retrieved 10 Oct. 2023. https://www.mind-the-gap.org.uk/wp-content/uploads/2021/05/Anna-Booking-Information.pdf.

Mindthegap.org (2021b) "Zara, About." Mind the Gap Studios. Retrieved 10 Oct. 2023 https://www.mind-the-gap.org.uk/project/zara/.

Mind The Gap (2024) "Our Goals." [Online] Mingthegap.org. Retrieved 11 Aug. 2024 https://www.mind-the-gap.org.uk/about/our-goals/.

Nielsen and RespetAbility (2021) "Visibility of Disability: Answering the Call for Disability Inclusion in Media." [online] Nielsen. Accessed 11 Nov. 2023. https://www.nielsen.com/insights/2021/visibility-of-disability-answering-the-call-for-disability-inclusion-in-media/.

Prooker, B. (2022) "Autistic Actor and Author Mickey Rowe Fights Ableism On and Off Stage." [online] Observer. Accessed 11 Nov. 2023 https://observer.com/2022/04/autistic-actor-and-author-mickey-rowe-fights-ableism-on-and-off-stage/.

Rowe, M. (2017) "The First Actor with Autism to Play Curious Incident's Autistic Lead Speaks Out." [online] Playbill. Accessed 11 Nov. 2023. https://playbill.com/article/the-first-actor-with-autism-to-play-curious-incidents-autistic-lead-speaks-out.

Rowlands, S., and Jean-Jeacques, A. (2019) "Sterilization of Those with Intellectual Disability: Evolution from Non-Consensual Interventions to Strict Safeguards," *Journal of Intellectual Disabilities*, 23 (2), pp. 233–249.

Sandahl, C. (2018) "Disability Art and Culture: A Model for Imaginative Ways to Integrate the Community." *Alter – European Journal of Disability Research, Revue Europé En De Recherche Sur Le Handicap*, 12 (2), pp. 79–93.

Snyder, S. L., and Mitchell, D.T. (2006) *Cultural Locations of Disability*. Chicago, IL: University of Chicago Press.

Soloski, A. (2016) "Actors with Disabilities Are Ready, Willing and Able to Take More Roles." The New York Times. [online] 29 June. Accessed 11 Nov. 2023. https://www.nytimes.com/2016/06/30/theater/actors-with-disabilities-are-ready-willing-and-able-to-take-more-roles.html.

Stein, C. H., and Faigin, D.A. (2015) "Community-Based Arts Initiatives: Exploring the Science of the Arts." *American Journal of Community Psychology*, 55(1-2), pp. 70–73. DOI: 10.1007/s10464-014-9698-3

Theodore, K., and Franklin, L. (2020) *Daughters of Fortune: Stories of Parents with Learning Disabilities Final Research Report*. Royal Holloway University of London and Mind the Gap, July.

Tilley, E., et al. (2012) "'The Silence is Roaring': Sterilization, Reproductive Rights and Women with Intellectual Disabilities." *Disability & Society*, 27 (3), pp. 413–426.

12 The Maternal Ground on Which I Stand

Developing a Solo Performance within the Harris Matriarchy

Aviva Helena Neff

Practice-as-Research Methodologies

Like many theatre and performance scholars, I was motivated by August Wilson's *The Ground on Which I Stand* (1996), which reclaimed "The American ground on which I stand and which my ancestors purchased with their perseverance, with their survival, with their manners, and with their faith" (1996). Imbuing Wilson's words with an emphasis on maternal lineage, I began an autoethnography with a consideration of the ground on which the women of my family stand. My maternal family, the Harris's, lived and died on the ground on which they were enslaved and later freed. We, the Harris family, had what American history would call a "good master," one who taught us how to read while simultaneously enslaving us and "fathering" children with an early woman ancestor of mine. There is no goodness in owning and raping people, no matter how well you teach them to write.

Because of my family's literacy, I had access to vital documents, land deeds, and birth certificates which helped trace our lineage – a gift that many descendants of enslaved people have not been afforded. However, even more critical were the living family members who shared stories, imprinting their lilting Southern accents on my Northern, nasal twang. My grandmother, Alma Harris Mayson, her sister, Doris Harris Carroll, and my mother, Heather Mayson Neff, were my only connections to my great-grandmother, Helena Harris, the force of nature who shaped the later generations of Harris women. Their words and humor unmistakably impacted my research and creative process. The ground on which I stand is matriarchal, community-focused, and brimming with creative energy. I come from a long line of musicians, artists, writers, and teachers – some of us chose to combine all of those professions. My solo piece, *Blood, Earth, Water* is an in-depth consideration of mixed-Black women's representation and an homage to these matriarchs.

It starts with a provocation borrowed from Alice Walker:

> And I remember people coming to my mother's yard to be given cuttings from her flowers; I hear again the praise showered on her because whatever rocky soil she landed on, she turned into a garden. A garden

DOI: 10.4324/9781003341802-20

> so brilliant with colors, so original in its design, so magnificent with life and creativity [...] perfect and imperfect strangers [...] ask to stand or walk by my mother's garden.
>
> (1983, p. 408)

Speaking these lines, I thought of what my family cultivated in plantation fields, the gardens of their homes, classrooms, and music rehearsals. These women, some of whom joined me on my site visits and some who allowed me to interview them, became the critical community that helped birth *Blood, Earth, Water.* While I will briefly discuss other elements of my process, such as literary analysis and archival research, this essay focuses on the role this community of women played in my attempt to create a more dignified, humanized, and complex depiction of Black women.

American filmmaker and visual artist Camille Billups once famously instructed bell hooks that the most revolutionary thing one can do is put yourself into your art: "Put all your friends in it, everybody you loved, so one day they will find you and know that you were all here together" (Qtd. in Greenberger, 2019). A core goal of my project was to position myself within the broader canon of stories about mixed-Black women within literature, history, and performance and thereby produce replicable processes that others may borrow and adapt for their work. By positioning the personal as critical, I gathered sources and materials that I wanted to embed within my work. Scholars, playwrights, historical figures, and artists such as Marie Laveau, Lulu White, Adah Isaacs Menken, Alice Walker, Toni Morrison, and Soyini Madison served as key players in my writing.

The theatre was one of the most powerful forms of mass entertainment during the Modern era, and the stock character of the "tragic mulatta" was a favorite of playwrights. The beautiful, pious Eliza Harris and star-crossed Zoe Peyton were the most recognizable leading ladies of the time, but, tellingly, a Black woman would never have graced the stage in one of these roles (instead they were played by white actors in makeup). The threads of Eliza and Zoe's tactics, objectives, and gestures were held by white playwrights who effectively used these characters as marionettes for furthering white supremacist sentiments. Unfortunately, to this day there are very few roles written explicitly about the mixed-Black experience that do not uphold Modern era "tragic mulatta" politics: narratives of "creole" women as temptresses, suicidal octoroons, or the duplicitous, guilt-ridden white-passing women. This piece granted me the freedom to re-present and challenge the archive of the mixed-Black identity crafted by writers such as Stowe and Boucicault. As I reveal in one segment:

> My superobjective is to refuse tragedy. To connect with my ancestors. To create a role for myself that isn't sad or suicidal or sex-obsessed. My superobjective is to grow plants in my garden that feed the bees and butterflies, to listen and make decisions with a clear head, to write the truth even if it kills me, to lead others into happiness, my super-superobjective is to—
>
> (Neff, 2021)

In addition to conducting academic research, I planned a trip with the help of my mother, great aunt, and grandmother that involved sites critical to my studies, but most importantly, my heritage: St. Augustine's University and Littleton, NC; The National Memorial for Peace and Justice in Montgomery, AL; and the Whitney Plantation in New Orleans, LA. Throughout my trips, I was accompanied by women who played integral roles in my life: my mother and my long-time artistic collaborator for over ten years, Janna Haywood. We share strong connections with our mothers. Haywood had also been present with me during times of grief, and, though I did not know it at the time, she would again reprise this supportive role during this trip.

I began to consider the act of embodied storytelling and how to bridge the gaps between archival research and personal testimony. While collecting evidence and research for this performance, I sought to intentionally and respectfully present a small performance at each research site by cycling through a series of gestures I developed while at home in Ohio. Before I departed for my psychogeographic research trip, I was fortunate enough to bring my mom into the studio with me and devise key lines of text, movement, and sound design. Together, we recorded her reading lines of text, although, the most verdant performance artifacts we generated were the candid snippets of our conversation, which greatly impacted the script I generated and provided elements of sound. Throughout my site performance, I played the flute and ukulele, while singing and dancing alongside the pre-recorded voices of friends and family who greeted me in the final scene. While traveling, I restaged material that I generated alone and with the support of my mother. Witnesses to these performance interventions were often passers-by; however, my intended audience was the spiritual ancestors for whom this work was developed and my mother. I allowed each gesture to change in response to the ground upon which I stood; while visiting Littleton, NC, I stood in the fields where the Harris women of my maternal family lived, loved, and died, allowing the uneven earth, humid air, and blazing sun to influence my movements.

Perhaps the most impactful collaboration with the Harris women was the ethnographic research. One of the key characters in my work is my great-grandmother, Helena Harris, a woman I never met but feel as if I know intimately. I interviewed my great-aunt and grandmother and was moved by one particular story: Helena was a fearless educator in Littleton, NC, where she taught Black students in the early 1900s in a segregated school. Every year, Helena would sort through the wealthy white school's trash to salvage discarded textbooks and supplies that she would use to enrich her impoverished students' education:

Helena poses for a photo on the steps of the gymnasium and thanks the photographer.

HELENA
Alright girls, let's get on home, it's getting late.
I know you're not tired, I'm tired! I'm ready for dinner and bed and—*phew.*

4 little girls, playin' in the cotton fields
8 white church shoes to match pretty Easter dresses
Doris Aurelia, Vivian Melba, Alma Marie, Emma Louise.
4 girls who see me scrape and bruise my knuckles—

She reaches into a rusty garbage can, fishing out textbooks.

She flips through them, marking out bits of vandalism on the pages, checking for water damage.

(Neff, 2021)

By embodying Helena's identity as an educator, community leader, and mother of four, I position her as a guiding spirit for "Golden," the character who represents me in the show. The characters, figures, places, and scenarios detailed in my research process are linked by a shared identity: mixed-Black womanhood and how they complicate dominant narratives about Black racial identity in literature, history, and performance. My representation of these women sought to challenge the "tragic mulatta" trope by exploring the multidimensionality of their experiences, most critically, their joy, tenacity, humor, bravery, and resourcefulness.

In 2019, this piece took on another complicated facet of this narrative: grief. When I first imagined myself onstage telling stories, my mind flew to a burlesque comedy, exploring how I have failed to sustain the semblance of racial tragedy expected of mixed-Black women. And then, I lost my grandmother. Alma "Goldie" Marie Harris Mayson was born on December 7, 1927, to Charles and Helena Harris. She was the second eldest of four sisters, and she was brilliant. A musician, educator, socialite, bishop's wife, mother, and grandmother, Goldie's presence loomed large throughout my life. She taught me how to cheat in almost every game, how to win the most impossible arguments, and how to dust myself off and bring the rage of a thousand armies when someone wronged me or a loved one. Goldie was not a smooth, quiet, cookies-and-milk kind of woman. She was bombastic and quick-tempered, a Southerner in a Northern city, and she burned with the intensity of North Carolinian summers her whole life. Her loss gave me the clarity I needed in shaping this project, for it became the axis around which *Blood, Earth, Water* revolved.

Most of my ethnography was conducted via informal phone calls and text messages. My great aunt Doris spilled gallons of "tea" about Goldie and her other sisters while chatting with me on Sunday afternoons. Before we lost Goldie, she and I spoke about drama within her social circles, stories about Detroit in the '70s, and raising two children who, in her words, were "too big for their britchidoos." My ethnography is simple, personal, and asks that the ethnographer practice a few key phrases, inspired by the Harris sisters' Black Southerness: "Mhm-mhm-mhm," "Huuuuush," "Lord, have mercy," and "You're kidding!" The key to speaking with my family was to not intervene or interject – to simply listen.

Goldie died while I was in Montgomery, AL with Janna Haywood, exploring the Museum and Memorial for Peace and Justice. While I did not speak at my Grandma Goldie's funeral service, I wrote all the words I wanted to say into *Blood, Earth, Water*, ending in an audio pastiche of messages left by friends and family, all framed by a recording I took of Goldie in 2018:

> Forgive.
>
> I've never tried to talk to the dead before. I've always been afraid, but, I'm not afraid of you. I'm afraid that we've lost you. I'm afraid of how quickly the months slipped by and how relieved I feel that I don't have to visit you in the hospital. I'm so happy that Mom can finally come straight home after work and that I am no longer afraid to answer my phone because it might be her calling with the bad news. But, now that it's happened, there's no more bad news to hear. Alma. I'm saying your name, even though no one called you that. You were Goldie, green-eyed Goldie. We have the same nose! You, me, and Mama. We have the same stone feet. You said that once, that we were all stubborn. I want to thank you and Ma for teaching me stubbornness. How to never let anyone topple me over, how to keep an even keel in the roughest seas, how to fight until my knuckles bleed because the crimson that breaks through my skin is the same as yours. The iron I taste in my mouth is the same that stained the earth you played in as a child. Before we lost you, you said, "I'm going home. I've been talking to my sisters." I want to talk to them too, is that alright?
>
> *She pours water over her head—baptized.*
> *Suddenly, a burst of yellow butterflies. The women from every scene appear. There is a circle.*
> *An audio montage of Goldie's voice, Heather's voice, and the voices of people who love the author. She dances with the butterflies. Lights fade. End.*
>
> (Neff, 2021)

While *Blood, Earth, Water* has been seen by hundreds of audience members virtually, the live staging (and filming process) was witnessed by four people – my sound designer, Matt Cantelon; my lighting designer, Megan Stanford; my filmographer, 'Drea Kirby; and my mother, Heather. While a rather limited version of the in-person audience for which I hoped to premiere my work, the film has allowed me to share this work freely with others, most importantly, students. My desire to create a blueprint for others hoping to write autoethnographic work is still a work in progress, yet, I have been fortunate enough to offer a small number of workshops on the subject of biographical and ancestral veneration in playwriting, followed by screenings or excerpts of *Blood, Earth,*

Water. Currently, my theatre company, Teatro Travieso, is assisting me with the effort to stage and tour this show in the coming year.

One of the most meaningful gifts in creating this work has been the opportunity to reconnect with my great aunt Doris Harris Carroll, who took up the mantle of storytelling on behalf of the Harris women after my grandmother's passing. For her help, I formally dedicated my work to my Aunt Doris, which she expressed was one of the greatest honors she has received. When I began this work, I envisioned it as an opportunity to learn about my history and how I wove into the fabric of our nation's past, but I was unprepared for how much I would need my mother, Aunt Doris, and Grandma Goldie to complete my project – not for their knowledge, but for the bonds that telling these stories created between the four of us. Goldie's illness, her daughter Heather's caregiving, and my fear of mortality became the underpinning of *Blood Earth Water*. Goldie once said that the three of us had "stone feet," that we were all too unyielding and stubborn – a personality trait that united us more often than it divided us. Both Goldie and Heather taught me about the importance of *me*. Goldie's excited, gossipy phone calls filled with narratives of Church Lady subterfuge and Heather's fastidious journaling and photography of life's minutiae taught me to remember and cherish every detail of my brief life. In the moments of writing, rehearsing, and filming that made me feel overwhelmed or defeated, I would hear Goldie's throaty croon – "Well, carry on."

References

Greenberger, A. (2019). "Camille Billops, Maker of Unflinching Documentary Films, Is Dead at 85," ARTnews. 3 June. Accessed 17 Oct. 2023. https://www.artnews.com/art-news/news/camille-billops-dead-12679/

Neff, A. (2021). *Blood, Earth, Water*. Premiered May 1st, 2021 via Zoom.

Walker, A. (1983). *In Search of Our Mothers' Gardens: Feminist Prose*. New York: Houghton Mifflin.

Wilson, A. (1996). "The Ground on Which I Stand," *AmericanTheatre.org*. Republished 20 June 2016. Accessed 14 Apr. 2021. https://www.americantheatre.org/2016/06/20/the-ground-on-which-i-stand/

Roundtable Discussion with Evelyn Diaz Cruz, Natalie Y. Moore, Aviva Helena Neff, and Winter Phong

Evelyn: Welcome and thank you for attending this roundtable. I would like to ask you all to share what connections or differences you saw across each other's essays.

Aviva: What I found interesting is that we had a mix of intentional and unintentional community-making that then became intentional. Typically, in my applied theatre practice, I am more process-driven and more interested in what we learn along the way versus what the destination looks like. Here, I started this project, then connected with a theatre company, and it snowballed into the final product. Winter and Natalie had different approaches to identifying the communities they were working with, but we all created a more "formal" theatrical product versus a more process-driven project.

Evelyn: With engaged theatre, we are typically more concerned with the message and do our best to present a worthy product that would potentially reach a larger audience. That's a hard balance. How do you approach that dilemma?

Winter: This excellent book called *Thanks for the Feedback* (Stone and Heen, 2014) outlines our ways of engaging with feedback. Our greatest response to feedback comes from how the feedback interacts with our identity. Movement, positive or negative, happens when we start to see our identity represented in the feedback we get. In acknowledging identities, we can better share our message and motivation for the work.

Natalie: As journalists, we're taught that our work should be going for the mainstream, regardless of someone's education level or socioeconomic background. Information should be getting to everyone. It's a public service.

Aviva: As educators, we think we want institutional support, and then that institutional support begins to make its demands. Ohio State University (OSU) had its expectations for what my work should look like. I had hoped to curate a space for predominantly Black

DOI: 10.4324/9781003341802-21

women or Black biracial women and non-binary folks. Because of institutional requirements and scarcity, I had to welcome people who did not fit into that community. They were excellent, and they took good care of me and my work, but I did lose a bit of control because I received a healthy amount of funding to research and produce this work.

Winter: As a first-generation college student not knowing what's acceptable, I often just do whatever feels right and hope for the best. It can certainly create mixed results but is a departure from the learned model of the passive audience. The Western theatre practice of sitting quietly in a dark room happened so that perceived nice middle-class, white women could go to the theatre, and their families would find it respectable enough for them to be entertained in these venues. But that doesn't make sense for us in today's theatre industry. That's not how we want to engage our audience. As a former managing director for a company that centers on disability, we want to open up questions, have a conversation, and create an action plan that generates new meaning, inclusion, and acceptance.

Evelyn: To that end, what are some of the ethical considerations that have come up with your work? How do you navigate the risk of trauma-mining, for instance?

Winter: Unfortunately, swaths of our communities have been taken advantage of. This is something that any artist, practitioner, or educator, needs to be constantly educating themselves about. By actively seeking out a better understanding of the world around you, you will do better. Of course, that's not always the case, but ideally, that should be what we are striving to do. The ADA [Americans with Disabilities Act] came into law in the 1990s, so everything is still rather new, and to assume that we're all going to do everything perfectly is unrealistic. But we still need to move forward.

Natalie: Everybody has blind spots. How do you put checkpoints in? Maybe that's done with a dramaturg, or through workshopping, or table reads. If you are entering a community that you're not a part of, educate yourself by reading and conducting background interviews. Although these things are subjective, they should be rooted in accuracy as much as possible.

Aviva: I'm thinking of these two influential pieces of writing on ethnography and applied theatre that influenced me: The first is Dwight Conquergood's (1985), *Performing as a Moral Act*. This piece discusses pitfalls that he's encountered in ethnography. And there's a fabulous book by applied theatre scholar James Thompson from the UK (2009), *Performance Affects: Applied Theatre and the End of Effect*. He looks back at his failures and successes, and argues, specifically when working with vulnerable populations, instead of trauma-mining, we should center pleasure, beauty, and joy. His institutional backers, such as the Red Cross and other global non-profits, have often wanted his project to do a sort of traumatophilia. He reflects on how that wasn't sustainable for these populations and that they didn't have any interest in it. It was a bad process and stained the project.

Natalie, you were talking about how accuracy is important to you as a journalist and as a playwright, but what I discovered is that accuracy is not important to me as a playwright and ethnographer. Since I'm writing about my maternal family, who are Black Americans and survivors of enslavement, Jim Crow, and the Trump presidency, I found myself in this weird space between memorializing and honoring my family's history by telling the truth, but also knowing that there were details my family does not want to be made available for public consumption. To honor my family, I have to honor that both of those truths exist. Another influential scholar, Diana Taylor, in *The Archive and the Repertoire* (2003), thinks about performance as an archive of repertoires and family history. I have to tell the truth but not necessarily the cold, hard, archival truth, rather the truth of our perception, the truth of our experiences. So, in a way, this project became about the fact that truth might not always be ethical, because it's not ethical for me to tell these stories that my family doesn't want mainstreamed for "white public consumption."

Natalie: If you're writing about the Civil Rights movement, you need to know when a specific march happened; or if your family is responding to the Civil Rights Act of 1964, you don't want to say it came out in 1972 because then you're hurting your credibility, and your audience could get distracted. So, in my case, if I'm going to write about an abortion protest set in contemporary Chicago, I need to know the laws in Chicago. I wouldn't want people who are entrenched in reproductive justice and civil rights work to see it and think that wouldn't even happen here. That's the kind of accuracy I am depicting, of a community rather than the interior lives of the characters.

Evelyn: Thank you for those distinctions. We learn from our failures as well as our successes; would you care to share an inspirational moment or failure that served you?

Winter: I once worked on a devised piece with a playwright who was speaking about people with disabilities in a way that I was uncomfortable with. It was as if the playwright felt settling was the best outcome for a disabled character. I was able to stop this narrative in the process, but how do I prevent that from happening in the future? How do I help instill values that aren't demeaning to people with disabilities? Especially, since I can't be everywhere to control everything. Instead of seeing my job as "rescuing" everyone, it's more productive if I help create a space where everybody feels confident in speaking their truth and being in a conversation.

Aviva: Well, my challenge was COVID-19. The pandemic emerged, and we shut down the world in mid-March. I had just started my fellowship that was funding this project. I had planned all my travel, etc., and we had to hit a giant pause button. I didn't know what was going to happen. My personal triumph came from turning to my community and turning to Black women in academia; I was fortunate to be working with Dr. Nadine George-Graves at OSU, who suggested I film it. That put me back on track to finish the project.

Natalie: For me, the real success was when I heard Black feminists involved in reproductive justice, especially the women from Dallas who put up that self-care billboard who flew to Chicago to see the play, say things like, "How did you get this so right? Were you eavesdropping on our conversations?" Which I was not. I was depicting the struggle and the intra-racial class dynamics. I was striving to capture the tension and the tenor of this work. Being told that I did that by people who are entrenched in this work was a great success.

Evelyn: What needs to happen for us to move forward as a theatre community?

Aviva: I think that depends on what moving forward means. We all need institutional support and funding. We want to pay our participants for their time, pay our vendors, and pay ourselves. But the institution can be an anchor that keeps us in a port rather than letting us go on a journey. On the one hand, as an educator, I want applied theatre to be recognized as a formal area of study. I want to teach applied theatre without having to explain to folks what that means. But, on the other hand, I resent that the ivory tower has to be the gatekeeper. I want there to be more workshops. I want it to be recognized as just as valid as the tickets you get when you purchase your season, but I also want it to have the freedom that we all experience from being under the radar. I want it all.

Natalie: I hope theatre becomes more accessible for new voices and new work.

Winter: During the pandemic, we found ourselves identifying with and coming together as communities. One of the biggest challenges that we are facing, particularly, in the disability community, is that people feel isolated. As we're thinking about and trying to move this work forward, we need to ask: "Who is our community and what do they need?" How do we build on that push to bring communities together in this time?

Evelyn: As we close this roundtable, what final thoughts are you taking away from this conversation?

Aviva: We're supposed to be preserving our histories, listening to each other's, and being in community with one another. The mainstream theatre has lost touch with the community aspect, of sitting in an audience and talking to the person next to you. Applied theatre is about embracing the mess and allowing ourselves to be *people* instead of *theatre people*.

Winter: The beauty of applied theatre is that there's always the opportunity to change, grow, adapt, and evolve. You can come back to the same group of people time and time again and create entirely new work. If there's a sense of trust and engagement with your community, there's an opportunity for something amazing to happen.

Natalie: I still feel new to this field. But this was great.

Evelyn: These conversations always give me hope for the world. Thank you.

References

Conquergood, D. (1985) "Performing as a Moral Act: Ethical Dimensions of the Ethnography of Performance." *Literature in Performance*, 5(2), 1–13, DOI: 10.1080/10462938509391578.

Stone, D. and Heen, S. (2014) *Thanks for the Feedback: The Science and Art of Receiving Feedback Well*. New York, NY: Penguin.

Taylor, D. (2003) *The Archive and The Repertoire: Performing Cultural Memories in the Americas*. Durham, NC: Duke University Press.

Thompson, J. (2009) *Performance Affects: Applied Theatre and the End of Effect*. London: Palgrave MacMillan.

Part V

Affirming Identity with Youth

13 Negotiating Gender (In)Justice

The Politics of Visibility in the Performing Justice Project

Megan Alrutz, Laura Epperson, Jasmine Games, and Faith Hillis

As applied theatre artists, we (the authors of this chapter) often frame performance and its potential visibility in the most positive light. After all, theatre is a powerful tool for representation, a critical vehicle for young people to make visible their stories, identities, and experiences that are often marginalized by society. For youth of color and LGBTQIA youth, however, visibility often results in vulnerability, danger, criminalization, or death. As we gather to write this chapter, gender justice for young people remains under attack across the United States. New legislation is targeting the removal of rights for trans and queer youth and families. Politicians are attacking the use of critical race theory, access to abortion and gender-affirming care, and the implementation of Diversity, Equity, and Inclusion efforts in spaces of teaching and learning.[1] In Texas, where we work, parents and teachers of trans youth are facing tough decisions about what it means to support their families in a state that aims to criminalize queer and transgender identities. Academics, educators, and artists are also navigating life-and-death politics of visibility as we employ theatre as a tool for social change. This tension thus invites us, and applied theatre practitioners at large, to reconsider our assumptions about our processes. With this essay, we hope to nuance our ideas and practices around visibility-making with and for youth populations.

More specifically, we examine the politics of visibility related to gender justice within the Performing Justice Project (PJP), an applied theatre model for devising critically engaged performance work with young people ages 13–21 (Alrutz and Hoare 2020). Over the course of a PJP residency (typically three to five weeks), participants engage in creative writing, storytelling, image and movement work, spoken word, song, scene work, and other creative modalities to express their views about living in a racialized, sexualized, and patriarchal society, as well as their hopes for creating a more just world. These "performance actions" are not merely games and dramatic strategies, but dialogic, creative, and movement-based exercises that activate critical thinking around race and gender (in)justice (Alrtuz and Hoare, 2020, p. 74). For example, participants might create and perform a scene about the

DOI: 10.4324/9781003341802-23

gendered expectations that get named in the first twenty-four hours after a baby is born, a monologue questioning the notion of support provided by the juvenile justice system, or an abstract movement sequence about what gender justice looks and feels like. The participants' devised pieces are carefully woven together and performed for an invited or public audience. These performances might also invite the audience to reflect or dialogue on the issues raised.

The authors of this essay have led PJP residencies with young people in a variety of settings, including schools, jails, foster care institutions, theatres, writing classes, and camps (both in person and virtually). Each residency is distinct, responding to the culture of the site, as well as to the experiences and artistic practices of the facilitators and the youth participants. While each residency has its own ways of working, projects all generate original performance material from three core questions:

> Who Am I?
> What is (in)justice and how does it show up in my life?
> How do I perform justice?
>
> (Alrutz and Hoare, 2020, p. 74)

By amplifying the stories and perspectives of the youth ensemble, PJP encourages participants and audiences to examine the individual and systemic issues of gender justice that shape the lives of young people.

In an article titled "Performing Citizen!: On the Resource of Visibility in Performative Practices Between Invitation and Imperative," Maike Gunsilius writes, "The resource of visibility can be used in performative practices to generate agency" (2019, p. 264), including allowing people the "possibility to choose a position towards visibility and performance, either to use this resource for public articulation and appearance, or else to reject a performative imperative through strategies of invisibility, disappearance, and resistance" (p. 266). In many instances, such as the color of one's skin, however, youth do not have the agency to "choose a position toward visibility." Furthermore, youth participants might face barriers around choosing a position toward visibility of their gender identity because of their age, life/family circumstances, and physical location (e.g. a foster home, among their families because of a pandemic lockdown). How then can theatre function as a space of possibility in a context where young people must adhere to adult and government-imposed limitations related to their gender identities?

As applied theatre-makers, and artists who work with youth, we have much to learn from Gunsilius' thinking about visibility as a resource. Who has access to this resource, and how are young people able to negotiate their own visibility or not? How do teaching artists and youth participants negotiate the politics of visibility within a PJP residency and ultimately support gender justice in the lives of youth and their communities? With these questions in mind, this essay offers two short case studies on the politics of visibility in highly monitored youth performance spaces, namely a group foster-care facility and an online Zoom-room. The PJP directors offer tools for navigating critical challenges that arise when centering gender justice with youth populations.

Supporting Youth Agency and Identity in Online Applied Performance (Voice of Jasmine Games)

Courageous Cadence[2] is a PJP residency that centers on the utilization of spoken-word poetry as a tool for social justice. Courageous Cadence 21′ was hosted in July 2021 and consisted of ten two-hour online Zoom sessions where youth participants explored their lived experiences with (in) justice through performance actions and drama-based activities. The youth participants devised and performed their piece – containing poetry, embodied sequences, and improvisational scenes – live on Zoom (from their homes) for an invited audience. All written work produced by youth poets had the opportunity to be published by one of our partner organizations, the Austin Bat Cave, in their annual anthology (Games, 2022, p. 13). While we worked toward a performance product, the real focus was on being in community with people who relate to experiences we might otherwise face alone.

With the support of Austin Bat Cave and the University of Texas at Austin, my co-facilitator, and I recruited queer youth of color through secondary schools in Austin and Humble, TX, past PJP participants, and colleagues in the field via Email, word of mouth, and social media (Games, 2022, p. 13). According to responses to a registration form for Courageous Cadence, the participants' pronouns, self-described by youth, were: (1) they/them, she/her, he/his; (2) anything but he/him; (3) she/her; (4) he/him (Games, 2022, pp. 24–25). The racial and ethnic makeup of the youth participants was as follows: (1) 50% Asian; (2) 40% Black or African American; (3) 10% Hispanic or Latino. The program topics were aligned with the PJP model, but my co-facilitator and I replaced some sessions with a specific focus on sexuality, a topic the youth participants requested after our first session on gender. Courageous Cadence 21′ was more gender and sexuality inclusive than our previous residency, which presented both a delight and a challenge to us as two queer facilitators.

The first session was an exploration of ensemble, which included an acclimation to the program and the first run-through of the session routine. Every session started with an access check-in where everyone was invited to express any accommodations they might need during the session whether technical, emotional, etc. We also rated our mood on a scale of 1–10, with 10 being the best possible mood to be in. By checking in, we took note of the session environment and accounted for what care could look like for that day. After checking in, we facilitated a "Name and Gesture" strategy, where everyone stated their name, pronouns, and performed a gesture to represent something they wished they could do for the day. We defined pronouns and modeled our own Name and Gesture for the youth. The exercise offered an opportunity for the participants to be called by the names and pronouns of their choosing.

After a presentation on PJP and the creation of group agreements, the youth participated in a performance action called "Mapping Geographies," which I adapted into a quatrain writing strategy (Alrutz and Hoare, 2020, p. 132). Using blank sheets of paper as a "map" and writing utensils, youth participants "marked" their place according to these prompts:

1 BORN: Mark the place you were born.
2 JOY: Mark a place where you felt immense joy.
3 DEFEND: Mark a time you had to defend yourself.
4 SAFETY: Mark a place where you are the safest.

Then the youth participants came up with a single line of poetry or a single sentence to encompass a feeling for each location. We asked the youth participants to describe that feeling, what was there, and to lean into sensory language. After writing our quatrains (four-lined poems), we shared them aloud. My co-facilitator and I renamed everyone on Zoom with a numbered order. I stated a prompt, and the first person numbered responded with their line of text from that prompt, followed by those numbered after them. We continued until all prompts were performed. The youth had the option to pass, and not share, at any point by making an "X" gesture with their arms, but no one did.

After this performance action, we reflected on the process, asking

1 Where does this live for you in your body?
2 Describe the color and shape it takes in your physical form, such as weight, sharpness, stickiness, etc.
3 What did you discover through this exercise?
4 What does location have to do with our personal experiences?

From these group discussions, the youth participants free-wrote poems with the option to write from the prompt "Where I'm From" or to write from their choosing. We later used this material as a part of the final performance.

A challenge, however, arose from the lack of privacy due to the COVID pandemic lockdown. As we progressed through this session, a grandmother – standing stoically and looking over the shoulder of her grandchild – peered straight into the Zoom camera. In a Zoom room of five high-school-aged participants and two facilitators, we all carried on without acknowledging the elephant in the room. My co-facilitator and I privately messaged each other while simultaneously leading the session. We were concerned. Many of the youth participants are non-binary and trans, and our session topics, namely gender and racial justice, have been widely criticized as inappropriate for children. Since we were working online, we did not have the usual circumstance of a parent or guardian dropping their student off and returning to pick them up. This grandmother showed curiosity about what happens in the in-between and continued to walk in and out of the space.

We became acutely aware that a level of surveillance was at play. Since we could not control what happens in their homes, we could not make the grandmother give our participating youth privacy. Furthermore, we could not assure them that everything they said aloud in the residency would not be heard by the occupants of their own homes. We began to consider what support and youth agency around their own visibility could look like within our residency and within the parameters of our Zoom-based program.

Ultimately, we realized that youth participants were taking their visibility and safety into their own hands by navigating how they could participate in PJP from their home spaces. They did not need an all-knowing facilitator to school them on (in)justice: These young poets were unsurprisingly aware of and informed about bigotry in society and how it affected their personal lives. They desired a space where they could talk mess, crack jokes, and explore their lives without censorship and surveillance of teachers, parents, and/or guardians. My co-facilitator and I thus took special care to build trust in our creative community by encouraging youth to make decisions about their level of participation. In the second session, we released a Google form survey link in the chat to see how comfortable participants were with the names and pronouns that were presented onscreen being stated aloud. This process invited them to control what names and pronouns were used and around whom. Participants also had the option to articulate anything they felt we should be aware of as we moved forward in the residency, especially now that they had an idea of what a PJP session would look like. This survey helped us know and respect our participants' boundaries around visibility and how invisibility, at times, may be necessary for them to participate safely or comfortably in the program.

Additionally, we were not attached to our agenda, and we often saw the off-topic as the on-topic. We provided an easily accessible, anonymous form for participants to share comments, critiques, and complaints at any point in the project. We acknowledged the power structures surrounding our program, such as facilitator vs. student, adult vs. child, organization vs. serviced participant, and we were transparent about where our power was non-negotiable (such as if a youth participant wrote about self-harm).

The young poet with the invested grandmother privately messaged us, offering clues for what name and pronouns we should use and when. In one instance, a young poet privately sent us a poem they wrote, inviting us to read it aloud anonymously, implicitly asking us to navigate the politics of visibility with them to protect them from a listening adult. As the program sessions progressed, our community knew how to interact with each other when one another's privacy proved vulnerable. As mentioned previously, the PJP poses three main questions to youth participants:

1 Who am I?
2 What is (in)justice, and how does it show up in my life?
3 How do I perform justice?

Moments like these, creating and performing in community with queer youth of color, remind me that we live the answers to these questions in our daily lives.

As a facilitator in arts educational spaces with youth, I am interested in theories around classroom radicalization, specifically the writing of bell hooks. In *Teaching Critical Thinking,* hooks (2009, p. 55) states, "'The personal is political,' [and] that experience is to be valued as much as factual information." She notes how classes often discuss curriculum without asking students how it shows up in their lives. However, youth in schools are often silenced for fear of lacking scholarship, which in this context is white academic knowledge. Courageous Cadence 21′ had the benefit of not existing under restrictive educational policy. This allowed us to center youth engagement and utilize visibility as a resource; however, we realized the ideal of visibility is in fact nuanced and contextual. We felt essentially free to protect students' choices and privacy in this project, but this freedom was not without challenges. If I choose to withhold information from a parent or guardian about their youth's sexuality or gender identity, have I committed an immoral act? I would argue no, although there are people who believe otherwise. I consider the line between a liberatory educator and a bad educator. As I ponder that line, I realize that I prioritize children being safe from the repercussions of unacceptance. We thus worked to not "out" youth participants by communicating through the chat feature on Zoom, by navigating proximity to visibility by renaming or not naming who authored personal writing, and by allowing the youth to create the audience list for their Zoom performance.

As artists and performers, we strive to make our work visible. Theatre practice typically dictates that theatre requires the presence of an audience of viewers. In Courageous Cadence 21′, rather than what some may say is hiding, we used in-visibility as a tool for freedom.

Navigating Youth Support, Safety, and Identity (Voice of Laura Epperson and Faith Hillis)

Starting in the summer of 2019, we began a multi-residency PJP with a residential treatment center (RTC) for young people living in foster care. Our partner site was both beautiful and complex. As an RTC, the site is dedicated to the care of young girls who have experienced emotional trauma, abuse, and neglect. Youth residents live and go to school together, accompanied to most or all places by at least one adult staff member. Residents also

Figure 13.1 Participants pose before their final performance. 2019. Photo by Kate Proietti.

receive counseling/therapy services and engage in a range of extra-curricular activities on-site. Trauma-informed and care-centered practices are threaded through all interaction and communication among youth, staff, and volunteers. The protocols and schedules for the youth and staff at this site are highly structured and very full. Yet the young people and our adult partners invited us into their space and dedicated their time, hearts, and energy to the explorative and vulnerable process that is PJP.

As our first rehearsals began, we quickly realized the nuanced nature of working within a site that has required rules and restrictions surrounding how young people are able to self-identify, specifically regarding gender. Though these rules are intended to keep the residents safe, at times the policies felt directly oppositional to the work and premise of PJP and raised questions about what and whose safety gets emphasized. For example, our partner site serves young people whom Child Protective Services identifies as female. Although those young people in fact possess a range of various gender identities/expressions, the site requires that all name and pronoun "changes" be approved by a case worker before they can be used. Accordingly, the staff dissuaded some PJP participants from using particular names and pronouns during our rehearsals while allowing other participants to self-identify. It felt unfair and confusing for us to navigate as persons not directly implicated by the rule, so we can only imagine the complex relationship some ensemble members had with the policy.

Figure 13.2 The full ensemble poses before the audience arrives for Our Voice: Imagining a New World. 2019. Photo by Kate Proietti.

As we navigated this tension, we began to learn that what is "safe and supportive" of these young people isn't always so clear cut. From our perspective as teaching artists, support felt like asking the ensemble what name they'd like to use during rehearsals, knowing that for a variety of different reasons, a young person might use a different name than we'd been given on our participant list. We wanted to make visible any and all identities that the young people shared with us. However, we quickly learned that a question as "simple" as "What name would you like to use?" might not be safe for the ensemble members to answer. We were nervous about breaking site rules, upsetting our adult partners, and jeopardizing our new partnership. Even more importantly, we worried about compromising the safety of the youth participants once they left rehearsals. We were unsure what consequences there might be for a young person if we openly referred to them by a name that had not been "approved." Though we made a point to never call any participant by a name or pronoun that they had not explicitly named for themselves, our fear kept us from engaging early in critical conversations with site staff about self-identification and gender justice. We sensed in ourselves, and in the ensemble, a need – a desire – to learn how to dance within the boundaries of the site *and* the self-designated boundaries of each individual to create spaces of visibility that support freedom and possibility but don't cause harm.

We wondered how this dance at the boundaries of visibility could be a way to create justice together. In *Emergent Strategy: Shaping Change, Changing Worlds*, adrienne maree brown offers, "We are socialized to see what is wrong, missing, off, to tear down the ideas of others and uplift our own. To a certain degree, our entire future may depend on learning to listen, listen without assumptions or defenses" (2017, p. 5). To move forward, we had to move past our initial disagreement and discomfort with the rules and procedures of our partner site. To begin the dance toward a solution, we had to do as brown suggests and not tear down or disagree, but listen to understand. We had to have conversations with our partners, the ensemble, and each other without defenses and without the objective of our own viewpoint being adopted by the other parties as the "correct" one. For example, during the conversation when a staff member told us about the name/pronoun rule, that same person expressed understanding and appreciation for the work we were doing to explore self-identification with young people. We learned from this discussion that when this staff member "corrected" the name or pronouns that a youth participant used, they didn't intend to subvert our journey toward gender justice. Rather, they were doing their own dance at the boundaries, navigating strict institutional rules that the staff were explicitly charged with upholding. Once we realized our goals were not fully at odds, we were able to better collaborate with the staff to expand the possibilities for youth expression within the context of this RTC. As we began to recognize the complexities surrounding the youth participants' lives, we began to practice an intentional curiosity about our own assumptions around the politics of visibility and applied theatre. Just as we encouraged PJP participants to embrace play and experimentation in their journey of self-discovery and collective creation, we put it upon ourselves to do the same.

This intention opened our collaboration to the possibilities that emerge when we center joy in the pursuit of justice as opposed to reluctance or fear. In *How We Fight White Supremacy*, author Akiba Solomon states, "Part of how we survived lies in how and why we laugh" (Qtd. in Solomon and Rankin, 2019, p. 84). Laughter is a crucial tool in surviving and thriving toward liberation. The transformative power of play and curiosity was especially palpable in one rehearsal midway through our residency. The focus for the day was "What is my understanding of and relationship to gender?" After an ensemble check-in and warm-up, we began our exploration with a performance action called "Alphabet Relay" (Alrutz and

Hoare 2020). This performance action asks participants to work in teams to respond to a prompt/question by generating words and ideas corresponding to each letter of the alphabet. Our prompt was, "What do we know about gender and attraction?" Leaning into the relay aspect of the action, we encouraged the ensemble not to overthink, not to worry about spelling or what's "appropriate." *Write down whatever comes to mind, and let's see which team finishes the fastest*. The youth participants embraced the challenge with enthusiasm, gleefully racing to and from the whiteboard where the alphabets were written, cheering on their teammates as each person took their turn. From "demisexual" to "Y-chromosome," we received a variety of responses. As teaching artists, we were happily surprised and a little overwhelmed by the direction and energy of the conversation emerging from Alphabet Relay. The room felt rife with curiosity, laughter, and possibility.

To build on this momentum, we went through each response from the different teams' alphabets as a full ensemble. Together, we discussed and defined the terms, concepts, and questions that participants had offered. The emphasis on impulse and speed during the race meant that for the most part, the ensemble did not know which individual had shared which responses. We hoped this layer of anonymity might support the group in being honest about what they did and didn't know about gender and attraction. As we went through each alphabet, everyone – youth participant, teaching artist, and adult staff – was encouraged to ask for clarity about language that was unfamiliar or new. Similarly, everyone shared whatever context or additional information they had about words and ideas on the lists. For some, this meant making themselves (or parts of themselves) visible by openly sharing their knowledge or experience. For others, this meant taking notes and approaching us privately with terms or definitions to share back with the ensemble later. In the moment, this conversation moved and twirled from person to person, as we all took on the simultaneous roles of learner and leader. We encouraged the ensemble to remember that just as language and terminology often shift, our relationship to these words and to gender can do the same. This moment was not about defining who we are, especially since for some members of our ensemble that was expressly not allowed. Instead, the moment was about expanding our communal understanding, being able to have an open discussion, and gathering tools to help us further understand ideas about gender and attraction. The dynamic between us, the staff at the RTC, and the youth felt collaborative as elements of the hierarchy in the room dissipated. There was little space for monitoring the youth's identities, as we all giggled through the wide variety of words that were on our alphabet lists.

Alphabet Relay was a pivotal moment. Together, we expanded opportunities for self-discovery and self-identification, which inspired curiosity and play later in our sessions. We rethought "visibility" not as a fixed asset but as a resource that we might choose to use or not, in a variety of ways. While visibility might be a young person publicly articulating who they are, in their own process of becoming, it could also be a youth artist privately sharing a story/poem with a teaching artist before anonymously contributing one line of that piece to a group composition.

In this partnership, we were fortunate to witness how some youth ensemble members would name and identify themselves as they gained knowledge, experience, and a justice-oriented community. In our final public performance, one ensemble member included a line in a group poem that identified himself as transgender, a term he had not used at the beginning of our rehearsals. Through his public performance, this young person was able to "acknowledge [his] understanding of the systems and institutions, or politics, that shape [his] life" (Epperson, 2020, p. 59). As educational equity expert Dr. Gholdy Muhammad writes, "Knowing self prepares young people to live joyfully in the world – a world that may tell them negative things about who they are" (2020, p. 80). Through the communal work of devising a performance in PJP, we worked together to decide if/when/and how to use our individual and collective resource of visibility to share experiences, learning, and relationship to gender justice. At this RTC, this meant that some participants relied on group performances of text to maintain personal anonymity, while others chose visibility by openly claiming their stories, poems, and performance texts as their own. In dancing at the boundaries of institutional policies that shape youth visibility, we hoped to support these young people in creating space to name who they are now and explore who they envision themselves to be in the future. By acknowledging the intersectional systems impacting the youth participants, the staff, and our own ideas about gender justice, we began to conceive applied theatre frameworks that allow for greater flexibility and fluidity.

Conclusion

While the PJP framework proposes and enacts possibilities for disrupting systemic oppression related to youth's gender identity and expression, it relies on performance, specifically the visibility of body and/or voice, to center or make visible the identities and experiences that are often marginalized by society. In our PJP residencies, attending to the messy politics of youth visibility within performance reveals the need for teaching artists to (re)negotiate these politics in both our devising processes and our performance products.

Visibility in performance is not inherently an agent of positive change; rather, we must engage with visibility as a resource that can be leveraged and navigated with nuanced attention toward gender justice with youth. Jasmine's project points to the possibilities of playing with shared visibility/invisibility (i.e. performing each other's narratives/identities), shifting one's proximity to visibility (valuing invisibility as a way to navigate justice and having private ways to communicate the consequences of visibility in different moments/contexts), and supporting youth to determine if/when/and how visibility offers a viable tool for performing justice. Laura and Faith's project demonstrates an intentional practice of curiosity about the politics of visibility already at play in the context of group foster care settings. By encouraging both teaching artists and youth participants to be expansive in how they choose to use visibility, they invite us to imagine how working with and within the youths' sites of living and belonging, might cultivate spaces of possibility for performing gender justice. Both projects ultimately work to center youth agency around their own visibility and practice a flexible approach to this resource. Taken together, these two residencies remind us that trust (in and among participants/facilitators), curiosity (about site, self, and others), and creativity (in our approach) can be critical tools for leveraging the resource of visibility toward gender justice with youth.

Notes

1 *The New York Times* reported on April 15, 2023, that "In the past three months, 10 Republican-led states have passed laws banning what is known as gender-affirming care for minors" (Paris, 2013).

2 I first piloted the Courageous Cadence residency in the fall of 2020 in partnership with several local nonprofits that support writing with youth: the Austin Bat Cave, Barrio Writers, and Speak Piece Poetry Project. I later co-led the Courageous Cadence 21′ residency solely in partnership with the Austin Bat Cave. Austin Bat Cave is a nonprofit organization that provides creative writing programing to youth. Additional project members are: (1) Parker Wozniak, Co-Facilitator; (2) Amber Whatley, Lighting Designer; (3) Co-Op Productions, Sound Designer and Video Editor; (4) Leticia Urieta, Program Advisor; and (5) Megan Alrutz, Program Advisor.

References

Alrutz, M. and Hoare L. (2020) *Devising Critically Engaged Theatre with Youth: The Performing Justice Project*. New York: Routledge.

brown, a.m. (2017) *Emergent Strategy: Shaping Change, Changing Worlds*. Chico, CA: AK Press.

Epperson, L. (2020) *Our Voice is Powerful: Toward an Aesthetics of Healing in the Performing Justice Project*. Unpublished Thesis. The University of Texas at Austin, Austin.

Games, J. (2022) *The Rhyme in Resistance: Youth Identity Development and Criticality in Courageous Cadence*. Unpublished Thesis. The University of Texas at Austin, Austin.

Gunsilius, M. (2019) "Perform Citizen! On the Resource of Visibility in Performative Practice Between Invitation and Imperative" in *Performing Citizenship: Bodies, Agency, Limitations*, (Eds) Hildebrandt, P. et al. Cham, Switzerland: Palgrave MacMillan.

hooks b. (2009) *Teaching Critical Thinking: Practical Wisdom*. New York: Routledge.

Muhammad, G. (2020) *Cultivating Genius: An Equity Framework for Culturally and Historically Responsive Literacy*. New York, NY: Scholastic Teaching Resources.

Paris, F. (2023) "Bans on Transition Care for Young People Spread Across U.S." *New York Times*, April 15. Accessed 21 Aug. 2023. https://www.nytimes.com/2023/04/15/upshot/bans-transgender-teenagers.html#:~:text=In%20the%20past%20three%20months,gender%2Daffirming%20care%20for%20minors.&text=Ten%20states%20in%20the%20past,Republican%20lawmakers%20across%20the%20country.

Solomon, A. and Rankin, K. (2019) *How We Fight White Supremacy: A Field Guide to Black Resistance*. New York, NY: Bold Type Books.

14 Queering Playback Theatre

Alejandro Bastien-Olvera

Introduction

This text reflects my process of designing and facilitating Playback Theatre (PT) spaces for queer populations. Queer Playback Theatre is not about revisiting the past but finding the strength in the present to share our narratives in a brave and creative space to co-create meaning, exercise our agency, and openly explore our queerness. While theatre is generally a welcoming space for queer[1] artists, it often requires us to leave our queerness outside the rehearsal room. Personally speaking, I've experienced internal and external regulation when my queerness has been deemed "too visible" when portraying a character. Moreover, traditional theatrical processes frequently reproduce patriarchal-vertical forms of collaboration and heteronormative relational expectations. Hence, queering Playback Theatre aims to provide a space for queer narratives and collaboration practices, bodies, and desires; queerness is a source of connection, joy, and curiosity, and is embraced as an aspect of the creative process.

One of my main intentions was to design Queer PT workshops where participants were willing to share moments of their lives that they'd never before told publicly. Jo Salas, one of PT's founders, says marginalized communities have been denied the opportunity to share their narratives in a supportive community as a form of testimony to create meaning and connection (Salas, 1993, p. 209). Therefore, I wondered, how can we tell our queer stories when most of us learned to live them in silence or feel guilt and shame in relation to them? What tools does a queer person need to articulate a moment of their life in a group forum? How does this process facilitate a creative, community-oriented, and risk-taking space rather than trauma-mining[2]? And how can we queer the rehearsal and performance room to receive these narratives? PT has been a useful methodology to address these questions due to its structured listening and performing model and its adaptability to different populations.

Casa de Muñecas Shelter

In the summer of 2022, I approached Casa de Muñecas Tiresias, a shelter for migrant transwomen in Mexico City, to offer a PT workshop. The administrators accepted the invitation, and we began an eight-session process. All the

DOI: 10.4324/9781003341802-24

cultural activities in the house were mandatory, creating some initial resistance, and the first two sessions went badly. The group said that they enjoyed the opening warm-up, where we played group-building activities. Their engagement was also evident through their laughter and spontaneity. By contrast, in the second part of the sessions, when I asked scaffolded questions and facilitated exercises about queer moments, their disinterest and reluctance were evident. For example, when I asked them to think of a moment during the last week that brought them joy, immediately, a participant asked me if I thought they had joyful moments living under hard circumstances in a shelter. That evening, I realized I had designed the workshop without acknowledging the participants' context. After that day, it became clear that participants needed a space to relax and connect through play rather than compel them to dive into meaningful stories. Subsequently, I encouraged them to participate by observing or making a hand gesture whenever they did not want to engage more actively. Once I dropped my initial intentions of applying PT methodology and focused instead on what was working for the participants, we were able to build a space where they felt a greater sense of agency and openness.

In the last two sessions, once we had built a space where spontaneity, consent, and play had been established, participants agreed to share some moments from their trans narratives to see them represented by other participants using PT. I gave them the prompt: "What is something you have done that you never imagined you would do?" One person told a story about the day she shared her trans identity with her family and their reaction. The atmosphere at that moment felt meaningful and attentive, yet at ease, with spontaneous laughter. I believe the participants' willingness to share their story created a sense of commonality as many group members had experienced a similar moment in their lives. Afterward, at least half of the participants shared their own stories.

After the experience at Casa de Muñecas, I understood I had initially enforced my agenda of sharing PT tools, thinking that our queerness alone would procure tangible points of connection. I realized that a fundamental part of queering PT was not forcing the need to tell queer stories and instead working to build a space of listening and spontaneity where any story could emerge; I also learned that practicing agency was fundamental, such as offering participants the option to observe or pass on an exercise. Creating favorable conditions to tell a personal queer narrative requires building a sense of group cohesion in a welcoming space.

Tlaxcala LGBTQ+ Festival

A few weeks later, an invitation came from the Cultural Office of Tlaxcala State in central Mexico. That four-day workshop allowed me to create a process with a diverse group of twelve participants from different disciplines who signed up for this explicitly queer space, as stated in the workshop's name. This time, in addition to starting with group-building activities, I decided to immediately teach short PT improv forms so participants could learn and gain confidence in the methodology before inviting our queer narratives. Hence, PT gave us a common ground to share everyday moments and gain trust as a group; they knew the group would validate their feelings and perspectives through the creative practice.

By the second session, we had co-created a tangible sense of group cohesion, evident in the high level of eye contact and laughter, the willingness to tell narratives, and the physical energy needed to improvise. In those two first days, we shared everyday moments as opposed to explicit queer narratives; nevertheless, the presence of beautiful and openly LGBTQ+ energies were present in the space.

Considering this sense of collaboration, I decided to give an encouraging speech to acknowledge that we were in a space where any of our queer narratives could take place, be listened to, and "playbacked" to us. This speech was remarkable because most of us, growing up in phobic systems, are used to regulating where, how, and with whom we share our queer stories. From my perspective, it made us feel extraordinary to be part of a group space where we could explore, share, and celebrate our non-heteronormative narratives. This opened the space for participants to give themselves permission to share any meaningful queer moment.

Narratives emerged with vulnerability and determination, including completing one's transitioning, being a teenage mother, and not having come out of the closet to a deceased father. The other participants played back the narratives, accompanied by laughter, deep tears, and spontaneous hugs. Participants realized how small moments can capture shared struggles and give them insight into their personal journeys. For instance, a young woman told of how her mother scolded her for watching cartoons with queer feminine characters. In telling the story, she realized that her mother had noticed something queer in her since she was a little girl, which is why she scolded her for watching those characters. To some extent, this story, which at first seemed an unpleasant sensation, ended up reinforcing the existence of her queer identity since her childhood.

This four-day workshop in Tlaxcala taught how fundamental it is that participants sign up with the intention of exploring queer narratives through PT, even though this excludes people who do not have the privilege or desire to share their life stories in a group setting. Also, I understood the importance of taking a moment to ground, acknowledge, and celebrate that this space was made to hold our queer narratives.

NADTA Conference

Queering PT also means queering its power structure. Along with Jisun Myung and Benedicta Akley-Quarshie, I led a workshop at the North American Drama Therapy Association Conference in 2022 to explore how queer theories can serve as an entry to sharing our stories. At the session, we explored four concepts: Queer Failure (Halberstam, 2011), Lesbian existence/

continuum (Rich, 2003), Queer Utopia (Muñoz, 2009), and Queer orientations (Ahmed, 2006)). This occasion was unique in the sense that most of the participants were connected to the drama-therapy field.

First, I presented the main concepts of each text to the participants, and then in small groups, they read and discussed whether these concepts gave them access to articulate moments of their queer lived experiences. Queer theory allowed participants to create a critical distance from their own lived experiences and transform a vulnerable, possibly disorienting process, into comprehensible narratives. By reflecting in small groups, we utilized queer theories as a lens to revisit our queer experiences. Afterward, the whole group came back together to add Playback Theatre techniques.

The group suggested that instead of having a single narrator for each improv form, we could start with a narrative, find the theme, and open up the narrator's role to other participants. For example, someone shared that it was their first time bringing their queer self into a professional space, and then, three more participants offered their experiences in relation to that sharing. In this way, stories came from multiple narrators and not one individual, as it is the norm in PT. This form of articulating and complementing stories as a group allowed us to notice common experiences and expand our sense of community. Moreover, when it came to improvising the story using PT forms, like "Pair," "Chorus," or "Fluid sculpture,"[3] performers spontaneously went beyond the regular improv structure to resonate with the collective narrative.

To queer PT, we sought to engage participants in the research by facilitating moments of reading, small group discussions, and consistently asking participants what they were interested in trying next. This mutual sense of curiosity helped build a tangible sense of community, as demonstrated in the shared comments after the workshop: "Just being in the space with other queer people, sharing our narratives was fulfilling, and honestly, healing" and "Thank you for making us part of this research."

Curious: Queering PT with Youth

For my MFA thesis in Theatre for Youth and Community at Arizona State University, I facilitated Curious: Queering PT with Youth, together with Rising Youth Theatre (RYT). The previous workshops prepared me for this undertaking with a broader perspective while adding multiple considerations, particularly intentional collaboration with youth and having a solid budget. The major collective achievement of this collaboration was the building of creative, flexible, and trusting relationships where a queer curiosity could emerge out of the process rather than external imposition.

I partnered with RYT, an organization based in Phoenix that creates art dedicated to social justice and community. Every RYT process is co-led by a youth and an adult artist. I collaborated with Sofia Fencken, a twenty-year-old who has been working with RYT for the past four years (I was twenty-nine years old at that time). This partnership was the first element that invited us to queer the leadership structure by making it more horizontal, diverse, and relationship-oriented. Given the difference in our ages, gender, and personalities, we were mindful to build a thoughtful collaboration. The planning phase lasted four months, during which time Sofia and I met weekly; the partnership felt relationship-centered, objective-oriented, and personally nourishing. We achieved this by checking in and checking out at every meeting, pausing to acknowledge and re-frame any resistance we were feeling, and taking the time to share and listen to each other's perspectives. We made decisions that felt right while holding ourselves accountable to the project's intentions. The biggest challenge was to maintain this non-hierarchical attitude and structure as we collaborated with the young creatives. As a society, we are conditioned to think that older people know more or have more power to make decisions. I had to constantly remind myself that we were all co-creators of our queer space. I had moments when I failed and said something authoritatively during a rehearsal; however, I deliberately took the time to hear everyone's opinions and feelings regarding group decisions.

To recruit participants, we shared an open-call poster through RTY social media and an Arizona State University theatre mailing list, and other local queer organizations helped us by reposting it on social media. We also held an info session to introduce us and our methodology before they committed. This session was crucial to set clear expectations, establish a sense of research, and let possible participants know we all would co-create the process and ultimately decide whether we wanted to open it to an audience. We ended up with a group of six queer and trans youth who engaged for the entire two-month process.

Once again, one of the most successful aspects of this process was engaging with queer theory. After several sessions, Sofia led us through a series of exercises to craft the questions that would guide our exploration of queer narratives. This was a significant change from my last processes because I now knew that co-creating the questions needed to be a group task so that participants would have agency over the themes and approaches to queer narratives. By the end of the session, we ended up with the following questions:

- How does it feel to be queer for you today?
- When is a moment in your life that you felt deeply curious about?
- What is a queer memory that brings you joy?
- When was a moment you were surrounded by allies/LGBTQ+ people?
- Tell us about a time when your queerness intersected with your religion.
- How was the journey of coming to terms with your identity?
- What spaces or people supported that journey?
- What is something that is still challenging about being queer?

Participants made it clear at the beginning of that session that they wanted to elicit a range of emotions to invite queer, joyful, and complex narratives.

Also, they created inclusive questions for allies in the audience to be able to also contribute as part of our queer space.

As we approached the performance dates, we thought about how we could prepare the audience to enter our queer space. Usually, in PT, performers begin by introducing themselves and sharing how their day is going; these are brief and meaningful statements that the rest of the group represents by embodying physical shapes. Instead, we decided to begin with the question: "How does it feel to be queer for you today?" This moment gave each participant space to ground and share the magic and complexity of being queer. It also clearly invited the audience to recognize that this was a space designed to hold queer narratives.

We also strove to make our performance space feel soft, fluid, colorful, and warm by designing a backdrop with rainbow fabric, placing colorful pillows on the floor for the audience, and adding playful blankets on top of the

Figure 14.1 The CURIOUS Ensemble (Ryn Mercado, Ray Anderson, S.C Mott, and George Hagelstein) embodies the prompt: "How does it feel to be queer for you today?" Directed by Alejandro Batien and Sofia Kencken. Spring 2023, Escalante Multi-Generational Center. Tempe, AZ. Photo by Jacob Buttry.

chairs. Every performer received a $100 stipend to dress as queer and colorful as they wanted to be, as opposed to a typical PT costume.

Looking for narratives around queer-joy and queer-hope was another critical aspect; J. E. Muñoz says, "Hope along with its other, fear, are affective structures that can be described as anticipatory" (2009, p. 4). Our choice of questions and deliberate design of the space felt like we were planning a queer gathering in our house. We held four performances in total; I noticed this project's strength, especially in the last two performances, as every audience member shared at least one thought or moment. We listened to narratives about coming out with supportive friends in high school and about the joy and complexity of a mother and their children both being queer; someone shared when her father came out as an adult and how that queered her heart, while a young adult shared how being Black and queer would never feel safe enough.

To synthesize this experience and the sense of queer community we co-created, I offer the following anecdote. One of the performers, S.C., eighteen years old, did not want their parents to attend because they were not completely open about their queer identity. They told their parents that there were no more tickets for the show, but their parents decided to go anyway. S.C. approached me and seemed very nervous. I told S.C. that we had several options and that the most important thing was that they felt safe and creative during the process. For instance, we could adjust the beginning of the performance; instead of answering the prompt, "What does being queer mean for you today?" We could look for something less explicit, or adjust their participation during the show, or even cancel the performance. S.C. thought about it for a few minutes, and then responded they did not want any details of the performance to be adjusted; if their parents had decided to come, it was their decision, and now S.C. wanted to honor the core of our work. Their determination was inspiring for the group. Hence, S.C. went out with the rest of the group to give a meaningful performance.

Conclusion

Upon reflection, Curious: Queering PT with Youth proved to be an effective means of validating and making visible the narratives and emotions that often have a negative association. Queer Playback Theatre showed us that reclaiming our narratives is less about revisiting the past and more about finding the strength in the present to share them. Queer PT was a risk-taking, creative, and social space where we could create meaning as a queer[4] community. During the process of co-creating with queer youth, the most important aspect was to take our time to build group cohesion and empower them to make decisions at every stage: crafting narrative questions, deciding whether to open our process to an audience or not, and choosing costumes and set pieces. By bringing our multifaceted queer narratives into the present, this creative space opened a territory where we can keep seeking, discovering, and sharing how it feels and what it means to be queer.

Notes

1 I understand queerness as a series of desires, impulses, and actions that re-direct the body in the space and allow us to question and dissent from (un)fixed heteronormative norms. When we dissent from those straight paths, we approach other spaces where other queer connections and transformations can happen. As such, queerness creates spaces for exploration, resistance, creativity, and performativity.
2 Trauma mining: "the process of creating an environment that demands that Black people, Indigenous peoples, women, Disabled people, members of the LGBTQ2S community share experiences of discrimination." (Nyangweso, 2020).
3 All these forms of improvisation last between two to three minutes and are performed by three to five performers. A Pair represents two emotions that are in tension; a Chorus represents a series of interacting moments; and a Fluid Sculpture represents the different emotions or moments that a narrator is going through.
4 "Community" is an ambiguous and abstract term, although community indicates a material reality. Usually, when someone speaks of LGBTQI+ community, they refer to an imaginary, utopian community, not a specific group rooted in practices or spaces. As Stephani Woodson says in her book *Theatre for Youth Third Space* (2015, p. 39), communities are built with intentional (although sometimes vailed) practices to make tangible what connects us to one another. In other words, communities are built through palpable practices, by knowing each other stories and interests. The queer community I refer to, is people of the sex-gender dissidence that have the accessibility both socially and individually to listen and share in group moments about how they became queer.

References

Ahmed, S. (2006) *Queer Phenomenology: Orientations, Objects, Others*. Durham, NC: Duke University Press.
Halberstam, J. (2011) *The Queer Art of Failure*. Durham, NC: Duke University Press.
Muñoz, J.E. (2009) *Cruising Utopia: The Then and There of Queer Futurity*. New York and London: New York University Press.
Nyangweso, S. (2020) QuakeLab. Accessed 5 Aug. 2023. https://quakelab.ca/blog/trauma-mining-do-you-really-need-that-hard-conversation.
Rich, A. (2003) "Compulsory Heterosexuality and Lesbian Existence (1980)." *Journal of Women's History*, 15(3), pp. 11–48.
Salas, J. (1993) *Improvising Real Life: Personal Story in Playback Theatre*. New Paltz, NY: Tusitala Publishing.
Woodson, S. E. (2015) *Theatre for Youth Third Space: Performance, Democracy, and Community Cultural Development*. Chicago: University of Chicago Press.

15 ART Built on Trust and Solidarity

Creating Applied Theatre with Girls and Nonbinary Teens

Dana Edell, Kailyn Oates, and Kit Bothum

"If boys were in it, I wouldn't do it," sixteen-year-old Kailyn says about her experience in The ART (Anti-Racism Theater) Project, a summer program for teenage girls and gender nonconforming teens in Wilmington, Delaware. In collaboration with adult teaching artists, the teens earn small stipends to write and perform a play for an audience of parents, teachers, family, peers, and community members. The Project, created by Dana Edell, and co-founded with Andrea Jacobs, is a deliberately gendered space: grounded in the belief that young people marginalized by gender crave spaces where they can express unique challenges, celebrate shared victories, and foster friendships with other teens dealing with similar experiences. This essay is written collaboratively by Dana, a white cisgender forty-seven-year-old woman; Kailyn, a Black sixteen-year-old cisgender girl; and Kit, a white seventeen-year-old gender-nonconforming, trans teen; we share our experiences creating theatre together during the summers of 2021 and 2022 with Dana as the director and Kit and Kailyn as part of the teen ensemble.

Over the years, ART has faced criticism for excluding cisgender boys from participation, in what has wrongfully been called "reverse sexism." Whereas boys need safe spaces to express vulnerable feelings (Way, 2011), be creative, and explore their voices through storytelling, we are committed to creating and fostering a space where girls and gender-nonconforming teens can express their feelings, opinions, and ideas without the judgment and power dynamics inherent in mixed-gender spaces. Together with other successful girls-centered theatre organizations such as viBe Theater Experience (viBeTheater.org) and Girl Be Heard (GirlBeHeard.org) in New York City, The Viola Project (violaproject.org) in Chicago, and A Company of Girls (acompanyofgirls.org) in Portland, Maine, we have found, along with applied theatre artists/researchers such as Ruth Nicole Brown (2013), Megan Alrutz and Lynn Hoare (2020), Kathleen Gallagher (2000), and Christine Hatton (2003), that girls and gender nonconforming teens benefit from spaces for themselves where they can use performance to strengthen themselves and their communities. As Kit and Kaitlin explain:

> We don't have cisgender boys here to keep this space safe and inclusive. While it's important to have everyone's perspective, it can be

DOI: 10.4324/9781003341802-25

> uncomfortable for our experiences to be undermined by cisgender males. Throughout my life, I have dealt with males dismissing me or presumptuously saying, "Oh, I understand." However, they don't. It's similar to how white people cannot understand the struggle of people of color. Cisgender men cannot understand how women and trans people navigate the world that they have molded for us.

Why We Participate

Many of us have little to no prior theatre experience, but we are passionate and committed to social justice. We recognize the world is challenging right now (far-right political extremism, economic injustice, systemic racism, gender-based violence, sexism, homophobia, transphobia, global wars, and climate injustice to name just some), so as teens, we have to know what's going on. We're socially aware because we have to be.[1]

We acknowledge that along with the ever-presence of social media, GenZ girls and gender-nonconforming teens have been struggling with mental health issues over the past decades, increasing in severity year by year. The *Sage Encyclopedia of Abnormal and Clinical Psychology* reports that adolescent girls are twice as likely than boys to report and receive diagnoses of depression (Dirks & Morningstar, 2017). From 2007 to 2017, girls experienced a 66% increase in depressive episodes, 36% of teenage girls reported high levels of daily anxiety, and 29% wished they had closer friends (Gadassi et al., 2021). Since the beginning of the COVID-19 pandemic, social isolation, increased social media use, fear of sickness, and remote schooling doubled these rising rates of depression and anxiety among teens (Racine et al., 2021). As we have been writing this essay, the Center for Disease Control and Prevention released a devastating report that finds teenage girls are experiencing "record high levels of violence, sadness and suicide risk," (CDC, 2023).

Adults often don't realize how the issues going on in the world affect teenagers, not just mentally but emotionally and physically as well. Despite our hunger for connection and support, getting teens to open up is hard. Kit notes the discomfort of having parents who "would try to force me to open up," while Kailyn offers:

> My parents always said things like, "because I said so" or "because I'm the adult." These statements gave me the feeling that no one cared about what it was I thought or had to say. I didn't know how to express my feelings about things because I was never given that opportunity as a child growing up. Writing is a way I get all my stuff out: I write rants and sometimes even pieces about life or anything I am going through at the moment. I am a person who doesn't like to talk about how I feel, but writing is a healthy way of coping.

As the playwrights of our stories, we have the power and control to decide exactly what we want to communicate and then use the rehearsal process to practice what it feels like to speak those words and eventually perform them for the public so that people know how we feel.

Our Process

In this section, we share some reflections about our summer 2022 project that included six teens (three girls, two nonbinary teens, and one who uses both she and they pronouns). We met four hours a day, four days a week, for six weeks. Our rehearsal process included social, gender, and racial justice education where we discussed and analyzed power and oppression and how and where it shows up in our lives and relationships. We analyzed media representations of gender roles. We used arts-based activities to discuss and share personal stories affecting teens (e.g. racism, gender, sexuality, mental health, peer and parental pressure, bullying, and suicide). We then strategized how to create scripts that amplify stories of gender-marginalized young people, offer alternatives, and encourage audiences to advocate for change. Using creative exploration, improvisation, movement, song, and poetry, we expressed how these issues impact our lives today.

Kailyn and Kit note:

> For us to open up about our lives and what we've been through, however, we have to trust the group. This trust comes from a slow and engaged process where we write and talk about our feelings and find solace in hearing others say, "I feel that way, too." As girls and nonbinary teens, some of whom are also Black, neurodiverse, queer, and trans[2], we connected over a mutual understanding of the struggle for power in our schools, families, and community. Bonding over issues related to gender gave us a head start in building the trust needed to explore, write, and perform the stories most important to us.

For example, one rehearsal activity was to create "An Ode to My Body," grounded in the theory of body functionality. This activity focuses on and celebrates what our bodies can *do,* rather than what they look like, contributing to more body-positive attitudes than conceptualizing one's body as an object (Alleva & Tylka, 2021). To this end, we drew pictures that celebrated our body's strengths and power, then wrote poems, and shared our work with each other. We also created "identity maps," which included a visual representation of how each of us sees ourselves on the inside and the assumptions about how we feel others see us on the outside. Through such exercises, we began to get to know each other, discovered connections, and fostered the trust we needed to create and perform a play together. After three weeks, we started developing an original script.

A critical tenet of ART is that the ensemble writes every aspect of the show: monologues and scenes, group poems and songs, and improvised movements.

"Our writing and ideas were never censored, instead, with attention to balancing power in this intergenerational collaboration, Dana offered feedback and support as we opened up to each other and dove deeply into the issues that impact our lives: the things that make us furious, make us laugh, and the things we want to change for ourselves, our friends, and our community." We created a seventy-five-minute play about a group of teenagers whose lives intersect at one high school. Each character has a personal arc where they reveal a challenge, and then throughout the play, the audience witnesses us address it, resolve it, overcome it, or learn to accept it. For example, Kit's character, Bobbi, feels pressure from their mother to do better in school. They eventually summon the courage to speak honestly with their mother about who they are and why they struggle. Another character, Phoebe, reveals how her mental health has impacted her ability to make friends, and she suffers from loneliness. She learns that by sharing her story, others can connect with her and support her. Eden struggles to come out as gay to her best friend, fearing it could ruin their friendship. Spoiler: It doesn't! Kailyn's character, Journey, is sick of the racist microaggressions she experiences at the predominantly white school and uses poetry to share her feelings.

The following scene illuminates many of the themes in both our process and performance. The situation included a storyline related to Cory, a girl dealing with sexism in her home. Her stepfather has been critiquing her appearance and making sexist comments to her about "crazy feminists." Earlier in the play, she expresses, "I just can't stand it. I have always had a fire inside me to stop gender stereotypes and how badly they affect society, but being around someone like him gives me no courage whatsoever to make that change." Then, after building closer friendships with other girls and gender-nonconforming teens and witnessing their courage, her own confidence grows:

CORY

Guys[3], since we're all here, I wanted to say that I am very sorry for being so closed off from all of you, just like Journey. It has nothing to do with who you are, it has to do with my home life…I trust you guys. So, I wanted to brag about an accomplishment I made last night!

BOBBI

TELL ME MORE!

CORY

Well, I finally had the courage to talk to my sexist stepdad. I don't want to go into major details, but I told him the things he said that made me uncomfortable, and we talked through ways he can be more careful with his words.

LAZ

I am so proud of you, Starlight!!

CORY

Thank you, I am surprised at how nice he was about it. I expected a lecture on why I'm crazy or something stupid like that. But yeah, it's definitely still going to be hard at home, but now I see that there is good in people, especially my stepdad, and I don't have to be so scared of everyone anymore and scared to stand up for myself and my gender.

EDEN

I am so proud of you, Cory.

The audience erupted in applause after this scene, celebrating Cory's act of courage and enthusiastic support from her friends. We appreciate that our peers felt seen and perhaps learned new tactics. We also hope that adults in the audience, such as parents, teachers, and community members, see the world through our eyes and can empathize more deeply with how we feel and what we need from them.

Successes and Challenges

The strength of this experience was our commitment to fostering an affinity space where teens can engage in dialogue and creativity. Our shared marginalized gender identities helped forge the connection needed to engage in sensitive topics with honesty, transparency, and humor. At the same time, we stress that gender affinity does not erase the potential tensions and ruptures that might still emerge, particularly related to racism. It is beyond the scope of this essay to explicate the ways in which racism was present and confronted throughout our process; though we spent several rehearsals discussing intersectionality and practicing how to speak openly, transparently, and authentically about the ways our race intersects with our gender to impact nearly every choice we make in the world. Subsequently, our play included narratives that address racism as well as sexism, transphobia, and homophobia. Creating, rehearsing, and performing scenes that directly reveal and confront racism is not simple or easy. It demands trust among the group, a commitment to honesty, and a sincere faith that performing such stories can show audiences paths toward potential solutions.

Theatre spaces can be a fertile ground for community-building as the process elicits conversation, creativity, and trust, as we collaborate toward a public performance (Edell, 2022, 2018). According to a ten year study that tracked more than 25,000 teens, researchers found that young people who participated in theatre activities showed "higher levels of empathy and tolerance for peers," among many other benefits (Catterall et al., 1999). We have experienced and witnessed this through our process and hope to add to this outcome.

Notes

1 According to data from the Pew Research Center (2019), young people born after 1996 are the most racially diverse generation, are more progressive than all previous generations, believe government should do more to help people, and have the most expansive understanding of gender in American history, with 21% of us identifying as LGBTQ+ and 60% demanding that official forms include gender options beyond the binary male/female.

2 Transgender girls would be welcome in our program, though none have signed up yet. We recognize the ways in which all trans youth have been marginalized by their gender identities.

3 As we analyze our script, months later, through the lens of gender justice, we acknowledge the ways we inadvertently perpetuate the centering of a male experience and identity, even among a group that did not include any boys or men. We now see how using the word, "guys" to refer to any group of people, regardless of their gender identities can reinforce male supremacy. At the time, we were so used to tossing this word around that we did not see the unconscious sexism. In hindsight, we might have considered replacing it with, "friends" or "folx," as examples of more gender-inclusive language.

References

Alleva, J. M. and Tylka, T. L. (2021). "Body functionality: A review of the literature." *Body Image*, 36, 149–171. https://doi.org/10.1016/j.bodyim.2020.11.006

Alrutz, M. and Hoare, L. (2020). *Devising Critically Engaged Theatre with Youth: The Performing Justice Project*. New York & London: Routledge.

Brown, R. N. (2013). *Hear Our Truths: The Creative Potential of Black Girlhood*. Champaign, IL: University of Illinois Press.

Catterall, J., Chapleau, R., and Iwanaga, J. (1999). "Involvement in the Arts and Human Development: General Involvement and Intensive Involvement in Music and Theatre Arts," in *Champions of Change: The Impact of the Arts on Learning*, ed. Edward B. Fiske. Washington, DC: Arts Education Partnership and the President's Committee on the Arts and the Humanities, pp. 1–18.

Center for Disease Control and Prevention. (2023). Youth Risk Behavior Survey Data Summary & Trends Report: 2011–2021. Accessed 15 Apr. 2023. https://www.cdc.gov/healthyyouth/data/yrbs/pdf/YRBS_Data-Summary-Trends_Report2023_508.pdf

Dirks, M. and Morningstar, M. (2017). "Depression in Childhood: Gender and Sex Differences," in *The SAGE Encyclopedia of Abnormal and Clinical Psychology*, ed. Amy Wenzel. Sage Publications, 1st ed. [Credo Reference].

Edell, D. (2018). "We Don't Come from the Same Background, ...But I Get You: Performing Our Common Humanity by Creating Original Theatre with Girls," in *The Crisis of Connection: Roots, Consequences, and Solutions*, eds. Way, N., Ali, A., Gilligan, C., & Noguera, P. pp. 363–379. New York: New York University Press.

Edell, D. (2022). *Girls, Performance and Activism: Demanding to Be Heard*. New York & London: Routledge.

Gadassi P., et al. (2021). "Connections during Crisis: Adolescents' Social Dynamics and Mental Health during COVID-19." *Developmental Psychology*, 57 (10), pp. 1633–1647.

Gallagher, K. (2000). *Drama Education in the Lives of Girls*. Toronto: University of Toronto Press.

Hatton, C. (2003). "Backyards and Borderlands: Some Reflections on Researching the Travels of Adolescent Girls Doing Drama." *Research in Drama Education*, 8 (2), pp. 139–136.

Pew Research Center. (2019). "Most U.S. Teens See Anxiety and Depression as a Major Problem Among Their Peers." February 20. Accessed 8 July 2023. https://www.pewresearch.org/social-trends/2019/02/20/most-u-s-teens-see-anxiety-and-depression-as-a-major-problem-among-their-peers/.

Racine N., et al. (2021). "Global Prevalence of Depressive and Anxiety Symptoms in Children and Adolescents During COVID-19: A Meta-analysis." *JAMA Pediatrics*, 175 (11), pp. 1142–1150.

Way, N. (2011). *Deep Secrets: Boys' Friendships and the Crisis of Connection*. Cambridge, MA: Harvard University Press.

Roundtable Discussion with Megan Alrutz, Alejandro Batien-Olvera, Evelyn Diaz Cruz, Dana Edell, Laura Epperson, Jasmine Games, and Faith Hillis

Evelyn: Welcome everyone. To begin this roundtable, thinking about each other's essays, were there any themes or points of resonance with your work that you'd like to share?

Dana: I found the piece that Megan, Jasmine, Laura, and Faith wrote about visibility illuminating because we often think of empowerment as simply telling your story and putting it on stage. It made me reflect on how we invite young people to be visible, which can be empowering but dangerous.

Evelyn: That begs the question of the ethical concerns inherent in applied theatre practices. Was there ever a moment when you had to shift gears because the work was not going in a principled direction?

Alejandro: When I was facilitating workshops with queer youth, I became aware that many people had stories they didn't want to share publicly. My response was, "You don't need to share." In thinking about my participants' visibility, I could feel their stories, even those that went unspoken. Stories become visible by witnessing them throughout our process. Not everyone has to perform them publicly.

Megan: Ethical concerns sit at the center of every decision we make in the Performing Justice Project. For example, in a juvenile justice setting where the state has tight control over gender expression, we often navigate the politics of inviting people to name their pronouns and their preferred names. We speak with young people about the very real consequences of doing this work and what it means to create a performance about justice within highly "unjust" places, spaces, and systems.

Faith: Identity can be very personal and complex, and no one person's entry point into these conversations will be the same. While engaging the ensemble, you might realize a better entry point for conversations around injustice and creating justice is discussing environmental issues, for example. It does the ensemble a disservice to force a conversation or performance action that's not

DOI: 10.4324/9781003341802-26

immediately resonating. Instead, we can find a point where environmental justice and gender justice intersect and see where that leads us. Being ethical in your approach sets the foundation for handling other ethical questions that are bound to arise during a residency.

Evelyn: With that idea in mind, how do you balance process and product?

Jasmine: I just finished my third Courageous Cadence program in the summer of 2023. The group ended up being all Black students, who were queer and out and some who were straight. Not all participants were interested in spoken word poetry. Some of them were not interested in writing at all. I can't force anyone to write, so I had to be okay with them coming up with the program for themselves. The polished finished project is never really the purpose. I privilege us coming together and being able to talk about things that matter to them, like interacting with their peers. They achieved that with a performance that was more like an open mic. People came up and told their stories with some theatre intertwined. It had an intimacy we wouldn't have gotten if I had steered them only in the direction in my head.

Megan: For me, the biggest threat to balancing process and product is when expectations and resources don't align. As a director and facilitator, I aim to manage expectations (for myself, youth participants, organizational partners, and audiences) by being transparent about time, experience/expertise, material resources, space, and funding. If time is short, I begin with the expectation that young people will hold scripts (in a beautiful, small black binder). If young people are performing for the first time, I might try to support them with elegant lighting or music to help hold the audience's expectation for theatricality. If the space is a gym, I lean into dressing in custom-made, matching t-shirts to remind young people that we are a performance ensemble no matter where we share our work. Lastly, we are clear with young people that there will be moments when we move from devising to scripting and then to performance. As we move through that trajectory, we become more inclusive of an audience and begin thinking about their experience and expectations for the product. The way a process moves and feels for participants remains front and center.

Dana: The process is always going to show up in the product. I don't believe you ever see a performance and not feel what the energy was like during the process. The process of the ART Project is intentional: The first three weeks of the seven-week program are for community building with a diverse group of young people. A group needs to have a shared language and just have fun together. In your essay, Alejandro, I appreciated the realization of the need for games and playing together. We have to have fun to build the trust to do anything that might culminate in a performance.

At the same time, our performance is product-centered because it's activist performance. We are deeply aware that we're creating work to impact an audience. So, our process includes thinking about who will be in our audience and what we want to say to those people. What change do we want to make with our work? The product also has the process built into it because we leave spaces for audience interaction. Sometimes, we'll play a game from rehearsal to engage the audience and bring the process into the performance.

Alejandro: Dana, your program is product-oriented, while in my program, we don't need to get anywhere. We're just trying to share a queer moment in our lives. I plan a ten-week process with check-in points to discuss whether or not we want to share this with an audience. If we don't want to, that's fine. In the second residency, we decided we did, and I caught myself thinking, "If we want public sharing, we need to get better at this." And then I was like, "No, no, no. The product should not determine how I approach each of the artists or get in the way of the curiosity and joyful lens." I realized I needed to change my approach. If we want a product to feel curious, exciting, and colorful, I need to ensure that I arrive with these elements every day. Ultimately, we prepared our space as if we were preparing our house to host a party. It felt like *we* were the party. We're just letting you (the audience) in for one hour. The audience isn't getting the whole experience, just a snapshot of our fantastic community.

Laura: How can we, as you're saying so beautifully, make the product so that people experience an invitation to the party of our process? I'm thinking about my first facilitation, not knowing what the final product would be like. I was working with new artists, and I was in graduate school. Although my ego felt it needed to prove something, I had to let go of my ideas about "quality." It was interesting how our attitude and that of the youth ensemble shifted once the performance became more real. The product and the process are both integral to doing this work, especially when we think about the vulnerability of young people being witnessed by adults who have control over their lives. This experience helped me interrogate my esthetics and how they connect to systems that tell us what is beautiful, what determines quality, and who gets to name and define that.

Faith: I often remind myself that uplifting and valuing the process does not mean you forsake the product altogether. Supporting the product does not equal rushing through the process and ignoring moments for adaptability, fun, and ease in the work. I find balance as a facilitator by constantly checking my own lens. Am I putting pressure on the product because I'm worried about external factors, for example, how people might perceive this work I care about so deeply? Or can we simply lean into the power of esthetics, joy, and beauty and trust that the work will be what it needs to be, what the ensemble feels good and proud of? Maybe I'm shying away from the product for some reason. That reflexive practice is what helps me find balance.

Dana: We did a show in the summer of 2022 where the teenagers had high levels of anxiety and depression, particularly the girls and non-binary teens. Half of them had attempted suicide at different moments in their lives. Part of what they wanted to say with the show was about the resources they needed and didn't have access to. Toward the end of the process, I panicked, thinking, "The show must go on. That's what they and the audience signed up for." But here, I needed to balance that with the fear of self-expressed anxiety and fragility. I had to ask, "Am I going to hurt them by pushing them to perform?" I used to be the kind of director who pushed the group to memorize lines and get ready to be onstage. But in this case, I felt it was okay for them to have a script in hand or if the narrative didn't make sense because we had to cut stuff to protect them. The day of the performance turned out to be beautiful: All of us engaged honestly about what everyone felt confident and comfortable sharing with an audience. Throughout the show, they had scripts on stage that they could sneak a look at if needed, and at the end, a monologue was performed with a script in hand. I could see the audience felt the care, effort, and courage it took to get them to that place of performance.

Evelyn: I'm hearing how you've all had to shift certain sensibilities. Can you share an inspiring moment when you knew you were successful?

Jasmine: During the pandemic, our workshop had to be online. The spirit of camaraderie of the participants was encouraging to me. They were connecting behind the scenes and sharing their work. Providing this space and process evoked the love and care they radically held for each other, which was truly inspiring.

Megan: I was working on a project where a group of young people were required to participate. In the beginning, I had significant reservations about requiring anyone to participate in applied theatre – after all, the work is about agency. On the last day of our time together, we had a reflection circle. Overwhelmingly, nearly all the participants said they were glad the project was required, as they would have otherwise quit or not joined. Several participants shared they had never followed through with a group activity, and they felt proud of themselves and the work. This reflection circle made me think deeply about required participation, agency, and success in applied theatre.

Laura: In our essay, Faith and I wrote about a group of young folks living at a residential treatment center. We had a performance at that site, but then we held one at the University of Texas, Austin, which is a big deal because these young people don't get to leave their treatment center. The event must be approved and scheduled; everything is locked up, and they must be signed out. They came to campus for two nights: one for a rehearsal and one for the final performance. We were in an actual theatre space as opposed to a room. It was overflowing with people, and we had to pull in extra chairs. A big part of the work is the exchange with the audience. The energy from the space and the audience buoyed their performance.

Faith: After the ensemble's final performance, no one wanted to leave. I was cleaning up and chatting with folks, and the ensemble lingered, laughed, and reminisced. They expressed their pride in their work and giggled about the thick layer of nerves that was in the air only seventy-five minutes ago. There were hugs and dancing and joy.

Alejandro: In my work, the main question is how do I invite queer narratives without just saying, "Who has a queer story that you want to share?" In the partnership with Rising Youth Theater, the co-leader, Sophia, came up with a simple yet effective facilitation: We read short excerpts from queer narratives that I selected, and then Sophia prompted them to come up with questions in response to the readings. They came up with about thirty questions, which we read out loud in a circle. One was, "When was a moment in your life when you felt curious." It was simple, yet it was so deep.

Evelyn: What do we need to move forward as an applied theatre community?

Faith: My hope is that we continue to support each other. Too often, the systems we work in can be disheartening. There's so much beauty in our collective love and commitment to creating and envisioning. There's so much space for all of us. I hope we continue to carve it out for and with each other.

Laura: As someone who works with young folks in applied theatre, I sometimes have to defend the quality of my work to theatre people at large. Theatre with young people isn't less than; it is just as beautiful and high-quality. Universities are engaging more in this work, but every theatre house should have more community-engaged practices as part of their programing.

Dana: Yes, Laura, I amply that by a thousand percent. And add an acknowledgment of the usefulness of the arts in social services and social justice spaces.

Laura: Part of the challenge is that the impact of these experiences isn't evident through the product alone.

Megan: I am hopeful that we will keep listening to young people and learning what theatre offers us in the way of change work. I also hope we will lean into esthetics and the possibility of theatre (product and process) to ignite dialogue, build relationships, and shift systems.

Jasmine: Theatres and arts organizations say they're trying to be more inclusive of people our society has marginalized and to include them more in their year-round programing, which I appreciate because I dislike the tokenization of applied theatre. As we continue to work with people who may or may not have experience with theatre, there has to be more patience, grace, and willingness to teach people and work with them from where they are. The spaces we're holding, designing, and facilitating are complex: It is the intersection of tensions, possibilities, joy, and trauma. We should also consider theatre's potential contribution to health, education, and well-being.

Evelyn: Thank you all for your time. We appreciate all your insights.

Part VI

Expanding the Definitions

16 Performing Vulnerability, Voicing Resistance

Women's Spoken Word Poetry in Trinidad and Tobago

Alyea Pierce

Introduction

As a poet and educator based in the northeast United States, my training in multi-disciplinary art forms, such as spoken word poetry, theatre, audio recording, and photography, has been integral to my research and preservation of Black and Afro-Caribbean oral tradition and collective memory. I share historical and personal stories to illustrate the struggles and triumphs of the African diaspora. Moreover, I use the language and theory of poetry as a form of activism to initiate conversations to dispel hegemonic narratives associated with Black, Indigenous, People of Color, and women-identifying folx. By implementing the gifts of theatre, including collaboration, imagination, and storytelling, and applying them in non-traditional settings to engage women with varying access points both domestically and globally.

Being an Afro-Caribbean-American woman poet informs my practice; therefore, when I entered my field study as a 2019–2020 Fulbright-National Geographic Storytelling Fellow, I used poetry and spoken word performance to examine the complex interplay of gender, spirituality, and socio-political relations within Trinidad and Tobago. My creative research focused primarily on workshops in partnership with the University of the West Indies' St. Augustine's Institute for Gender and Development Studies and the WomenSpeak Project: an online community-building forum that highlights creative work, personal reflections/survivor testimonies, and issues impacting women's lives in the Caribbean. WomenSpeak facilitates networking among activists and organizations, engages in research and community arts workshops, creates opportunities for learning and capacity-building, and supports women in telling their stories of surviving violence and discrimination. With these community partnerships, I facilitated my Write to Speak Spoken Word workshop on November 16th, 2019, to spread awareness about the *16 Days of Activism Against Gender-Based Violence*: a campaign that begins on November 25th, International Day for the Elimination of Violence against Women, and culminates on December 10th, Human Rights Day.

This essay looks at how the inclusion of women's voices and bodies in poetic spaces can embrace vulnerability to conjure hope and effect change.

DOI: 10.4324/9781003341802-28

In her article, "Troubling Aesthetics: Mapping Vulnerability as a Generative Force in Community Theatre" (2022), Elsa Szatek explains that "vulnerability is encountered as a structural and situational matter, related to class, ethnicity, place, and gender" (p. 42), and as such is "politically and socially produced" (p. 43). While all beings are vulnerable, "in the sense that we could die or be exposed to harm, some will be more exposed than others and therefore be more vulnerable" (p. 43). For instance, as with my workshop, "participants might be marked by violence, discrimination, and/or injustice. Thus, when creating a performance based on their experiences, the aesthetics will partly arise from experiences of vulnerability." She further maintains that while vulnerability "is often connected to passivity and lack of agency," as Judith Butler (2016) argues, "vulnerability can potentially inform actions" to resist the power structures that limit participants' lives (p. 42). Applied performance can create a space away from daily life to share experiences, expose structures producing vulnerability, and collectively shape a "generative space enabling new ways of becoming" (p. 48). Since these workshops are not public displays, the women are not performing their vulnerabilities for a voyeuristic audience. Instead, they can find solidarity in common experiences, contextualize these experiences, and reimagine their subjecthood.

Context

Having one of the largest diasporas per capita, Trinidad is one of the most cosmopolitan societies in the Caribbean (Tidwell, 2001). The city of Port-of-Spain, Trinidad is colorful, bustling, and at the center of arts and business; Caribbeans, Caribbean migrants, and Americans of Caribbean descent comprise a diverse array of customs, characters, history, cultures, races, religions, and languages unto themselves. However, it is also in a flux state with a dramatic spike in the national murder rate over the last fifteen to twenty years being attributed to underserved neighborhoods; growing crime rates against women and girls; class tensions as residents of "crime hot-spots" increasingly reject marginalization; protests by residents in low-income areas; and rising ethnic, socio-economic disparities. Other factors include spatial conflicts as Trinidad experiences a mass influx of people from East Asia for work, citizens from Venezuela in need of sanctuary, and others from various Caribbean islands.

As a response to these significant socio-economic challenges, a new generation of poet-performers of Trinidad and Tobago have revitalized the spoken word poetry movement with hard-hitting lyrics, esthetics of word play, authenticity, and theatrical movement and body language. Spoken word poetry has a way of responding to the immediacy of the moment, whether that be the global Black Lives Matter movement or women's rights in Trinidad and Tobago. The movement has evolved from the art of oral storytelling and music genres that African and Indigenous ancestors used traditionally to entertain and educate, like Kaiso music whose rhythms trace back to eighteenth century West Africa, then Trinidad and Tobago's Calypso of the mid-nineteenth century, and Rapso in the 1980s.

Spoken word poetry was and is still used as a platform to articulate the struggles, joys, histories, pains, and triumphs of the African diaspora. It is a vessel for remembrance, drawing on a rich literary and musical heritage. As stated by the Smithsonian's Center for Folklife and Cultural Heritage, "The oral tradition carried African narratives across continents and sustained them through bondage. As a political catalyst, speech defined the struggle for freedom and moved ordinary people to extraordinary acts of courage." Although "institutions of slavery, colonialism, and racism attempted to silence generations of Africans in the Caribbean, oral history became a means of maintaining identity, surviving and resisting oppression and exploitation, as well as a tool for achieving freedom" (Smithsonian Institute, 2024).

In an interview with Patricia J. Saunders, the acclaimed Trinidadian writer Earl Lovelace suggested that "when we think about culture, we have to think about cultivation. One cultivates culture through practice; it's a lived experience" (1999, p. 11). We create and cultivate culture in three main ways: the stories we tell, the language we use, and the practices we engage in. My practice evokes an awakening of the body, voice, and spirit, creating a space for dialogue, exploration, improvisation, and interruption. What follows is a detailed description of the workshop, how it led to the women's creative writing/performance, and the effect this experience had on the participants.

Practice

Goals and Learning Objectives of the Write to Speak Spoken Word Workshop

Participants will be able to:

1. Develop verbal fluency, confidence, and communication skills to lead effectively in their community through public speaking and theatre exercises, and the construction of their own original creative piece.
2. Promote activism, women's empowerment, and leadership through uncensored writing and performance poetry.
3. Understand and appreciate poetry as a literary art form and how to use art as a form of self-reflection and freedom.
4. Analyze the various figurative elements of poetry and incorporate them in their writing, such as diction, tone, form, genre, imagery, figures of speech, symbolism, theme, etc.
5. Identify a variety of forms and genres of poetry from diverse cultures and historic periods, such as haiku, sonnets, dramatic monologues, free verse, etc.

Simone Leid, founder of the WomenSpeak Project, opened the session with a conversation about *16 Days of Activism Against Gender-Based Violence*,

Figure 16.1 Workshop Group at the University of the West Indies. 2020. Photo by the author.

and participants discussed the various ways in which women experience violence in their daily lives. Additionally, participants learned about how women are even more vulnerable to violence in the contexts of natural disasters, terrorism, and migration.

After Simone Leid's conversation with the group, I took participants through various exercises to help them create impactful images in their poems and to identify different ways to express their feelings about being a woman. The women then engaged in a sharing exercise where they responded to various word association prompts. They also had the opportunity to write a short piece and receive one-on-one feedback from their peers before presenting their piece to the whole group.

At the beginning of every workshop, we create a social contract to foster a space where participants feel comfortable and supported in this intimate process. To prepare, I hang a large sheet of post-it-pad paper labeled "Ground Rules." I open the activity by explaining the purpose of ground rules and asking the participants about their importance. I propose the following ground rules (in no particular order):

1 Maintain confidentiality.
2 Actively Listen.
3 Participate as Fully as Possible.

   a Participation can look different – you can raise your hand, write and share with a partner, engage with the activities, show engagement through body language, etc.

4 Use "I" Statements.
5 PEMI (Please Excuse/Educate My Ignorance).

6 Don't Yuck My Yum (No sounds of displeasure, laughter, and/or judgment of fellow artists).
7 Have respect for yourself and everyone in the room.
   a Avoid labeling individuals or groups and honor how folx identify.
8 Uphold a safe and brave space.

Once these are explained and outlined, I check if the participants have any suggestions for additional ground rules. After we compile the full list, the entire group claps once in unison to show that they are all in agreement with this social contract. This exercise can be used as a foundation and opportunity for the group to reconnect with the learning goals and objectives of the workshop at any point.

I then inform participants that they will engage in holding a space of openness and greater compassion to explore topics and identifiers around gender, language, culture, lived experiences, etc. It's essential to recognize that each participant/writer has a different life experience and may feel more or less comfortable discussing them. Since this can be a sensitive area for individuals, I want everyone to approach conversations with the following practices:

- Ask open-ended questions (e.g., begin with "How…" and respond with "Can you say more?") to draw out the perspectives of the participants.
- Use active listening skills (e.g., paraphrasing, mirroring, summarizing) to ensure everyone's comments are clearly understood.
- Calling in vs. Calling out

  "Calling in" encompasses the facilitator/individual taking a compassionate approach and having a conversation with the participant. (If the facilitator needs to have this conversation as a sidebar, an assistant, additional staff member, or teacher present, could remain with the group).

Example language:

I noticed you used a phrase or word that made me uncomfortable. Did anyone else have a reaction to the word that was used at that moment?

"Calling out" may include abruptly stopping what is happening and addressing the issue at hand in front of the entire group. This may lead to feelings of rejection, shame, guilt, denial, or "othering." It may involve an abrasive approach.

Example language:

- "You are wrong for saying or doing …"
- "You shouldn't say or do …"
- "This is problematic …"
- "You should know better …"

After I facilitated this discussion, I reminded the participating writers that spoken word allows us to witness the truth in our fellow human beings, especially those whose voices have been historically and systematically marginalized; and build community by showing support for one another's perspectives; engage in political, cultural, and social discourse; and most importantly, reopen ourselves to the nuances of our emotions, like passion, fear, anxiety, depression, joy, and love, which often go neglected due to cultural expectations.

For the first activity, I used a collection of charms as an opportunity for participants to reconnect with their imagination, engage with transparency, and map their memory. This gave me a barometer to understand the group's dynamic, as well as where individuals are in the process of vulnerability.

Example prompts:

1 Pick 1-3 charms that represent(s) how you feel as a woman in this society.
2 Pick 1-3 charms that represent(s) what makes you feel loved and appreciated.
3 Pick 1-3 charms that reflect(s) if you ruled the world, what are the first things you would change? Why?

This warm-up exercise aimed to connect with implicit and explicit memories through visualization, "where the participants collectively share and explore difficult themes from their everyday by" utilizing the charms (Szatek, p. 43). Through imagery, participants expressed an appreciation for helping them flex their muscles of imagination, which many have not used since they were young children. For example, a participant who was rather quiet for the duration of the workshop chose a charm with wings. When it was her time to share in front of the group, she expressed how she lost her older brother

Figure 16.2 Photo of Charms. 2020. Photo by the author.

to police violence. She later shared that she never had the space to express her emotions and how this activity allowed her to focus on the image of her brother rather than the devastation the event caused her family.

The second activity was a vulnerability exercise created by Project Adventure Inc., a non-profit organization that uses movement, play, and laughter to think creatively, solve problems, and build resilience. As a scholar, artist, and educator with a background in leadership education, I am conscious of how the academic discourse on resilience has often dismissed the existence of communal survival strategies and how those strategies have been passed down generationally. The overemphasis on resilience can have adverse effects, causing individuals to cling to coping mechanisms that bring them away from addressing vulnerabilities. Therefore, when approaching "Sneetches," an activity in which participants respond to a series of questions ranging from low to high risk, I made sure to remove resilience from the conversation, and instead, focus on individual and group trust, cohesion, and vulnerability. For this activity, every answer given should be taken as absolutely right; no one should question it. The group proceeds around the circle, starting with a different person each time. If a participant cannot think of an answer at their turn, they can say, "pass," and the facilitator will come back to them.

Directions for participants:

- Please speak loudly so that everyone can hear you. Try not to change your answer once you decide what it will be or what you think will be a "more appropriate answer." Stay as honest as possible.
- While each member is answering, watch that person carefully. We can learn a great deal from the look of a face, the movement of the hands, the head movement, and by what people do not say, or hesitate in saying. We are concerned with discovering good things about each other, including strengths and characteristics.
- We must listen. This is *not* a debate. We are not here to disagree. We are here to seek out the person that is each of us. Too often we defend our own words without listening to all the hearts beating around us.
- As each person answers, collect those various answers in your mind and begin developing an idea of each person in the group.
- If we all do this, perhaps a few of our invisible boundaries will melt, and we'll get to know each other better.
- Reminder: We must make sure that we take care of each other and each other's stories and be ever mindful of who we share these stories with when we leave the room.

Sample low-risk questions:

- When did you last sing to yourself?
- If you could choose to be an animal (other than a human), what would you be?

- What is your favorite place?
- If you could wake up tomorrow having gained any one quality or ability, what would it be?

Sample medium-risk questions:

- What culture(s) has most influenced who you are?
- What is your strongest emotion?
- What is your favorite thing about being a woman?
- What is the most important quality you expect from a friend?
- What is the most beautiful thing that you know? And why?

Sample high-risk questions:

- If you could destroy anything, what would it be?
- What is your greatest accomplishment?
- Complete this sentence, "I wish I could …"
- What is your best quality?
- What is your worst quality?
- If you could relive any day of your life, what day would it be?
- What is your biggest fear?
- What is one thing you are most grateful for?

Processing questions:

Do not get into heavy discussions, just ask the questions and listen to the responses.

1 If you could ask any member of the group about any answers they gave, who would it be?
2 Who would you like to get to know better?
3 Who surprised you the most?
4 Who do you identify with the most?

All participants dove right into the Sneetches activity, and we found that even some of the low-medium risk questions brought forward intense memories and feelings for individuals. As a result, upon conclusion of the activity, I asked all participants to stand, inhale/exhale, and then stretch or shake it out. Those who needed a break were welcome to get a drink of water or take a brief ten-minute walk for fresh air. Throughout the activity, the group was mindful of the instructions (e.g., that participants could not speak unless it was their turn in the circle) and used non-verbal cues and body language (e.g., snaps, smiles, head nods, steups [sucking one's teeth], eye contact, and even, hugging) to express camaraderie and trust. Rather than seeing vulnerability and agency as binary opposites, the group experienced "vulnerability as a resource for collective action" to "become both an artistic expression and a mark of resistance" (Szatek, p. 43). It was a reminder that we have similar fears and experiences, and most importantly, we are not alone.

Figure 16.3 Workshop participant writing at the University of the West Indies. 2020. Photo by the author.

Show, Don't Tell Exercise

Like theatre, spoken word poetry needs a speaker and a listener. In this exercise, I have participants focus on using the five senses to enrich their poetry with vivid imagery to help the audience feel immersed and engaged, providing details that help them enter the world built by the speaker. Through this exercise, participants have an entry point to the comprehension of figurative language, like similes and metaphors. See the example below created by Participant B:

------------------	Smells like...	Sounds like...	Tastes like...	Looks like...	Feels like...
Being a woman...					

Being a woman ...
Smells like ... *delicious dandelions*
Sounds like ... *a sweet melody*
Tastes like ... *Hershey from the jar*
Looks like ... *the gentle waters greeting the shore*
Feels like ... *a heavy bag on your shoulders*

The Show, Don't Tell exercise built on the previous activities by operating as a structured framework for connecting emotion and experience. It gave

Figure 16.4 Workshop Participant Performing at the University of the West Indies. 2020. Photo by the author.

participants a realistic goal to achieve without the pressure of performing before a large audience. Instead, the group approached the final exercise of writing an original poem and sharing it in front of their small cohort of writers, with an understanding that poems must be built one line at a time, grounding it in an image and a feeling.

Additionally, I delineated and examined the imaginary line between written and spoken word poetry in a decidedly Caribbean space. Dr. Kevin Browne's paper, "Mas Movement: Toward A Theory of Caribbean Rhetoric," inspired me to encourage "the major modes of Caribbean Rhetoric like code-switching, call-response, wordplay, circumlocution, boasting/shaming, proverbs, the sermonic, and nonverbal/visual semantic" to authentically express their story (2009, p. 20).

See full-length poems inspired by the workshop below:

Alyea Pierce (after ELSZ)[1]

DEAR GUILT,

where were you born? was it after the first war? after the win? after my
mother's mother's mother handed her husband her sword? were you born
for his win to occupy history books and hers, a foolish tale told among
drunk captains on the sea? or was your birth for a world hungry for beautiful
instead of blood? how long have you shadowed in the backs of women's
throats? filled our mouths with water to drown ourselves in ourselves?

I cannot remember the last time I said *no*. we give and the world takes or maybe, we all have a choice.
But when expectation has extended generations is choice silenced?
yet, still, I wanted *my* world to look me in the eye and say *thank you* and mean it.
but that's not how the story ends.

Akhela G. (Workshop Participant)
Untitled.

Vulnerable and weak
I let you take and take
I used to love when you say you loved me
Longing for those fingers to massage my scalp
Opened my legs because maybe that would make you stay

Simone Leid (Founder of The WomenSpeak Project)
Etiquette for Fine Young Cannibals

A woman walks into a bar and says
What's for dinner?
The bartender says
Ma'am, we don't sell food here
She kicks off her high heels and sits on a stool
What about that bowl of cherries? You
think I'm a fool?
The bartender says
Those aren't cherries, they're women we've raped
The woman says
You think I'm a fool? I know the difference
between food and rape
Rape is bloody, is hung up in display cases
at the front of restaurants
People walk by and pick out the one
that looks overdone
have the waiters take it to the kitchen
chop it up and serve it with a side of white rice
Ma'am, says the bartender, this is an elite
establishment
we don't deal in dead. All our rapes are 100% guilt-free
tiny bite-size murders

dressed in machismo and
apathy
buried
left to ferment
in a bed of self-doubt
and silence.

Participant A. (Workshop Participant)
No More Apologies

I am not sorry for being all this woman.
I am shape,
a shape you cannot play'doh into whatever your heart desires. I am
curves. I am
battlefield. I am
the war
the win
and the freedom.
I am stretchmarks. I am
stretching and you cannot fit me within this poem
anymore.

I am not sorry
we, women take up too much space for *you*.
How we, women uncrossed our voices too soon for *you*.
How we, women stand loud
too loud
too often
Who said they could dream?

I am not sorry.
I am not sorry my color will always speak louder than anything I say.
I am called a color more often than human because I am too hard to label
in [his]tory.
But I am not an issue.
And I refuse to be sorry.
I am me.

Participant B.
Where does a woman go when she is too scared to go out at night?

Yuh make a party all alone

and laugh with a pint of ice cream to make yourself feel better
and whine to Meg's, *Body-ody-ody-ody* in panty and bra
and peer pressure 25 crunches out of yourself
and starfish on yuh favorite couch exhaling today's unsaid fuck yous
and pass the Puncheon between both hands to not drink all alone
and when enough Puncheon passes pain speaks
and naked in the mirror you stand
and pull every inch of *"fatty thigh"* the family critiques into the trash to make yuhself feel better
and peek through living room windows to see how bright the night really is
and how people with people wander in glee
and maybe you can be one of those people
and maybe the moon can streetlight even the softest corners
and maybe it is safe

but is it *really* ever safe for a woman?

Conclusion

Spoken Word Poetry evolves from the oral tradition, providing "a way of remembering, a way of enduring, a way of mourning, a way of celebrating, a way of protesting and subverting, and, ultimately, a way of triumphing" (Smithsonian Institute, 2024). This qualitative creative research demonstrates how spoken word offers useful creative and critical tools for generating viable alternatives. "The performance may not have changed the structures producing vulnerability, but they have been reworked and critiqued by the [women and] girls who put them on the agenda" (Szatek, p. 54). In this sense, vulnerability "can, thus, be a resource that strives toward political equality and justice becoming linked to knowledge production enhancing the ability to take on the world" (p. 53).

After reviewing the post-workshop survey, participants gained an awareness that "to build community requires vigilant awareness of the work we must continually do to undermine all the socialization that leads us to behave in ways that perpetuate domination" (hooks, 2003, p. 36). They shared:

> The most important thing I learned about spoken word is that it's a way to give women a voice to speak their opinion and their story especially when it comes to activism.

> [Violence against women] should not be accepted as a norm. Women must speak out, express themselves, and be able to feel safe.

> I've learned that natural disasters can also cause women to be subject to abuse, [e.g. in 2020 – during the COVID-19 pandemic – there was a 9.7% increase in DV calls].

According to founder Simone Leid, WomenSpeak provides women-safe settings where women-identifying folx feel free to speak: "I think many women feel relief that they have that space and they are understood and supported; especially when engaging with poetry, women come forward in creative spaces. Many Caribbean women poets continue the tradition of using written form poetry to bring awareness and talk about issues of grooming, sexual assault, and other forms of gender-based violence, and have always done so" (2023). This essay demonstrates how the creative process can bring forth a different understanding of vulnerability and, thereby, a re-articulation of self, community, and power.

Note

1 In written poetry, this is how a writer gives credit to another writer for inspiring their piece.

References

Browne, K. (2009). "Mas Movement: Towards A Theory of Caribbean Rhetoric." Ph.D. Thesis, The Pennsylvania State University, Accessed 2 May 2024. https://etda.libraries.psu.edu/catalog/9746.

Butler, J. (2016). "Rethinking Vulnerability in Resistance." In *Vulnerability in Resistance,* edited by Butler, J., Gambetti, Z., and Sabsay, L. pp.12–27. Durham, NC: Duke University Press.

hooks, b. (2003). *Teaching Community: A Pedagogy of Hope*. Routledge, New York, NY.

Leid, S. (2023). Email to Alyea Pierce. Nov. 20.

Saunders, P.J. (1999). "The Meeting Place of Creole Culture: A Conversation with Earl Lovelace," *Calabash* 1:2, pp. 10–22.

Smithsonian Institute. (2024). "Say It Loud: African American Spoken Word." Smithsonian Folkways. Accessed 8 July 2024. https://folkways.si.edu/say-loud-african-american-spoken-word/struggle-protest/article/smithsonian

Szatek, E. (2022). "Troubling Aesthetics: Mapping Vulnerability as a Generative Force in Community Theatre," *Research in Drama Education: The Journal of Applied Theatre and Performance* 27:1, 40–56, DOI: 10.1080/13569783.2021.1985990.

Tidwell, C. (2001). *Trinidad and Tobago: Customs and Issues Affecting International Business*. Conference presentation. 28 June. Andrews University.

17 Tools for Equity and Collaboration

Nicole Perry

As a dance educator and choreographer, introduction to the consent-forward work[1] of staged intimacy inspired me to examine how power dynamics impact my teaching and creative work. First, the body that I present in my roles as an intimacy professional and dance educator holds perceived power because I fit the typical Western and commercial stereotype of a "dance teacher" or "choreographer:" white, cis-female, thin, and middle-aged. Moreover, as I viewed my pedagogy through the lens of consent, I realized the systems in which I trained and perpetuated in my classes, denied full humanity to students. Spaces in which I asked them to be vulnerable and creative were also the spaces in which I tried to be in control, hold the "right" answer, and craft students' bodies and ideas into what I thought they should be. Instead, I could validate autonomy by creating opportunities for students to connect with their bodies and needs.

In Western performance, women's bodies are objects; women are often on stage in dance but underrepresented in leadership. Moreover, we scarcely see the bodies of trans, nonbinary, and/or gender-fluid dancers on stage, and rarely in stories that center them. While *The Nutcracker*'s Mother Ginger or Les Ballets Trockadero de Monte Carlo provides representation, these depictions are often comedic parodies, suggesting we do not take these artists or their contributions to our field seriously. In response, this essay offers a toolkit, inspired by intimacy direction, to increase belonging and confidence for all, particularly students and performers of marginalized genders.

Tools for Creating Consent-Forward Spaces

Consent cannot occur without acknowledging everyone has control over their own body and what happens to it. A failure to accept bodies as they are – in race, gender, age, size, or ability – is a denial of humanity and personal agency.

Tool 1: Boundaries

Often in performance and training the framework for boundaries is: "Don't touch my ___." However, personal boundaries encompass not only choreography-related points of contact but also the context in which contact happens

DOI: 10.4324/9781003341802-29

and the content it conveys. We cannot assume someone's gender, sexual orientation, age, or any other demographic determines their willingness to engage in touch, staged intimacy, difficult or traumatic content, risky physical activities, or any other performance-related action. We can encourage performers to express needs and boundaries around:

- What they are willing to have their body do
    - I.e., physical actions they will perform (or, in the case of simulated sex or kissing, be seen as performing)
- What are they willing to consent to have done to their body
    - I.e., receive touch, be lifted, etc.
- What they are willing to have their body do (with consent) to the body(ies) of others
    - I.e., give touch, perform a lift, etc.
- The content presented in the action
    - I.e., is this topic activating, within lived experience, etc.
- The context (physical and psychological) of the choreography
    - I.e., how close is the audience, visibility of the action, level of trust between dancers, etc.
    - Especially important for consideration in this essay is the personal context of "Who am I in this group?" If a performer is the *only* trans, nonbinary, or gender-fluid person in the space, this will likely affect their boundaries (Perry, 2020).

Tool 2: Dialogue

Beginning a collaborative experience with a time for acknowledging and sharing boundaries, strengthens ideas of bodily awareness, concepts often dismissed for trans, gender nonconforming, and nonbinary people, as well as women. For conversations between peers, or as a tool those in power can offer those who are not, I have developed a three-step boundary conversation (2020):

1 Know that you can speak up. Everyone has boundaries, which should be respected in the workplace.
2 Ask their boundaries first. I model this as, "Hey, partner. We're working together today with contact/difficult subject matter/etc. I was wondering if you had any boundaries or needs, I should know about?" In this, I demonstrate:

    a I want to be a good collaborator.
    b I want to create work in which we both feel confident.

c I believe boundaries are normal, and I expect people to have them.

Furthermore, many performers feel more confident sharing "needs," rather than "boundaries," so this script creates an easier entry to conversation with that addition.

3 Share my boundaries. Hopefully, after I complete that step, my partner will ask, "Do you have any boundaries?" But even if they do not, I still have an opening to say, "Thanks for sharing. Here are mine."

While this conversation formula is not foolproof (performers are conditioned to say "I don't have any boundaries"), it creates space for conversation.

If we are ethical creators in performance spaces, we are inclusive of all genders and bodies, at all points and positions in the creative process. Therefore, dialogue shouldn't just happen at the top of a process, or only when harm has occurred – it should be ongoing. In my own teaching and creative process, conversations occur throughout, and usually start with one of the following:

- "What do you need to be successful in this space?"
- "What do you need in order to bring your most creative self to our work today?"
- "How would you feel about ..."
- "How would it work for you if ...."
- "How did that feel?"
- "Tell me about ...."

These open-ended questions ask for reflection, not a quick "yes" or "no." They center the experience of the collaborator, not the power-holder's perceptions or desires.

There are challenges to ongoing dialogue. Open-ended questions and boundary conversations require reflection, trust, and may take time away from the schedule. Dialogue may challenge the power-holder in the room to change typical methods of working or speaking. Ultimately, however, I find investment in people worthwhile. Having boundary conversations saves time in later rehearsals, as performers are clear and confident with the material. Ongoing dialogue reinforces trust and builds community, supporting a joyful, compassionate workplace, and excellent performance.

Tool 3: Choice

Many students coming out of commercial dance studios have never been asked to contribute their own embodied knowledge to their learning. They have reflected that making choices in dance class awakens playfulness and creativity rather than a focus on perfection. For performers who have experienced trauma, particularly at the hands of dance teachers or choreographers, the opportunity to make choices bolsters safety. For those of marginalized genders, decision-making is a reminder that their bodies and their experiences of their bodies are valued, and that their needs are valid.

With the ability to choose, performers practice agency and see its impact on their bodies and creative work. Similarly, opportunities to make choices dismisses the hierarchy of "one right way thinking" (Okun, 2022). When we dismantle the idea that there is one way, or only a choice between binary options, to move, perform, or be in performance spaces, we start to destroy that idea outside these spaces as well.

Practically speaking, I do not offer choices constantly. Instead, I ensure that each section of class (check-in, warm-up, technique, combination, cool-down, and check-out), or a rehearsal (check-in, work of the day, and closure) includes an opportunity for choice. By balancing structure with freedom, students and professionals develop trust in me, their own embodied knowledge and creativity, and in the ensemble as a place where they can take risks.

The check-in is based on choice. Drawn from the work of Molly W. Schenck (2024), I begin with a personal somatic check-in where students or performers spend two minutes giving themselves what they need. The goal of this time is to engage in a physical activity that brings awareness to their bodies, regulates their nervous systems, and/or creates presence and attention. Then, there is time for any boundary conversations the day's work may require. These steps early in the creative process ask performers to bring their embodied knowledge to the rest of our work.

Choice may look like reminding students/performers they can decide the number of turns they attempt, remove arm choreography from a complex footwork pattern, or adjust levels in space to protect knees or backs. For challenging combinations, I often give a choice of tempo, i.e., at tempo vs. half speed. Additionally, offering modifications for injuries or physical issues in class reminds students that all bodies can dance but that they may look different.

As we reach the cool-down, students can include a stretch they feel their body needs at the moment. Finally, they check-out with the option to share from the work that is sticking with them. In rehearsal settings, these physical and/or verbal rituals are part of the closure practices that are a pillar of staged intimacy work (Sina, Richardson, and Rodis, 2016).

Tools for Disrupting Binary Structures

The emphasis on the gender binary in Western dance training and performance, particularly in ballet, does not allow for full humanity to be recognized. While the above section focused on tools to create opportunities for embodied power, this section offers tools for dismantling structures (at a class or organizational level) that hinder those experiences.

Tool 1: Remove Common Binary Examples

In 2019, after Chase Johnsey, a gender-fluid dancer who uses he/him pronouns, danced female roles for the English National Ballet, *Pointe Magazine* featured three other trans, and/or nonbinary dancers. *Dance Magazine* featured three additional trans and/or nonbinary dancers in 2022 (Matthews-Guzmán, 2022). While these trans, nonbinary, and gender-fluid representations are important to the industry, the dancers were presented as individual exceptions. Making day-to-day changes in language, facilities, and dress codes, can create equity, not for one dancer at a time, but for all.

Change Vocabulary

Ballet has a binary gendered movement vocabulary. In classes, instead of "the men's step" or "the woman's variation," I discuss movements and/or movement qualities: i.e., a movement employs Strong Weight or Light Weight,[2] or that one phrase has more jumps and the other more turns. Dancers may try all the options and then make their own choices.

Similarly, partnering is often expected to be male/female, with the male leading and/or lifting. Many cities now host queer social dance events, in which gender does not determine the dancer's role; instead, partners decide who is leading or following. In fact, "lead" and "follow" now become the roles, rather than "man" or "woman."

Change Daily Structures

Many dance classes have binary dress codes. Instead, dancers could be encouraged to wear anything that allows a range of motion that fits the movement esthetic and does not distract them or others. In my syllabi, I show photos of various bodies in acceptable attires,[3] to demonstrate what is available.

Classes and performance spaces frequently have binary facilities. I, with the Dance Education Equity Association, conducted an as-yet unpublished audit (2023) of websites of fifty dance conventions in the United States.[4] We discovered that only one publicly offers dressing spaces dedicated to trans, nonbinary, and/or gender-fluid dancers. In fact, seven conventions still base awards, either regional or national, on binary genders. Removing these binaries will create space, physically and metaphorically, for inclusion of dancers of all genders.

Tool 2: Offer New Expectations

In workshops with teachers and choreographers, I encourage them to interrogate their use of the word "empower." While it may seem beneficial, it's actually disempowering, because it means that power must be granted or permitted by someone who holds it, rather than something to be embodied by all. Mary Parker Follett, management consultant and educator ([1933] 1973) writes, "I do not think that power can be delegated, because genuine power is capacity" (p. 109). She clarifies later, "Power is not a pre-existing thing which can be handed out to someone ... You cannot confer power, because power is the blooming of experience" (p. 111). Instead of "empowering" as teachers, we create space for others to practice their power.

This bodily control via language also shows up with possessive language, like "my dancers," "my students," etc., which is a hierarchical practice and denial of autonomy. A challenging yet effective shift can occur in acknowledging personal power by simply calling them "dancers," "students," "performers," etc. A switch to "collaborators," could reinforce equality within the ensemble.

Conclusion

While changes are and can be made for inclusion of all genders in dance training spaces, there is work to be done in the field at large. The @feminists_in_dance account on TikTok shared videos of female dancers lifting other female dancers. Unfortunately, the account has been inactive for about a year, possibly because of the vitriolic comments left on videos, mocking the young women. Similarly, there are audience members who are unprepared to confront their own biases around gender on stage, evidenced by reactions to the casting of Johnsey, and pieces such as Matthew Bourne's *Swan Lake* (Foster, 2019; *The Lowry Blog*, 2018; Sulcas, 2018). A question for the field may be, "How can companies and artistic leadership educate critics and audiences about gender inclusivity, and publicly support performers of all genders, in all roles?"

Pedagogic and performance practices that center consent and collaboration center humanity and equity. While this essay focuses on dance, its lessons are applicable to other mediums. With small, purposeful changes, the performing arts can become more just, for people of all genders.

Notes

1 "Consent-forward" is used by Intimacy Directors and Coordinators, through whom I am certified. According to Colleen Hughes, Director of Core Training, this language positions consent as an ongoing process.
2 In the Laban/Bartenieff Movement System, Effort qualities are capitalized.
3 See one example here: https://www.discountdance.com/search/mylist:603490. My own syllabi also use photos of former students who have agreed to be photographed, in order to be more inclusive of genders and disabilities.
4 This audit is expected to be published on http://www.instagram.com/danceequityassociation in 2024.

References

Follet, M. P. (1973) *Dynamic Administration: The Collected Papers of Mary Parker Follett*. Medcalf, H.C. and Urwick, L., eds. London: Pitman.

Foster, R. D. (2019) "Cue the Homoerotic Swans." Cultural Daily. Accessed 1 Sept. 2023. https://culturaldaily.com/cue-homoerotic-swans/.

Matthews-Guzmán, J. (2022) "Beyond Male/Female: Nonbinary Dancers Forging Their Own Paths." *Dance Magazine*. Accessed 9 July 2023. https://www.dancemagazine.com/nonbinary-dancers/.

Okun, T. (2022) "Characteristics." White Supremacy Culture. Accessed 30 May 2023. https://www.whitesupremacyculture.info/characteristics.html.

Perry, N. (2020) "Power, Consent, and Agency" and "Protecting the Performance: Boundaries and Closure Practices." Momentum Stage Guest Artist Workshops.

Schenck, M. W. (2024) "Introduction to Trauma Informed Creative Practices." Grey Box Collective. Accessed 25 Apr. 2024.. https://podcasters.spotify.com/pod/show/molly-w-schenck.

Sina, T. S. Richardson, and A. Rodis. (2016) "The Pillars." Accessed 9 Sept. 2023. https://www.idcprofessionals.com/blog/the-pillars-of-intimacy-in-production.

Sulcas, R. (2018) "He Wants to Be a Ballerina. He Has Taken the First Steps." *New York Times*. June 8. Accessed 25 Apr. 2023. https://www.nytimes.com/2018/06/08/arts/dance/the-first-man-dancing-in-a-female-corps-de-ballet.html.

The Lowry Blog. (2018) "Five Things You Didn't Know about Matthew Bourne's *Swan Lake*." October 22. Accessed 1 Sept. 2023. https://thelowryblog.wpcomstaging.com/2018/10/22/five-things-you-didnt-know-about-matthew-bournes-swan-lake/.

18 The Art of Genderbending

Fighting Hegemonic Gender Ideology with Chinese Martial Arts

DeVante Love

"I'll be honest with you DeVante," Joe remarked after performing what I call the Underworld Qigong form, "I am feeling extremely moody. But I'm not afraid of being in this state. Is it strange that I want to linger in these messy emotions?"

Joe (they/them) was a student who had been coming to my Qigong meditation classes for a couple of seasons and had rarely spoken, except to note they "don't do emotions." They are a genderqueer person who grew up socialized as a man. From childhood, they were taught to privilege reason over emotion, which was reinforced by classmates who called them "sissy" anytime they used hyper-expressive facial expressions, hand gestures, or body language. But this momentary outburst signaled something new for Joe. They not only recognized being in an emotional state but also validated and articulated those emotions to the group. Joe even expressed a desire to become more familiar with their emotions so they could ultimately accept them. Performing the Underworld Qigong form in a room full of supportive folks had opened up access to a part of themselves that society had spent years teaching them to abandon.

Seconds after Joe's comment, other students in the room noted how different they felt after performing the Qigong form, as though "some type of transformation was happening within themselves." Rae (she/her) particularly caught my attention, as she was lovingly hugging herself on her yoga mat while calmly swaying side to side as if a smooth jazz song were playing. Sensing what was going on in the room sparked a bonfire of joy deep within my chest as it reminded me of the healing and revelations these Qigong movement meditations have inspired in my queer students. This group's performance of the Underworld Qigong filled the room with sacredness.

Nearly two decades ago, I joined a Kung Fu studio in Northern California to begin my training in Qigong and other styles of Chinese martial arts. The training was, at first, a method to learn how to protect myself from bullies. Gradually, martial arts became the tool for me to explore the depths of who I was and who I am. Each training session gave me more insights into my personality, desires, and hopes. Some of these realizations were harder to accept than others, especially living in a white heteronormative society.

DOI: 10.4324/9781003341802-30

Still, the training inspired more courageousness and helped me heal within that society. Once I received the highest ranking in the martial arts system (a black sash), I began a journey to discover what more might be possible through committed training in Chinese martial arts. I traveled for the next decade, learning under masters of various Kung Fu lineages and competing in international tournaments. I saw how the Kung Fu movements could be used to help other queer folks of color improve their mental and emotional health by discovering and embracing a genuine self. I began applying what I had learned from my master's degree in clinical psychology to develop a trauma-informed approach to the practice of Chinese martial arts, highlighting its therapeutic potential. My theory found a way into practice when I competed and performed in martial arts at the 2018 Gay Olympic Games in Paris. After I won, judges and competitors alike talked to me about the "therapeutic" effect my performance elicited and asked me if I could teach my philosophy and movement practices. The door was open for me to create a new approach to martial arts that emphasized healing the self rather than destroying and breaking an opponent.

Two years later, when the COVID-19 pandemic hit, many folks came to me feeling disoriented. The call for help led me to open Healing Kung Fu, a healing temple with spiritual martial arts classes and ritual performances empowering queer people of color. It achieves this through an emphasis on embodiment.

Embodiment is essential for queer folks of color. We face a lifetime of our bodies, desires, and sensations being policed by social norms that are not designed with our well-being in mind. We forge awkward identities that conform to forced societal ideologies. In *Body/Meaning/Healing,* medical anthropologist Thomas Csordas posits that embodiment is the way to "overcome the dichotomy between the body as an object of ideology and the body as an experiencing subject" (Csordas, 2002, p. 62). This notion exemplifies why integrating Chinese martial arts and Qigong practices is so important for Healing Kung Fu's students. Class discussions center around liberatory spiritual philosophies derived from Buddhism, Daoism, African mysticism, and Native American shamanism to name a few. Every topic is taught alongside related spiritual martial arts practices that connect to the body and heighten students' awareness of the subtle physiological responses that arise from their thoughts and feelings. The movement into specific embodiment practices allows us to break away from these conditioned behaviors and devise new ways of being more aligned with our conception of who we are. I crafted this mind-body pedagogy to meet the holistic needs of Healing Kung Fu's queer population.

We are a community of educators, lawyers, college students, clinicians, farmers, nomads, artists, and many other walks of life, united in our desire to overcome societal challenges to our race, gender, and/or sexuality. Some of us exist at the intersection of marginalized identities, which means we face scrutiny from multiple communities that aim to micromanage our manner of being. As genderqueer people of color, most of us must also contend with the queer community, which privileges whiteness, and our racial community, which frequently takes a sexist or homophobic stance. To cope with the difficulty of navigating through our intersectionalities, many of us have developed limiting beliefs, anxiety-ridden habits, or debilitating coping mechanisms.

Students who come to Healing Kung Fu are ready for a change: They want to shift from surviving each day to thriving. Spiritual martial arts practices allow us to courageously disrupt social norms and heal the wounding incurred from living in our society. The curriculum is infused with positive psychology and notions of PERMA (Positive emotion, Engagement, Relationships, Meaning, and Accomplishments), well-being, and flourishing, as theorized by Martin Seligman (2012). Training involves an embodied practice of martial arts and a space for each person to verbalize what they experienced through the practices. Students engage in what Linda Lantieri (2017) calls "Spiritual Active Listening": a type of listening that occurs from a state of deep mindfulness in which the listener can develop an empathic response to what is shared. Healing Kung Fu builds a community that celebrates individual differences and acknowledges points of connection that draw us together.

The genderbending workshop in which Joe and Rae participated was part of a series offered by Healing Kung Fu to decondition the self from debilitating gender ideologies. In the first workshop, students contemplated notions of femininity. They used the Underworld Qigong form to explore what it felt like to embody a healthier understanding of their femininity. We began with a lively discussion about our culture's attitude toward femininity and how it both prescribes and restricts folks' behavior. After analyzing how our culture often disregards the feminine, I discussed Chinese philosophy and how Asian societies have interpreted Daoism's Yin Yang ideology. Daoism takes a structuralist view, suggesting that the world functions on a system of interactions governed by a force of nature called the "Dao." As a philosophy, it theorizes the way energetic forces and our actions intersect to bring about harmony or chaos. Yin and Yang are understood to be complementary energetic essences that contain traits we can observe in our everyday lives (e.g. light/dark, quiet/loud). What most folks take away from this theory is that each essence requires the other to maintain balance and avoid chaos. However, scholars such as Lisa Raphals (1998) and Robin Wang (2012) have critiqued how ancient Chinese society utilized the Yin Yang theory to perpetuate constrictive sexist and heteronormative notions.

The Yin is oversimplified as "feminine," "soft," and "emotional," while the Yang is "masculine," "strong," and "rational." Ancient societies gendered Yang masculinity as a male-bodied characteristic and Yin femininity as a female-bodied characteristic. In these societies, a strong and rational man should know how to assert himself by way of controlling the soft, emotional feminine woman. A woman is expected to maintain balance by pacifying herself and submitting to a man's dominant power. In this view, men and women work together to build a harmonious family unit. Women are domestic and will use their emotionality to tame a man's recklessness. The students of Healing

Kung Fu instantly recognized how these ideas also show up in Western, heteronormative culture. After voicing their frustrations, we spent time examining how gendered power dynamics are maintained through our sociopolitics, infosphere, and everyday activities. Students articulated how these ideas have disoriented their life experiences rather than foster the harmony that Daoism promotes.

I then introduced the work of Zhenevere Sophia Dao (2020), a trans scholar and playwright who founded post-Daoism and created Qigong forms based on its ideology. Post-Daoism aims to reinterpret traditional Daoist philosophy by putting traditional texts in conversation with Romanticism, contemporary depth psychotherapy, and modern antiracist, feminist scholarship. In post-Daoism, the Essential Yin is a feminine essence understood to be a wise power that gathers strength through its experience of emotions. The Yang is a masculine essence that gains power through taking vulnerable and passionate actions. In post-Daoism, the Yin doesn't need the control of the Yang but perceptively knows when to draw from the Yang energy to achieve harmony.

After providing a list of ways post-Daoist thought redefines the Yin, I informed students that though the Yin is feminine, it is an energetic force that all bodies experience. The same is said for the Yang and its masculine force. No matter what race or gender we identify as we can all embody both Yin and Yang energy. Since training in the Chinese Martial Arts movement is one of the ways we can gain such experiences, I continued the workshop with a comprehensive teaching of Qigong through the Underworld form, which Joe and Rae found to be transformative. This form helps a person embody the fullness of Yin energy (as defined in post-Daoist thought).

As the students imitated my repeated movements of the form, I recounted anecdotes about the Underworld, self-love, and nature's way of enduring harsh conditions. At key moments, I encouraged them to be conscious of how their organs, muscles, and joints reacted to the stories and the movements. Doing all this at once allows students to break away from their habitual mind. Once they have that freedom, their mind, and body are in an expansive state where they can mythologize their performance of the Underworld form. According to scholars such as James Hillman (1997), mythologizing an experience stimulates the development of novel perspectives that can be used to recontextualize our past experiences. As a result, we begin to imagine new ways of acting in the present that correspond to the new perspective. We then begin to form new neural networks, which help determine our future behavior. In this way, the performance of the form ignites a journey in which one begins to rewrite the way they perform their own identities out in the world. The guided teaching of the Underworld form, combined with an empowering discussion of the feminine, allows students to achieve a more legitimate expression of femininity that aligns with their way of being.

After about fifteen repetitions of the form, I brought the room into contemplative stillness. Each person crossed their arms over their heart and took deep breaths. I advised them to sink into their bodies and recognize the surfacing physical sensations and thoughts. This moment of stillness was crucial to allow the mind, body, and spirit to synchronize and ritualize the collective performance. I then gave them a chance to journal, prompting them to reflect on their experience in the Underworld Qigong form as it intersects with their understanding of femininity. A few minutes later, Joe launched into their unexpected comment about their moodiness and the desire to explore that state. Still seated on her yoga mat swaying side to side, Rae took a few deep breaths before responding to Joe. "When you shared that, I noticed my chest and lower Dan Tien (an esoteric energy center located below the belly button that correlates to personal power) became really light and soft, which is unusual and a little scary if I'm honest." In previous workshops, Rae shared that people often think she is "too sensitive and overly emotional." After someone called her "hysterical," she started believing that her emotions were too overwhelming for others. She felt it best to perform for the world by presenting a tough, emotionless exterior to defend themselves from the verbal abuse of others. "I'm used to toughening myself," she continues, "and the fact that I feel a need to be soft right now is strange. As I went through the form, I kept hearing and seeing bees swarm around me as if I were a flower and they were waiting for me to bloom into a state of softness." I supplemented her comment with an interpretation of bees from a shamanic perspective that seemed to help her feel more comfortable exploring softness. "Yeah, I'm definitely going to meditate on that further and see how I can own my emotions while staying soft. Seems important."

A month after the workshop, Rae reached out to me and shared that she had seen a lot more bees lately. Each time they caught her eye, she intentionally paused, took a deep breath, and actively softened her body while letting herself relax into the emotions bubbling up inside her. "My mental health has improved a lot this past month," she shared, "This state of being soft is not only helping me be more in touch with my emotions, but it's also attracting more people to me. Random people are giving me compliments, and my friends say I'm glowing. When they ask me 'what's my secret,' I give them a cryptic answer that I think you'd understand. I say, 'Oh well, I'm just allowing my emotions to soften my being, and it's attracting a lot of happiness and good fortune.'"

I did, in fact, understand what she meant, as her transformation is similar to the healing process many queer folks face when increasing self-acceptance. After years of being told by the media and our surrounding communities that our desires are bad and harmful, we learn to bottle them up. The more we hide our desires away, the more we signal to ourselves that we disapprove of who we are. This belief then prevents us from recognizing and accepting opportunities that would be fulfilling to our whole selves. We reject these opportunities and become cold, cynical, and locked into our unhealthy psychological habits. Rae's acceptance of her feelings has allowed her central nervous system and body to relax. She isn't constantly on high alert, fearful that her emotions will drive people away. Instead, she is channeling that post-Daoist essential Yin magnetic quality, which leaves her feeling powerful, soft, and emotional and attracting expressions of the Yang toward her.

As we repeated the Qigong form, the students all became more aware of how the feminine Yin essence moves through their bodies to bring about harmony. The journaling and discussion afterward was a critical moment for them to think through how they might integrate what insights came through with what they will experience in the world once the workshop is over. Every student had a different experience and myriad takeaways. But one commonality was that each person, no matter race, gender, or sexuality, was able to embody their sense of femininity without the pejorative ideology that our culture attaches to it.

Healing Kung Fu has also created scripted plays, such as *Healing the Broken Heart* (a subject for another essay). Still, the workshops are just as connected to applied performance: For, about, and performed by queer folks of color, they allow participants to embody and integrate a reclaimed sense of self. Sociologist Erving Goffman (1976) explains how playing into our expected gender roles affords us access to the social sphere. As humans who desire connection, we perform those roles despite their negative impact on our well-being. In Goffman's terms, the workshop provides participants with an expanded set of social scripts they can reference when performing their identities out in the world. This challenging work requires awareness of how culture has conditioned their behavior, recognition of what behaviors feel authentic, and the courage to embrace these behaviors in a world still plugged into a heteronormative matrix. The workshops provide space to experience these three things by imbuing us with new scripts to engage authentically with society while nurturing our own mental and emotional well-being. The wellness we cultivate as individuals will fortify us as we care for the well-being of our communities.

References

Csordas, T. J. (2002). *Body, Meaning, Healing*. New York, NY: Palgrave Macmillan

Dao, Z. S. (2020) "The Post Daoist Yin." Mogadao Institute, School of Mythosomatics and Queer Ontology. January. Santa Fe, New Mexico, USA.

Goffman, E. (1976) "Gender display." *Gender Advertisements*. New York, NY: Harper & Row.

Hillman, J. (1997) *The Myth of Analysis: Three Essays in Archetypal Psychology*. Evanston, IL: Northwestern University Press.

Lantieri, L. (2017) "Strategies for Cultivating the Inner Life of Students." Columbia University Spirituality, Mind, Body Summer Institute. July. New York, NY, USA.

Raphals, L. (1998) *Sharing the Light: Representations of Women and Virtue in Early China*. Albany, NY: State University of New York Press.

Seligman, M. E. (2012) *Positive Psychology in Practice*. Hoboken, NJ: John Wiley & Sons.

Wang, R. R. (2012) *Yin Yang: The Way of Heaven and Earth in Chinese Thought and Culture*. New York, NY: Cambridge University Press.

Roundtable Discussion with Lisa S. Brenner, DeVante Love, Nicole Perry, and Alyea Pierce

Lisa: Thank you for being here. What excites me about this section is it expands what's considered applied theatre. Given that you are all working in multi-disciplinary art forms, what connections do you see in each other's work?

Devante: The first thing I noticed about this section is the idea of helping folks gain awareness, and through that awareness, find the healing potential or the potential of showing up in space differently.

Alyea: The words that came up for me were "truth-telling" on a personal and societal level. In Devante's work, I was moved by the discussion about Daoism and Yin and Yang: how an ideology can be misinterpreted or misrepresented, and how a cultural belief system may be in us in ways we don't realize. Nicole's work made me think about asking open-ended questions.

Nicole: We are all writing about personal practices that might end up on the stage at some point, but that wasn't necessarily the purpose. This work is behind closed doors, preparatory, reflective; as Alyea says, "not for public display." The workshops aren't really for public consumption. They are internal, which informs both the process and the performance.

Lisa: In thinking about the internal nature of this work, what is the power of creating rituals in these spaces with a specific group of people?

Nicole: We often enter with fear as to whether our expectations will be met, or because we don't know what to expect. Having rituals holds space to help manage those expectations, at least for me, and helps manage anxiety by setting a tone.

DeVante: Ritual is an opportunity to remove some of the standards of how things should be because ritual is, for me at least, about going into the liminal space where anything is possible. And with gender and sexuality, there are defined binaries. Ritual becomes a key to breaking them down. Ritual also delineates the space as not just a casual place where we're just chatting, or whatever. It's a space in which we are bringing the most of ourselves and being intentional about what we're doing here. Ritual is a chance to say, "This space

DOI: 10.4324/9781003341802-31

is important," which allows for some sort of change, even the potential for deep-level transformation.

Alyea: I love what Nicole said about expectations and what DeVante offers about building a new structure for the group. Ritual also gives a moment to pause, reminding us of what our bodies feel like: What room are we in? Are we breathing? It gives us a moment to reflect and ground ourselves.

Lisa: Can we circle back to Nicole's observation about process? You all wrote about a process that's really more for the participants, yet there is often a project you are working toward. Perhaps, it's not binary.

Alyea: I struggle with this because I'm a forward-thinking person: I need to have a goal. But then the writer in me is like, "No. It's never been about the product, right?" In spoken word, we approach our work from a lens of brainstorming, then drafting, then revising, and then editing. So, the process is almost never-ending. The poem is never done. That's what we're taught. Even once it is produced onstage, it's not the end. There is always going to be a product, but I'm more concerned about the process: How are we allowing ourselves to be vulnerable? How are we holding space for one another? How are we preparing the space?

Nicole: I struggle with this, too. When I'm in teacher mode, I recognize that learning takes time. But when in choreographer mode, that urgency of opening night starts to enter, even though I resist it. It gets in the way of caring for the artists and ourselves in the way that we most want to. The opening night is approaching: It has to be ready for other people, and now we have to care about those other people.

Devante: Before I do anything, I sit down and intentionally dream about the thing I'm working toward. I'll envision a thousand different potential outcomes. And then I use that to inform my process. So, I think the process is laden with these dream outcomes. Then when I'm teaching, I'm just focused on being in the moment and not caring so much about the product because everyone's going to take away something different. People will latch onto a word, a movement, or a breathing pattern. I can't know what they will latch onto, but I trust that people will take something away. I don't have to know exactly what it is.

Lisa: It's like this mantra that I learned: "The plan means everything; the plan means nothing." You think it all through, and then you allow for flow and adaptation.

Earlier, you talked about the word "awareness." Alyea, your essay argued that part of awareness is recognizing how the society in which you live has made you vulnerable. And Nicole, you mentioned the word "care." What are the ethical considerations when working with vulnerable populations?

Alyea: First and foremost, I never tried to attempt an intervention. I am not trained, so I always have an advocate in the room. For the workshops in Trinidad, the Women Speak organization had an advocate and the founder in the room. I'm adamant that what you share is what you want, and that you can leave the room at any point if you do not feel safe. I also make it clear that we don't take notes on people's experiences. I don't want people scribing as a person is sharing their poem.

Also, in Trinidad, in the Caribbean, we're dealing with mixed populations, predominantly South Asians and African diasporic people. For example, how do you refer to Black people? Do you, as a South Asian person, feel like you can say the N-word? How we choose to write about the "other" is something I discuss a lot so that we can approach the workshop with an ethical and cultural lens. And then we have to think about the "Englishes" that we use. Because when you're dealing with the Caribbean, there's this idea of what's "proper."

Devante: Because I am a trained mental health professional, I recognize that I have the potential to provide interventions. I make it clear to the people who come to my workshops that I have this training, but I'm not going to be doing that because it is a group space. I'm not going to single out one person to have a moment of intervention. I believe it provides a little bit of safety because I'm holding the space, but I'm not going to delve into someone's traumatic past. Even when I respond to people, I say something like, "This can be a deeper thing for you to explore." I'm saying this can be a potential intervention, not to work with me but with somebody else. (I refer people out if need be). Which I think helps to normalize the importance of therapy.

Nicole: I start classes, workshops, or the first cast meeting with a community agreement. One expectation is that we honor others when they need a moment.

Lisa: Thank you. Let's switch gears and talk about joy and success. Can you tell me about a moment that brought pride or joy?

Alyea: Spoken word is similar to public speaking: Few people can speak their story. So, participants being able to just write something and come into the room is joyful. I'm especially proud because a lot of the folks in my room are people of color, predominantly Black women. Just speaking their story is enough. They don't have to do anything more.

Nicole: Ballet has very gendered approaches to steps. Certain things are expected of the people who are considered male and the people who are considered female in the room. When I am teaching steps, I present them as different qualities of movement – a light quality or a strong quality – and we try to explore all these qualities. Having students realize that their bodies have so much range and capability is exciting. I'm creating a piece with a class of all cis-gendered female students, and they are partnering with each other. They are lifting each other. They are turning each other. And they're telling me, "I didn't know that my body could do this, that this was a possibility in ballet." It's nice to set up rules and norms, and it's also nice to tear some down.

Alyea: Your comments made me think about how people approach poetry by only connecting to Shakespeare. When I ask in my workshop, "What do you think of when you think of poetry?" It's usually old white men. It's unfortunate that the education system doesn't teach different kinds of poets.

Devante: For me, what's exciting is when I'm working with students on the Qigong form, and they're lost and not sure why this movement makes them feel this way, or what is this new sensation that's coming up, or this memory that's budding. I'm always interested in these moments of confusion because they become clearer as time goes on. There's a part in which people are sort of moving their arms in a specific way that sometimes feels awkward. And then, as they go through it four more times, that awkwardness becomes a story that awakens within them. These moments of confusion and strangeness, then become normalized and then become something else, which excites me.

Lisa: What are the ways that this field needs to move forward? I'm thinking specifically about applied performance, but it can be about the arts as a whole. What are the rules we need to break or reconstruct?

Alyea: I'm thinking about who's telling these stories and how we can bring in more communities. For example, Shakespeare, let's go back to that. Yes, his work is important, right? When we think of the rules of building a sonnet, that is important to know. But how might poetry not just fit within the rules and constraints of the sonnet but bend them or build something new? For example, the free verse poem isn't as respected as the sonnet. As a creative writing instructor teaching free verse, students ask, "Shouldn't we be learning sonnets, limericks, or ballads?" My response is that you can do something different.

Nicole: I am teaching Dance Appreciation, and I've been saying all semester long that ballet is not the foundation of all dance. "Technique" and "ballet" are not synonymous, interchangeable terms. Every dance form has its own technique, and we have to learn what its rules are to value it. We can break the rules. We can write new rules. We are in the business of creating worlds. So, let's make the one we want.

DeVante: For me, it's how we intentionally get people to use their imagination. I think of the imagination as a muscle that needs to be grown, developed, and practiced over and over. Social media withers away our imagination, where we see images all the time, but we're not necessarily creating images ourselves. So, within our practices, we're encouraging people to go into memory, their imagination, and different kinds of thinking to bring forth awareness. For me, to go against the constructs of society, such as queerness, gender, race, and class, we have to begin to imagine or dream something beyond what's presented in front of us.

Lisa: To wrap up, what is something you are going to walk away thinking about after this conversation?

Nicole: I'm holding onto what Devante said about how they dream of the product ahead of time. I do that too, but in the sense of the worst-case scenario! I was like, "Oh, dreaming and worrying are not the same thing!" So that's a new practice for me that I'm going to try.

DeVante: I'm left with this strong feeling of hope, and from the very bottom of my heart, I think it's reading the essays, hearing you all talk about your work, and realizing there are other people out there doing this. I feel very hopeful, which motivates me to do more work. So, thank you.

Alyea: I guess that the term "applied theatre" is restrictive. I'm grateful to you for allowing our stories to be in this anthology. In spoken word, you just need a speaker and a listener, and that, in essence, is theatre. This conversation has allowed me to expand my mind and see how I may be restricting myself, which then restricts the groups I engage with.

Lisa: Thank you all so much.

Extending the Conversation

A Supplemental Roundtable

A Roundtable Discussion with Quenna Lené Barrett, Jasmin Cardenas, and Alyssa Vera Ramos

Alyssa: Let's begin by introducing our work.

Quenna: I first had the idea for *Rewriting the Declaration* on a bus. Organizers from Chicago went down to Cleveland for a Movement for Black Lives convening. We had all literally just de-arrested a young Black boy who was sitting on a train platform, and police were antagonizing him and arresting him. I had also recently read the Declaration of Independence as part of a training. The language in there is highly violent toward Indigenous folks and people of color. Mariame Kaba, an abolitionist organizer on that trip, was like, "Well, you're an artist; rewrite it."

I wanted community folks, organizers, and artists to all be involved. Then the pandemic happened in 2020, and we pivoted to a devised piece on Zoom. After the uprisings in response to the deaths of George Floyd, Breonna Taylor, and more, my mentor suggested this would be a great topic to explore, especially as we were having the presidential election. In the final piece, we invited audience members into healing rituals, ancestral invitations, movement, singing, and literal acts of rewriting the Declaration.

Alyssa: Quenna and I work with For Youth Inquiry (FYI), a participatory theatre company. I was the artistic director for several years. Currently, FYI is a program of the Illinois Caucus for Adolescent Health (ICAH), a Reproductive Justice nonprofit focusing on young people. Our first plays were made to help young people explore conversations about sex, with invitations to think about who influences you, practice having difficult conversations, and help characters in the play do something, that maybe, you might need to do later. (Laughs) We have since supported ICAH's education and organizing priorities, including abortion access for young people and policy change in Chicago Public Schools.

Jasmin: The group WorkersTEATRO exists because I felt the need to apply my work as a Theatre of the Oppressed practitioner to real-world issues. The participants are not professional actors. They are

DOI: 10.4324/9781003341802-33

temporary workers on factory lines (who sometimes also happen to be the union representatives). As immigrant Latino workers and African American workers, we use our stories of wage theft, workplace abuse, and discrimination to amplify our power and push for change. The catalytic "we can change policy" moments happen when we are directly linked with a workers' rights organization that we can support using theatre.

For example, one time we were able to grow power by being on the picket line. We created a participatory theatre experience in front of a Victoria's Secret flagship store on Michigan Avenue, the same day as the VS models were striking in LA and New York, #VictoriasSilence. Rather than go out there only with signs, we acted out a scene of harassment that happened inside the factory. We theatricalized the working women's story, and it made the evening news. This got the owner's attention, who had avoided their requests for a meeting, but finally said, "Okay, stop it. Stop going to Victoria's Secret on Michigan Avenue. What do you want? We'll meet with you." (see Cunningham, 2020).

Quenna: People in social justice theatre sometimes say there shouldn't be a focus on esthetics. But I'm like, no, we *have* to use the tools of culture! To bring people in, because people like entertainment, right? That's what's going to make the news.

Jasmin: I would add that we're not doing the work right if we're not centering women and trans folks. So those are the people on my team.

Alyssa: I'm linking it to grassroots organizing: The people who are affected are the people who need to be moving the work.

Quenna: For *Rewriting the Declaration*, I leaned into what I learned from the Black, queer feminist lens of movement organizing: To free us all, we have to free the Black, queer femme, or trans person, who is the most oppressed in society.

So we put out a call and cast seven Black women and one nonbinary person of color. Our process involved interrogating the document itself and then devising what I called Black Queer feminist theory teachbacks. I invited them to bring in folks they considered theorists, this included not just academics but also the people in their lives with lived experience.

Alyssa: The "community" of *Rewriting the Declaration* was the ensemble.

Quenna: Absolutely. We were transformed by being a part of it.

Alyssa: That is also a form of organizing.

Quenna: Anytime you make a play, you are gathering a new community. And you build relationships with people.

Alyssa: I am training new organizers with this work, too: the actors. For one FYI play I stewarded, *Expectation*, we taught the actors all about Title IX[1], so they could then hold informed facilitation. Afterward, they had a stake in the fight and were moved to do more for the young people in their lives. The play was rooted in young people's experiences: Devising started with thirty-plus interviews of young Chicago parents and pregnant folks to explore the times when it would have been nice to have somebody in your corner. I also gathered a council of young parents to consult on the script. Throughout the production, audience members could choose to follow one of three young characters who are pregnant or parenting. With their supportive squad, that character goes to the doctor's office, a family meeting, or the counselor's office. So, the audience builds a relationship with the character while learning, for instance, what Title IX laws entail and what type of interruptions can happen. Then, the audience practices advocacy by literally doing it.

Quenna: It's practice for real life. As Boal says, "rehearsal for the revolution."

Alyssa: This work is a cultural shift by changing people's points of view, and then inviting them to act on that new, more inclusive, liberatory understanding that they will remember because they embodied it.

The other FYI play I want to mention is *This Boat Called My Body*. Quenna was one of the writers and co-director with our collaborator Nik Zaleski. It centers on a young person trying to access abortion, amid challenging, even hostile laws. Youth and adult organizers were working to repeal a notification law in Illinois. We taught the audience what that meant, while the characters asked: "How do I have conversations with my mom? What are the kinds of care I need other than this procedure? What's gonna give me comfort?" Ultimately, there's an invitation from the lead character: "Please come help me." The audience has the opportunity to show up for her by joining her on stage and giving her physical support, gifts, and things like that.

Quenna: Before we even got to the playmaking process, there was a period of "data" collection, stories from young folks who had gone through abortions. The storytellers were paid for their time, and some were also in our devising process.

Alyssa: ICAH youth organizers did a lot of coding to identify interesting and recurring themes.

Quenna: We invited specific folks to a reading: Chicago Abortion Fund and other Reproductive Justice folks, judicial bypass attorneys, and our abortion storytellers. To make sure that we were getting the story right, we received feedback both from people impacted and people who work with folks impacted by this issue. I don't think that happens in typical play processes. I think the goal also has a lot to do with what makes a piece applied theatre or not. The goal wasn't merely to produce a play about abortion access for young folks but to move folks toward legislation. At the end of the play, we have a call to action to write a letter to your legislator.

Jasmin: I think of WorkersTEATRO as having three audiences. The workers themselves are our first audience. Together we create the story and develop the capability to tell difficult stories. I would never ask Quenna to tell me her story of trauma and then expect Quenna to perform that story over and over again. But through Image Theatre (see Boal, 1992, pp. 174–203), we create a theatrical narrative that's built upon multiple real stories. We're not a therapy group. I have no way of bringing people back from a dark place if I crack an egg. I often only have forty-five minutes, so it's very incremental work. As people are comfortable to share, they offer more details.

The second audience is the community. Sometimes those people are actual low-wage workers as well. Sometimes those are affluent professionals who have invited us to their event and might have some power to put us in front of stakeholders, policymakers, and researchers. The third audience, then, is the lawmakers in political power, the owners of the factory, or the board members who can change a situation. We tell the stories in all three of these markets because that's how change will happen.

Quenna: I love that. Inviting all stakeholders into our practice is how theatre does collective liberation struggle.

Jasmin: Theatre is just one tool. It's not more important than traditional organizing or union building, but powerful when used in combination. Sometimes as theatre artists, we forget that we should be a part of a larger liberation struggle.

Quenna: In applied theatre work, if the community is also the ensemble, how do we mitigate harm within our own community?

Jasmin: One partner organization actually pushed for more trauma stories. It was up to me to tell them: "We're not only pulling the workers' horror trauma stories for you."

Alyssa: Telling folks in power at the nonprofit, "No"! That is an important cultural shift.

Jasmin: We also need to work on celebratory things and show how beautiful and capable we are.

Quenna: Absolutely. That's community care. It's a different way of making theatre. Also, how do we resist urgency? According to Tema Okun (2021), that's a characteristic of white supremacy culture. But it's also a habit of the theatre industrial complex, right? "Oh, we only have four weeks to get this thing staged and put up." So? And? (Laughs) It's a focus on the people and not just on the project outcome.

Jasmin: I remember clearly, in my theatre training, "You check your shit at the door." We are creating in the most humanistic form, but do we have to cut ourselves off from part of our humanity? That's impossible with WorkersTEATRO. When the workers are coming to the group, we have to deal with the fact that there might not be any childcare, so today's workshop suddenly has three little children in it. At times the needs were so great we didn't get any rehearsing done. We had to hold each other because of a death or a loss of work. How do we make space and structure for the emotional and well-being of the communities we collaborate with? You have to meet the whole person.

Quenna: We have to intentionally carve out space and time for people's lives to enter the process because we're humans.

Alyssa: As the person who's holding the space, when you do have that power, what can you adjust?

Quenna: Our foundation is us being together. *Playing* together. That's what gets us through. We were all in rehearsal when we got the news of Ruth Bader Ginsburg's passing. People just needed to take time to process. I said, "Everybody, take what space you need, and we'll gather in another thirty minutes." But only because we had spent so much time just playing together, could we allow ourselves to say, "Actually, I can't be here right now." You have to engender comfort for people to be able to say that.

Jasmin: I couldn't agree more about the importance of play. Life is hard, and especially with the community I work with, they never play. That's how children learn. That's how adults learn. We need to be in a playful place to be open to new ideas. Play neutralizes the power dynamics.

Quenna: Part of my process is to always invite the group into leadership. I shouldn't be leading everything, even if I'm the director. One day, an actor led a twerking meditation. She put on some twerk music and said, "We're gonna warm up our Sacral Chakra." And that became a part of the play.

Jasmin: I want to warm up my Sacral Chakra!

(All laugh.)

Alyssa: How do we bring ourselves back to our bodies? *That* is the world we want to live in!

Quenna: Having Black women and non-binary people of color in that ensemble allowed us to bring in spiritual practices. These were people who had practices building altars, drinking water, and moving their bodies as meditation.

Alyssa: A pleasure coach, Rashida KhanBey Miller, taught me this: Our bodies learn habits. We get used to waking up and going straight to work. We get used to feeling sexy only in a certain way. And then we have to make active, embodied shifts to move differently.

Quenna: Practice allows us to build the muscles that we need.

Jasmin: The relationship between imagination and action is just the ability to do. If I see a piece of theatre, and I see a woman who's just like me, and she speaks up, suddenly, in my imagination, I see what's possible, and the gears begin to shift. Our workers in our team are no longer the same submissive workers.

Quenna: How do I imagine myself doing something if I've never seen it? And then what does it mean to put women and trans folk into the forefront of that? That's why I became a theatre artist, so that brown and Black girls could see themselves.

After *Rewriting the Declaration*, the ensemble reflected, "This was the first time I had a full people of color team," or referring to working with a Black woman director, "Now, I'm only going to work in and create in spaces like that."

Alyssa: It's like adrienne maree brown's *Emergent Strategy* (2017) concept of fractals, which multiply. More people are going to continue the work.

Quenna: I'm also thinking about abolition as a practice of imagination. We have to dream that space that we want to see. In theatre, we literally build new worlds every day on the stage. We build a set. We build a new reality. How do we do that in real life?

Note

1 A 1972 US Constitutional amendment protecting against discrimination in education based on the basis of sex.

References and Further Reading

Boal, A. (1985) *Theatre of the Oppressed*. Adrian Jackson, trans. New York, NY: Theatre Communications Group.

Boal, A. (1992). *Games for Actors and Non-Actors*. Adrian Jackson, trans. London and New York: Routledge.

brown, a. m. (2017). *Emergent Strategy: Shaping Change, Changing Worlds*. Chico, CA: AK Press.

Cardenas, J. (2021) "Theater of the Oppressed and Labor Organizing: Possibilities and Limitations." *Pedagogy and Theatre of the Oppressed Journal*. 6(6). Available at https://scholarworks.uni.edu/ptoj/vol6/iss1/6/.

Cunningham, B. (2020) "Women Confront Ugly Harassment at Beauty Product Plant," Labor Notes. 21 Feb. Accessed 2 Feb. 2024. https://labornotes.org/2020/02/women-confront-ugly-harassment-beauty-products-plant

Okun, T. (2021) "White Supremacy Culture – Still Here." 1 May. Accessed 2 Feb. 2024. https://www.WhiteSupremacyCulture.Info/Characteristics

Spont-Lemus, M. (2021) "Beyond the Page: Quenna Lené Barrett," Sixty Inches from Center. 25 Jan. Accessed 19 Feb. 2024. https://sixtyinchesfromcenter.org/beyond-the-page-quenna-lene-barrett/

Stanley, J. (2018) "CHOICE/LESS 405: Their Bodies, Their Boats, Their Play," Rewire News Group. 14 Sept. Accessed 19 Feb. 2024. https://rewirenewsgroup.com/2018/09/14/choice-less-405-their-bodies-their-boats-their-play/

Index

Note: Page numbers in *italics* refer to figures; and those followed by "n" refer to notes.

For Product Safety Concerns and Information please contact our EU
representative GPSR@taylorandfrancis.com
Taylor & Francis Verlag GmbH, Kaufingerstraße 24, 80331 München, Germany

www.ingramcontent.com/pod-product-compliance
Lightning Source LLC
Chambersburg PA
CBHW050346270326
41926CB00016B/3629

* 9 7 8 1 0 3 2 3 7 7 6 3 6 *